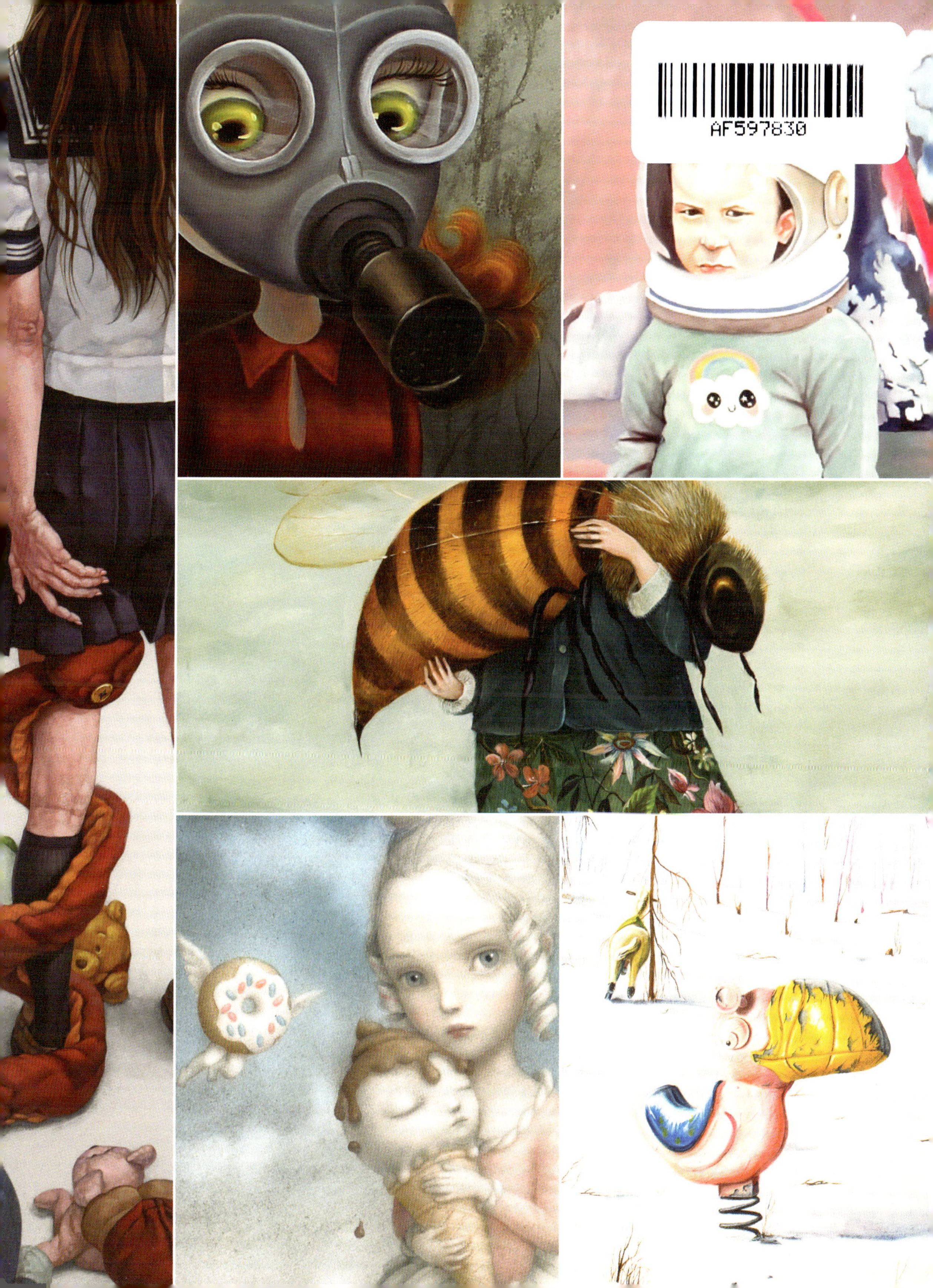

Sweet & bizarre

Editor, concept, and project director
Anna Minguet

Project's selection, design and layout
Carolina Amell (Monsa Publications)
Cover design
Carolina Amell (Monsa Publications)
Introduction and text edition
Monsa Publications
Translation
Somos traductores

Cover image by Victor Castillo
Back cover image by Nicoletta Ceccoli

INSTITUTO MONSA DE EDICIONES
Gravina 43 (08930)
Sant Adrià de Besòs
Barcelona (Spain)
Tlf. +34 93 381 00 50
www.monsa.com
monsa@monsa.com

Visit our official online store!
www.monsashop.com

Follow us!
Facebook: @monsashop
Instagram: @monsapublications

ISBN: 978-84-16500-53-6
D.L. B 11806-2017
Printed by Cachiman Grafic

BY CAROLINA AMELL

Sweet & bizarre

monsa

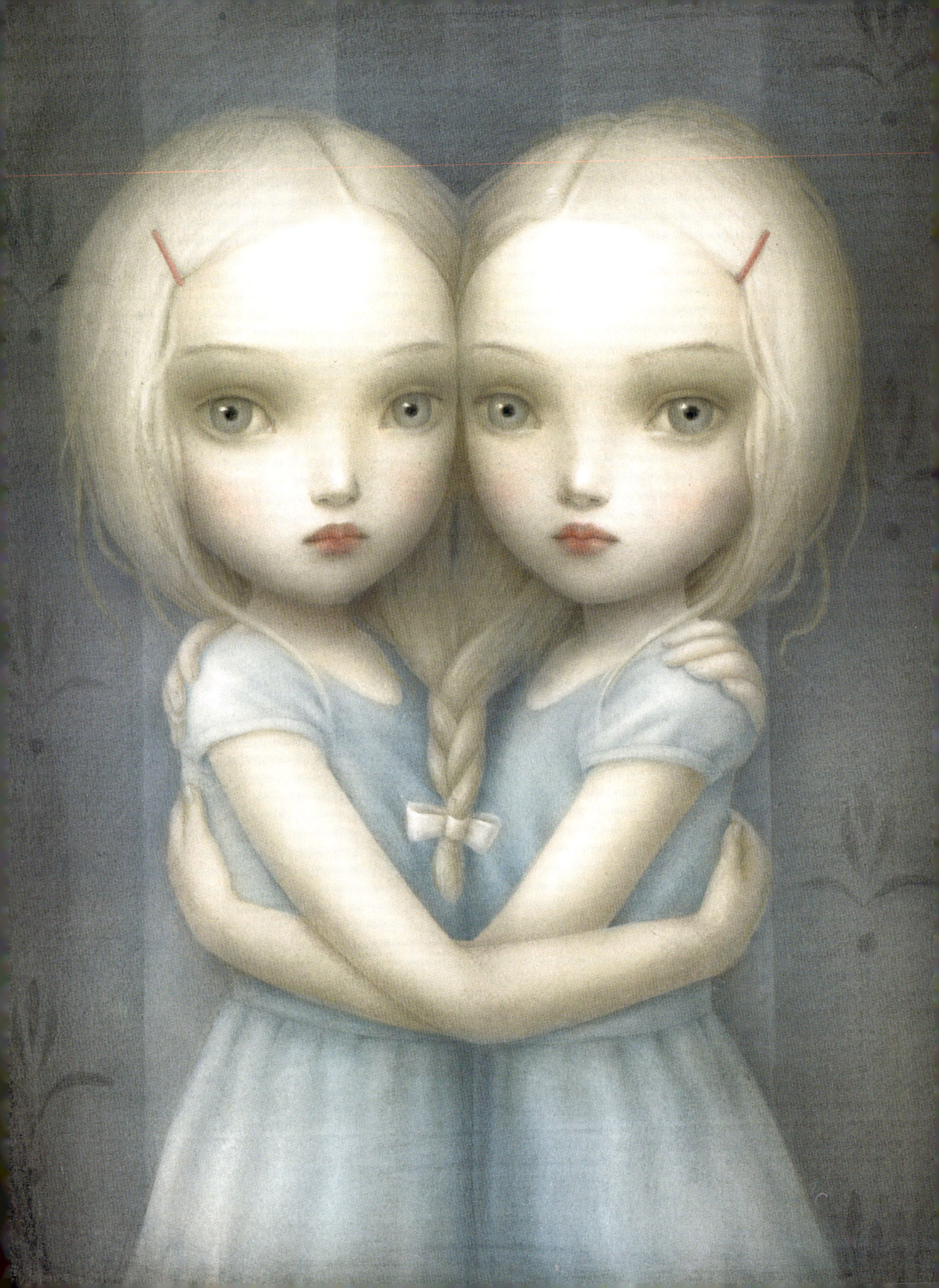

Intro

Sweet & Bizarre is a way of describing works of art from the Lowbrow - also called Pop Surrealism - movement.

The "Lowbrow" movement arose in 1979, led by artist Robert Williams after various art analysts struggled with categorising his works. Many artists are now associate with this new concept, including Mark Ryden, Nicoletta Ceccoli, Gary Baseman, Takashi Murakami, Sara Sanz, etc.

Museums, art critics and "mainstream" galleries have been adamant in their rejection of Lowbrow art, although this has not stopped collectors from buying them. There are art critics who hesitate to label Lowbrow as an artistic movement because many of the artists are self-taught and they started their careers not in art schools but in in the worlds of illustration, tattoo art, comics.

In the following pages you will find fantastic works that will make you feel something sweet and bizarre at the same time, artists like Kazuhiro Hori, Xue Wang, Nicoletta Ceccoli, Marion Peck, Brandi Milne, Dilka Bear...

Each artist tells us about their trajectory and their more personal styles.

Sweet & Bizarre, es una forma de describir las obras del movimiento Lowbrow, también llamado Pop Surrealism.

El movimiento "Lowbrow" surgió en 1979 de la mano del artista Robert Williams, después de que diferentes analistas de arte no supieran donde encajar sus obras. Surgió entonces este nuevo concepto, con el que ahora se identifican muchos artistas como Mark Ryden, Nicoletta Ceccoli, Gary Baseman, Takashi Murakami, Sara Sanz, etc.

Los museos, críticos de arte, galerías del "mainstream" se han mostrado firmes al mantener su postura de rechazo al Lowbrow, lo cual no ha impedido que los coleccionistas compren obras. Hay críticos de arte que ponen en duda que el Lowbrow sea un movimiento artístico, debido a que muchos de los artistas son autodidactas, y el origen de sus carreras se aleja de las escuelas de arte y se encuentra en campos tales como la ilustración, el tatuaje o los cómics.

En las siguientes páginas encontraréis fantásticas obras que os harán sentir algo dulce y bizarro al mismo tiempo, artistas como Kazuhiro Hori, Xue Wang, Nicoletta Ceccoli, Marion Peck, Brandi Milne, Dilka Bear...

Cada artista nos habla de su trayectoria, y sus estilos más personales.

▸ Soulmate by Nicoletta Ceccoli

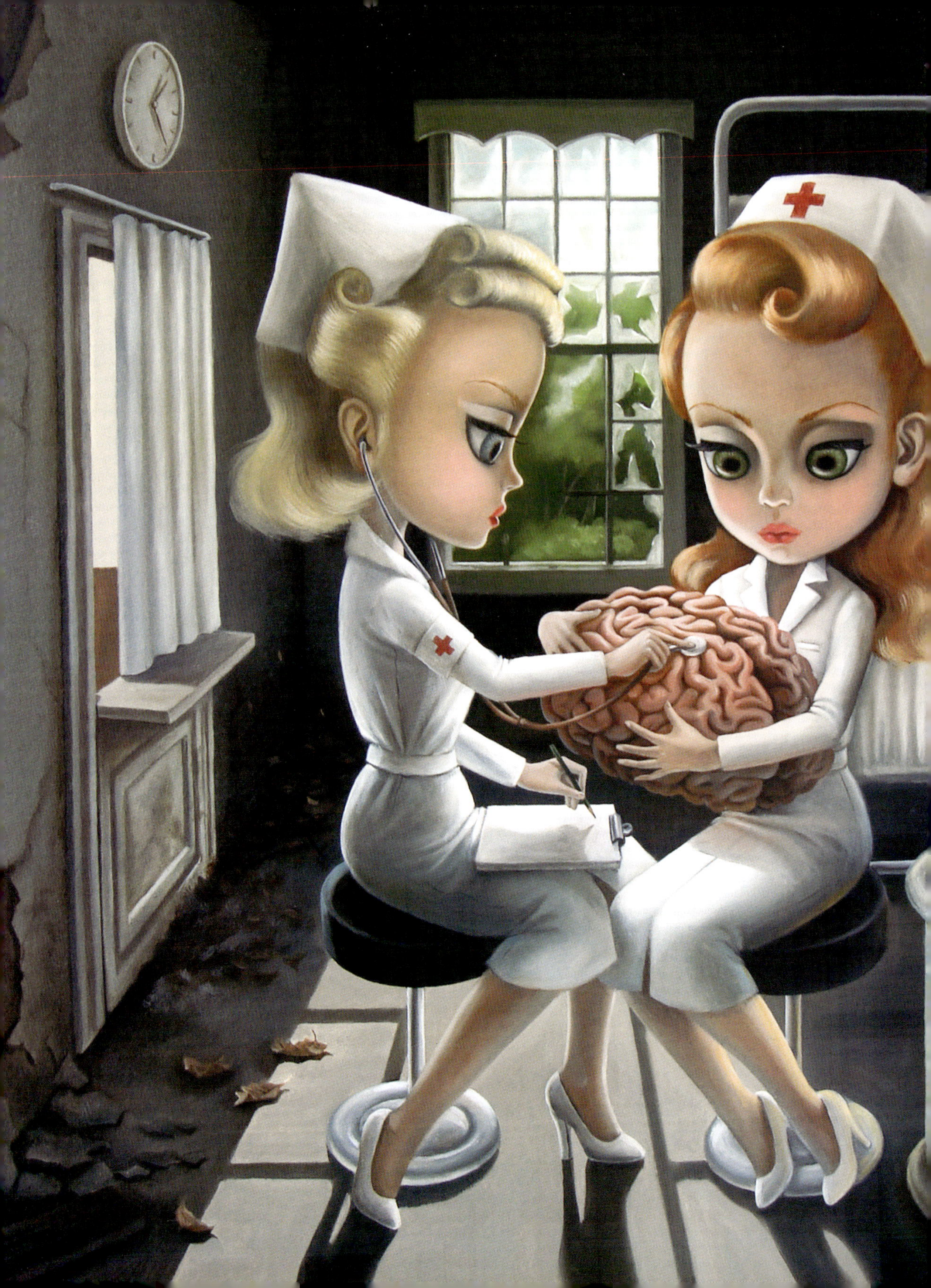

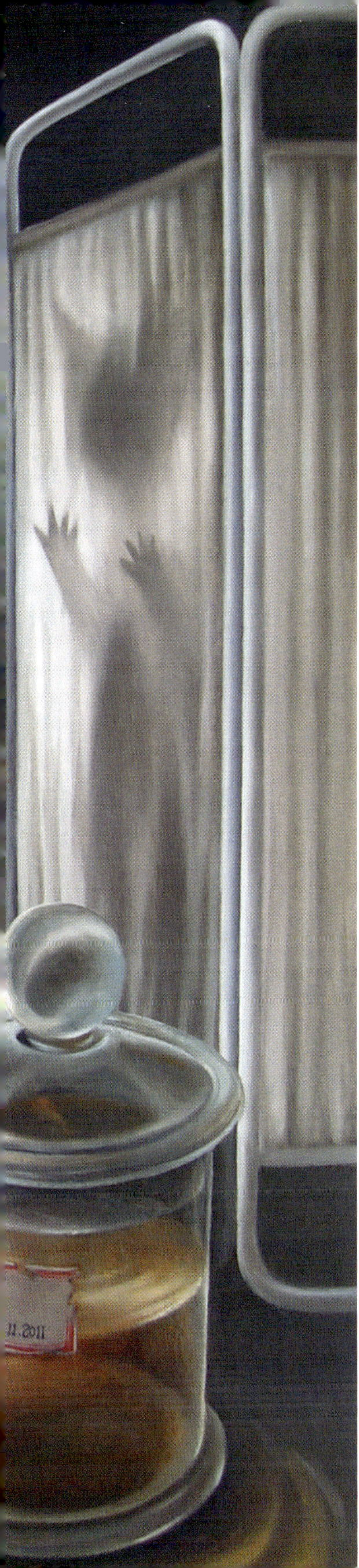

Index

▸ Intimate Thoughts by Xue Wang

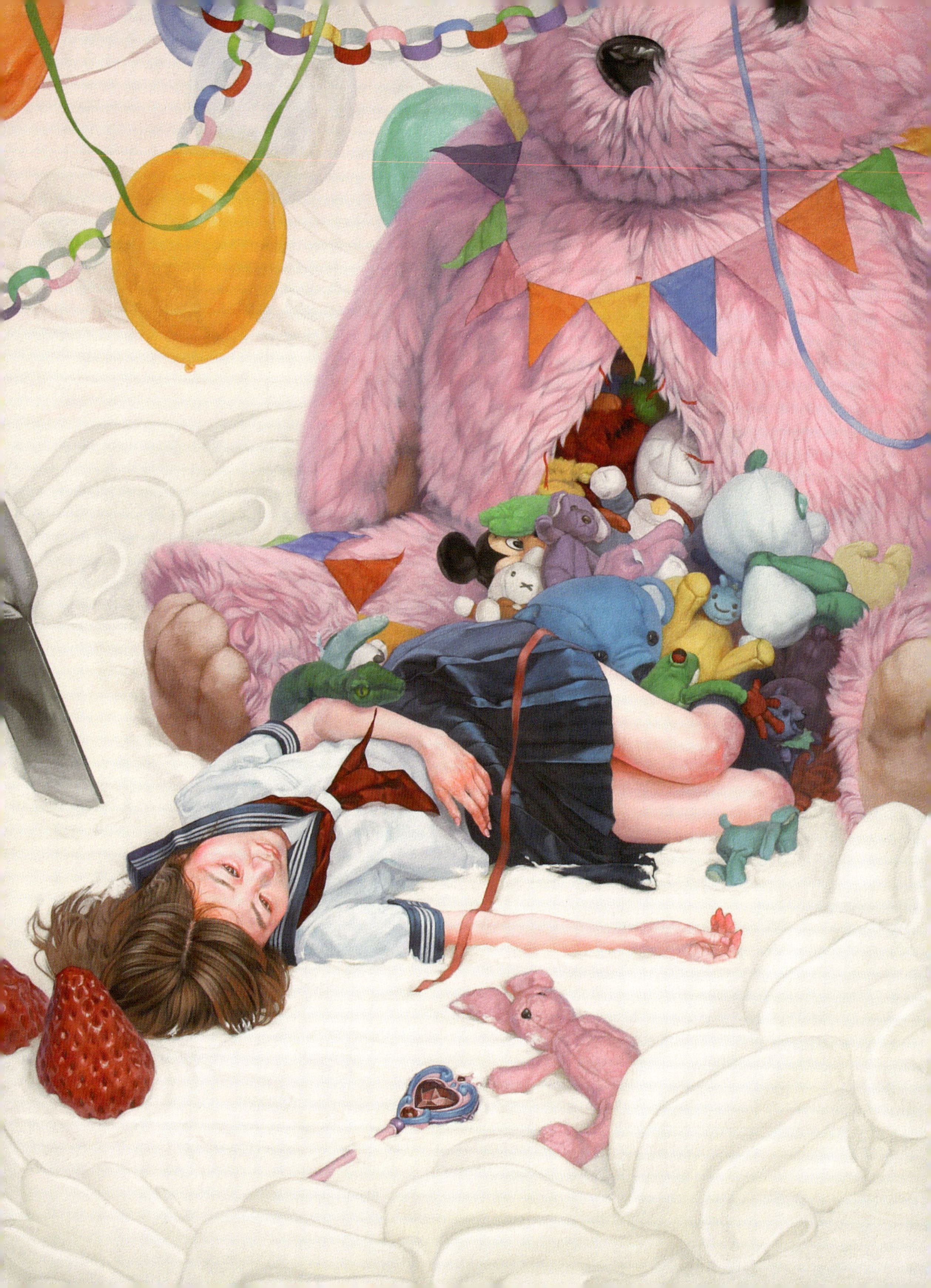

www.facebook.com/chardinchardin
instagram: @chardinchardin

Kazuhiro Hori

Japanese Junior High and High School Girls - recognizable by their school uniform - are living a dazzling and radiant existence. Surrounded by fashion, music, cute things, and sweet confections they like; they smile together and spend their time with their friends. But, at the same time, their minds are filled with anxiety, and their hearts are held down by dark thoughts and feelings. They study the things they might never find useful in the future, they want to belong in a clique, they don't want to be outcasts, and they want to maintain their relationships with their peers. They are anxious about the things that await them in the future when they finally enter "the real world". That is the bitter and sweet circumstances of their lives. Seifuku - their school uniform - represents modern Japanese girls' complex situation. Seifuku is a symbol of purity; yet, at the same time, is also a symbol of sexuality. This is something most Japanese people understand without needing to hear a lot of additional explanations. School uniform is much more than the clothing Junior High and High School girls have to wear. Their uniform binds them with a certain organization (namely: their school), defines their roles, and gives them a sense of community as well as a place to belong. Being a part of a community reduces their individuality; yet, at the same time, protects them from attacks and ridicules. But, school uniform is not necessarily bland and generic because - within certain limits - these girls are allowed to customize and style their uniform to express their uniqueness as well as their affiliations with their cliques. Girls can only wear their seifuku for a limited number of years. The world they are living in would not last forever. As they grow, their sweet confections and fluffy teddy bears are going to be further and further away from their lives.

Chicas japonesas de escuela - Reconocibles por su uniforme escolar. Están viviendo una existencia deslumbrante y radiante. Rodeadas de moda, música, cosas lindas y dulces que les gustan; sonríen juntas y pasan su tiempo con sus amigos. Pero, al mismo tiempo, sus mentes están llenas de ansiedad y sus corazones están sujetos a pensamientos y sentimientos oscuros. Estudian cosas que podrían no ser útiles en el futuro, quieren pertenecer a un grupo, no quieren ser marginadas y quieren mantener sus relaciones con sus compañeras. Están ansiosas por las cosas que les aguarda el futuro cuando finalmente salgan al "mundo real". Esas son las circunstancias agridulces de sus vidas. Seifuku - su uniforme colegial - representa la compleja situación de las niñas japonesas modernas. Seifuku es símbolo pureza, sin embargo, es también un símbolo de la sexualidad. Esto es algo que la mayoría de la gente japonesa entiende sin necesidad de escuchar un montón de explicaciones adicionales. El uniforme escolar es mucho más que la ropa que las chicas de la escuela de Japón tienen que llevar. Su uniforme les vincula a una determinada organización (es decir, su escuela), define sus roles y les da un espíritu comunitario, así como un lugar al que pertenecer. Formar parte de una comunidad reduce su individualidad y al mismo tiempo, les protege de ataques y burlas. Aún así, el uniforme escolar no es necesariamente soso y genérico ya que, dentro de unos límites, a estas niñas se les permite personalizar y diseñar el uniforme para expresar su singularidad, así como sus vinculaciones a los grupos. Las niñas sólo pueden llevar su seifuku durante un número limitado de años. El mundo en el que viven no duraría para siempre. A medida que crecen, sus dulces confecciones y los ositos de peluche amorosos van a estar cada vez más y más lejos de sus vidas.

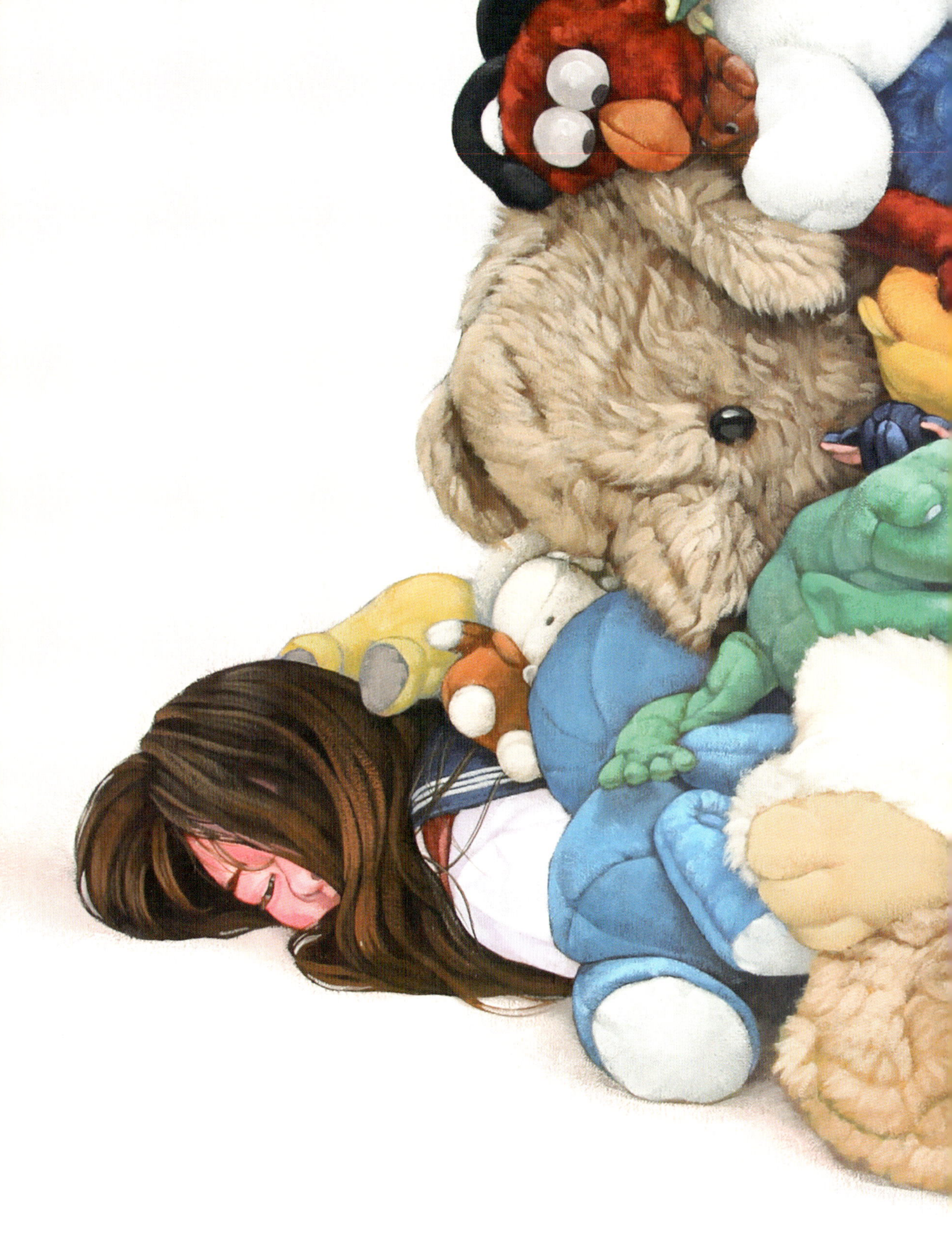

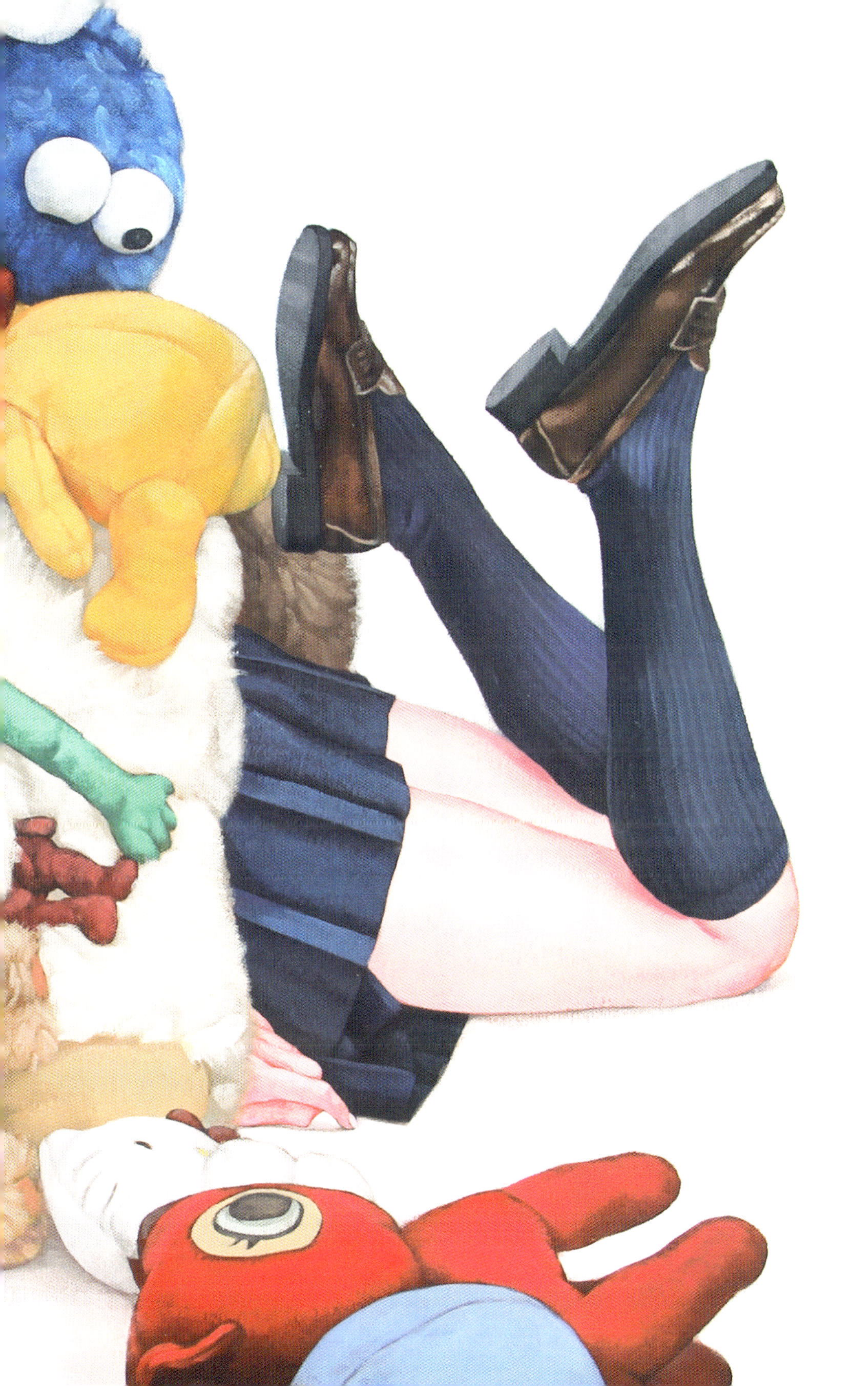

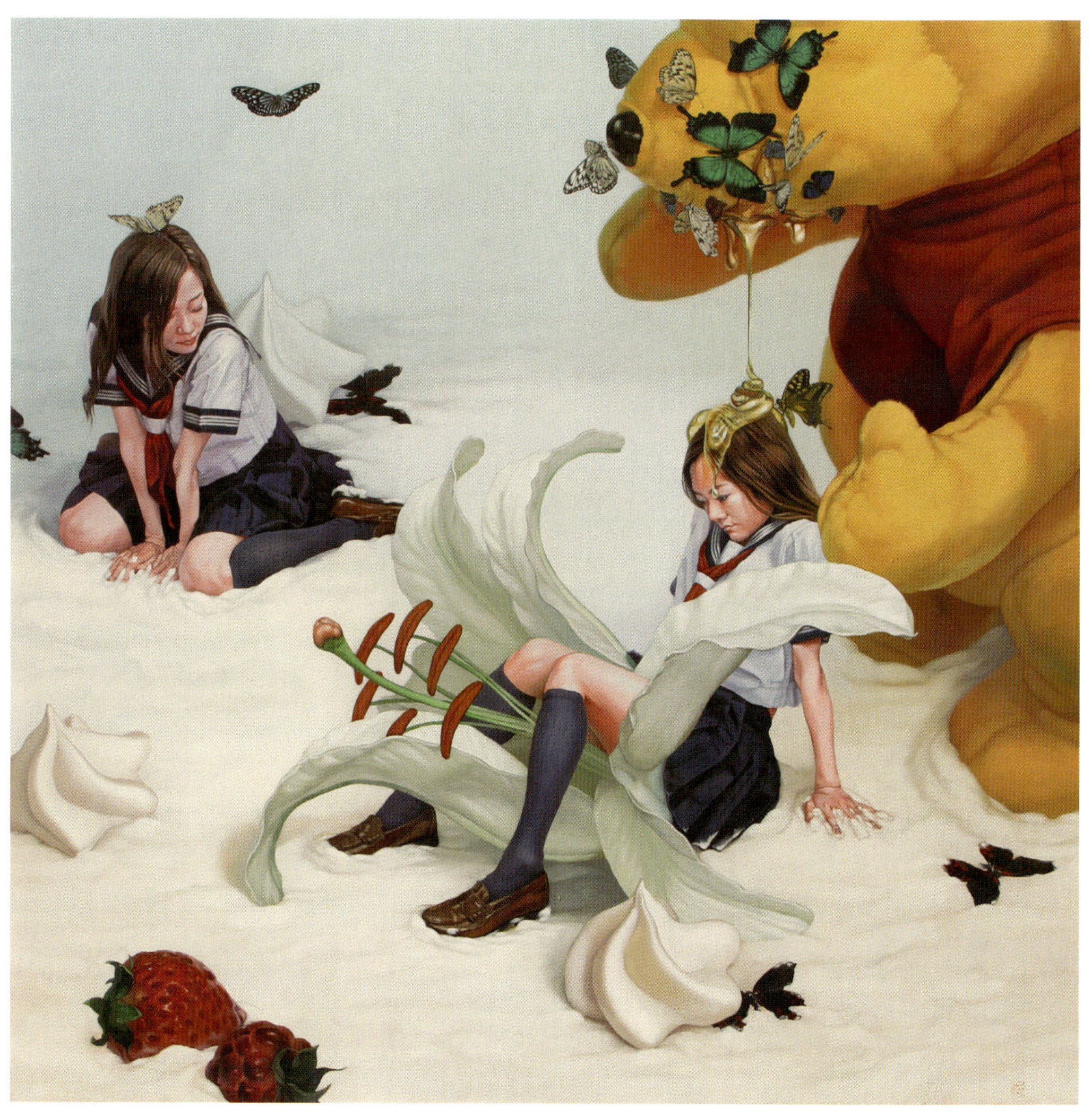

Honey trap

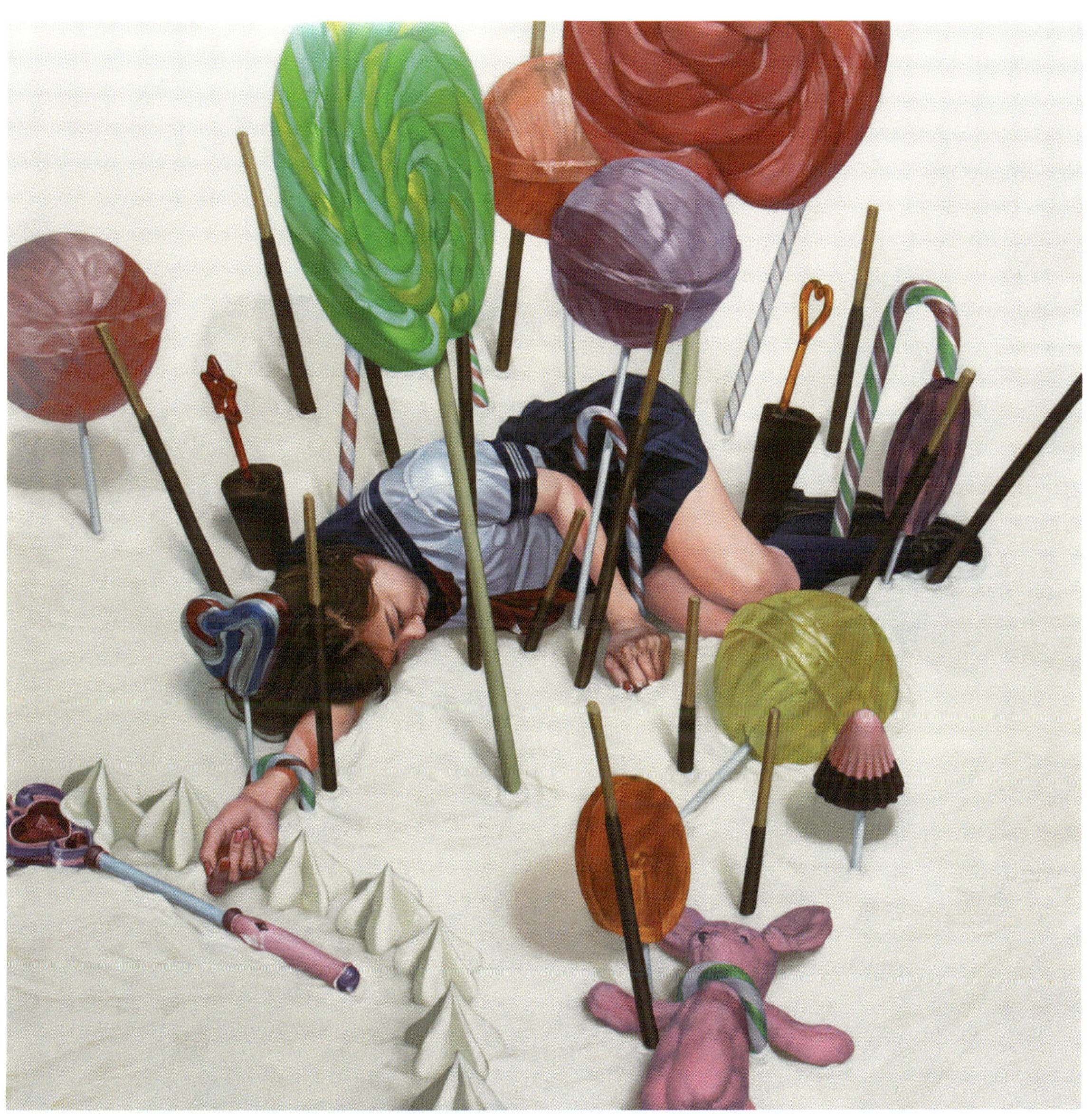

Magical girl captured

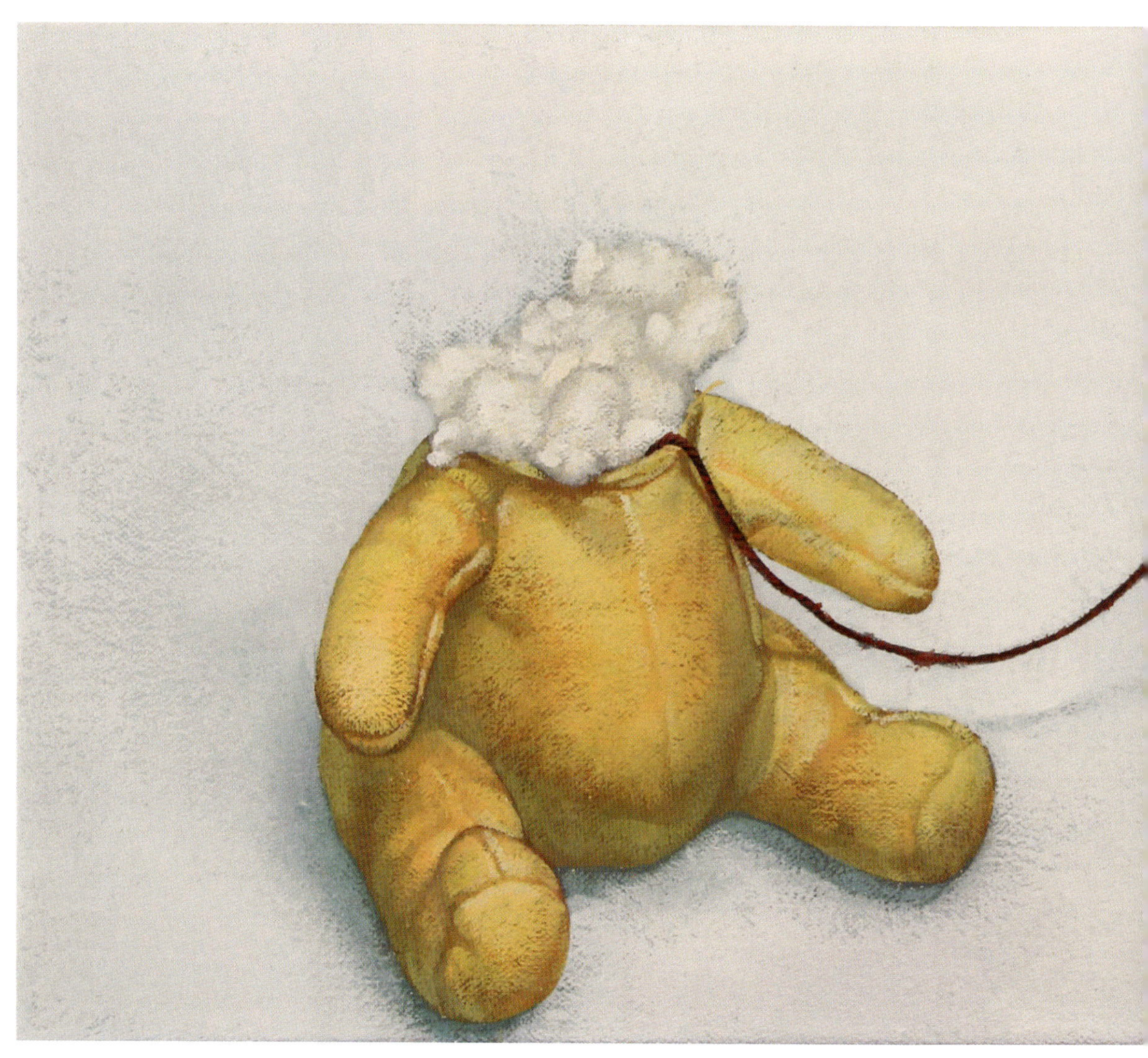

No face

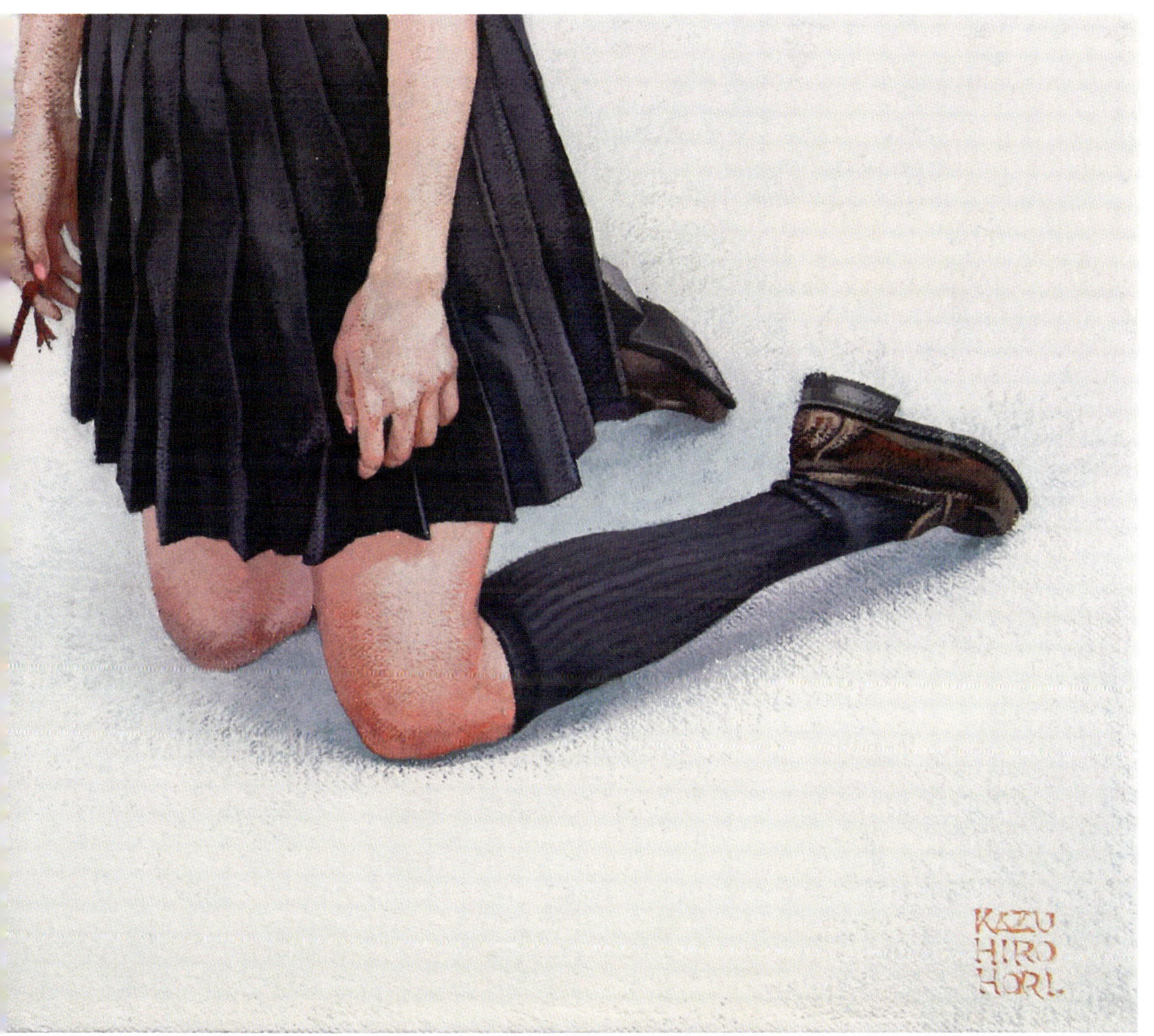
KAZU
HIRO
HORI

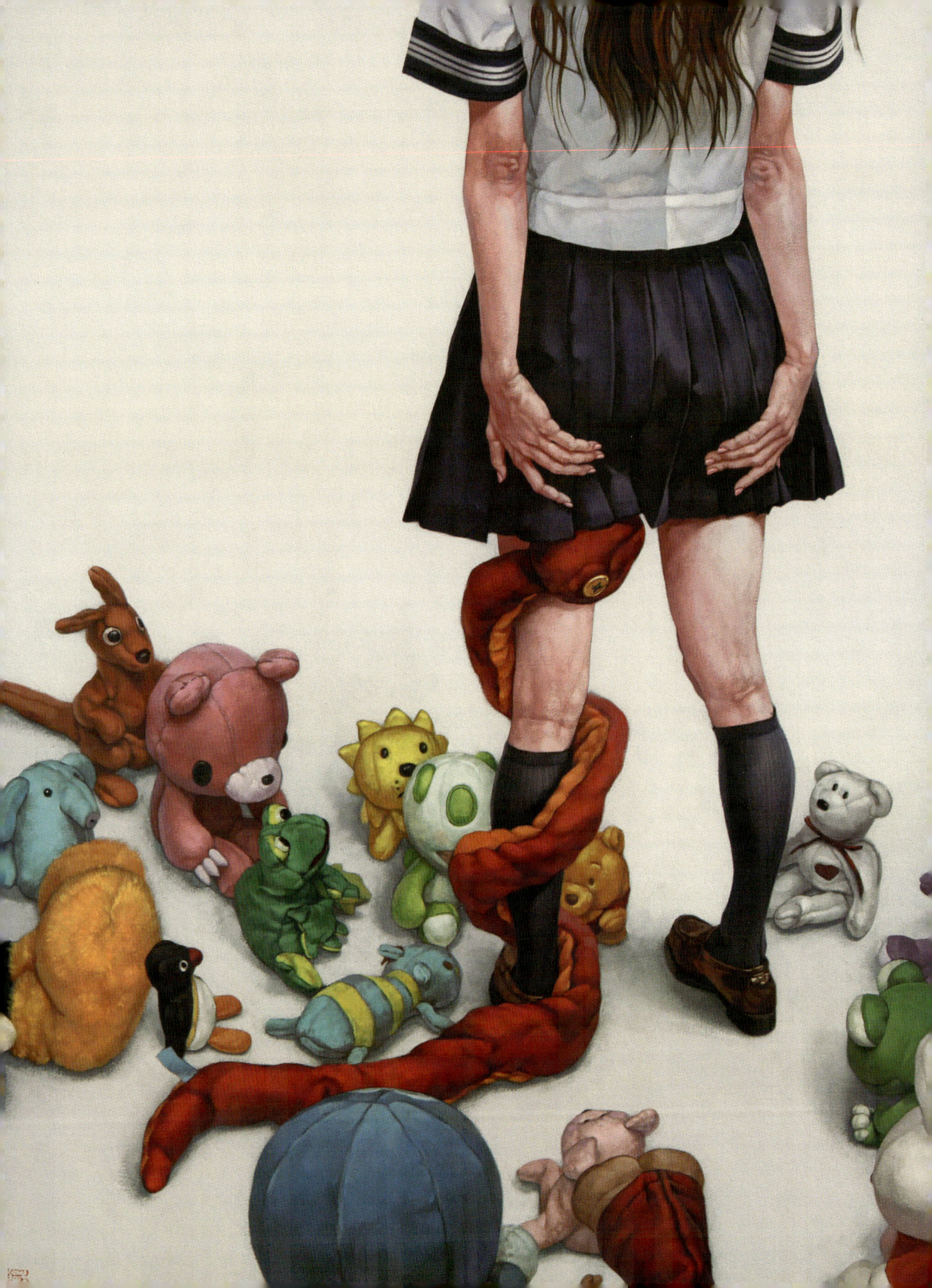

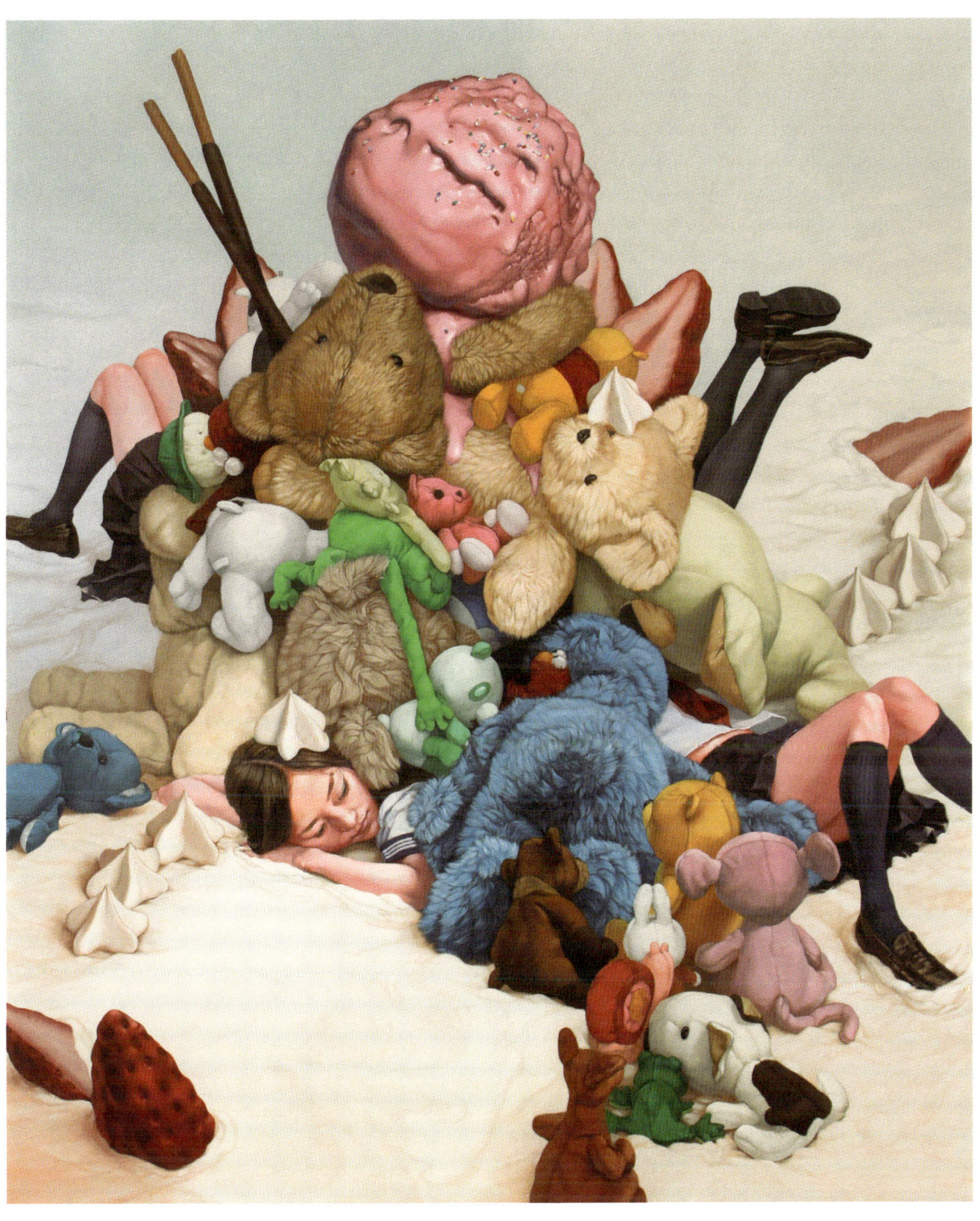

left: Sneak // *right:* Sweet life

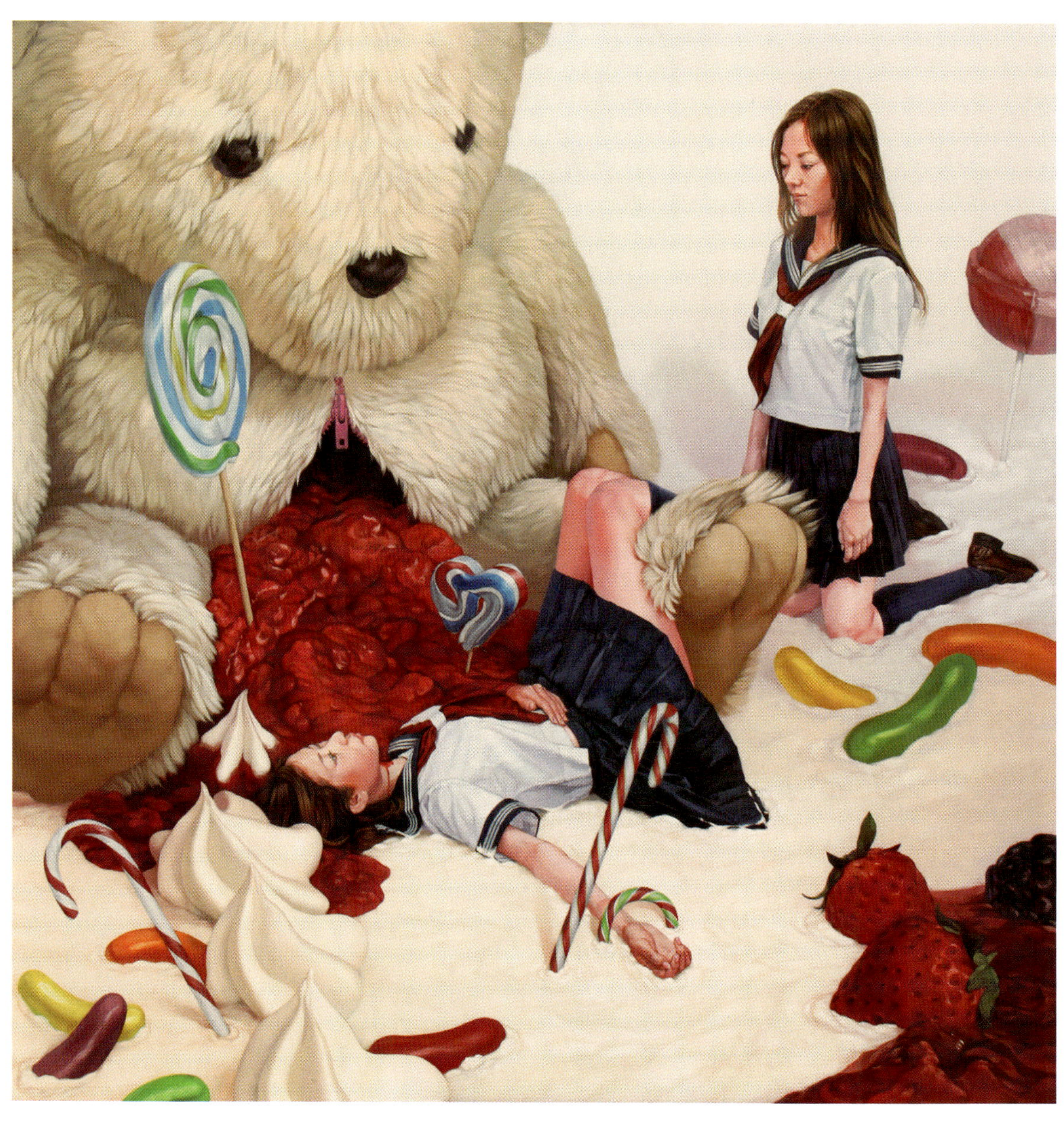

left: Tender Binding // *right:* Tender Binding

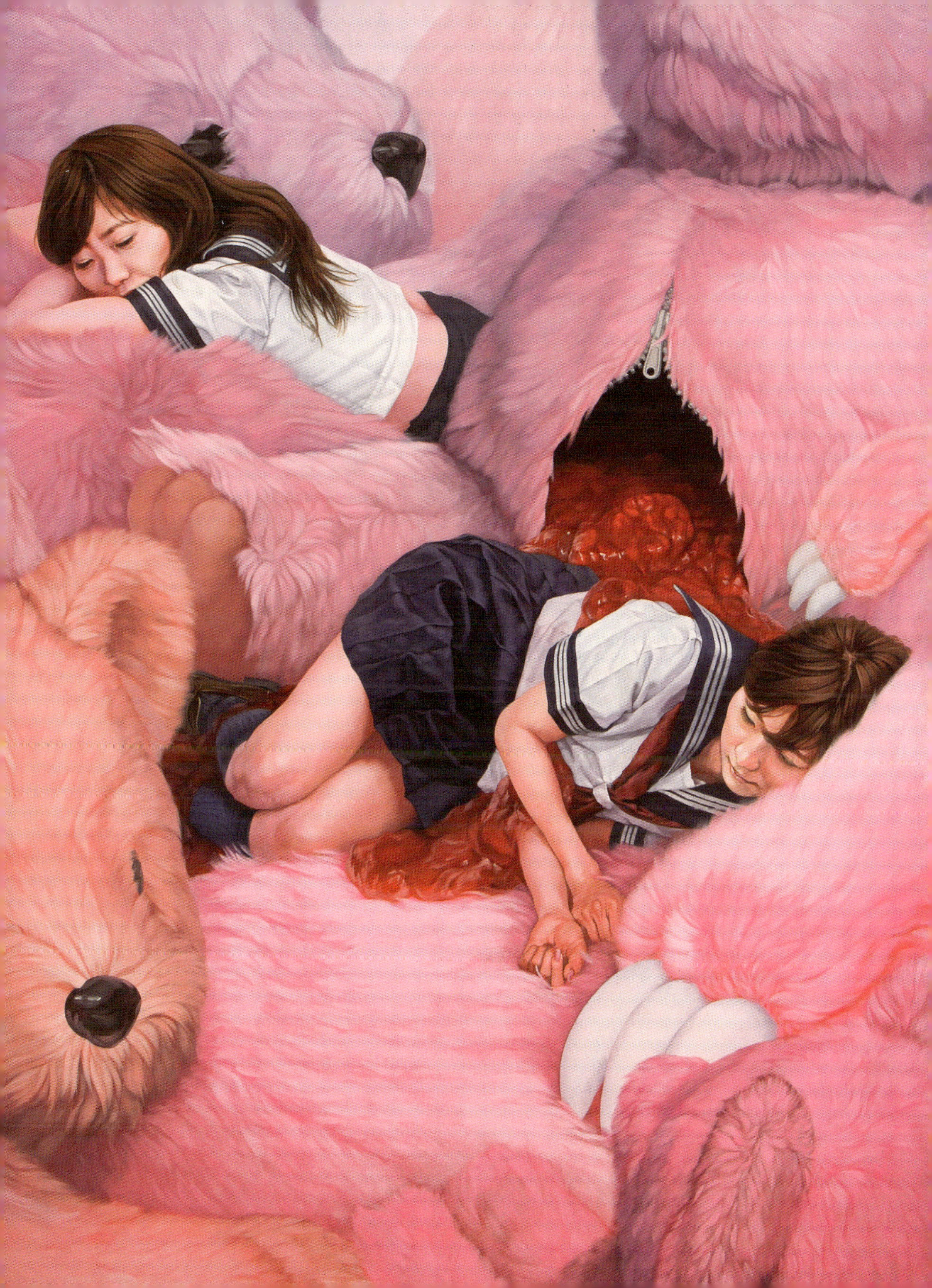

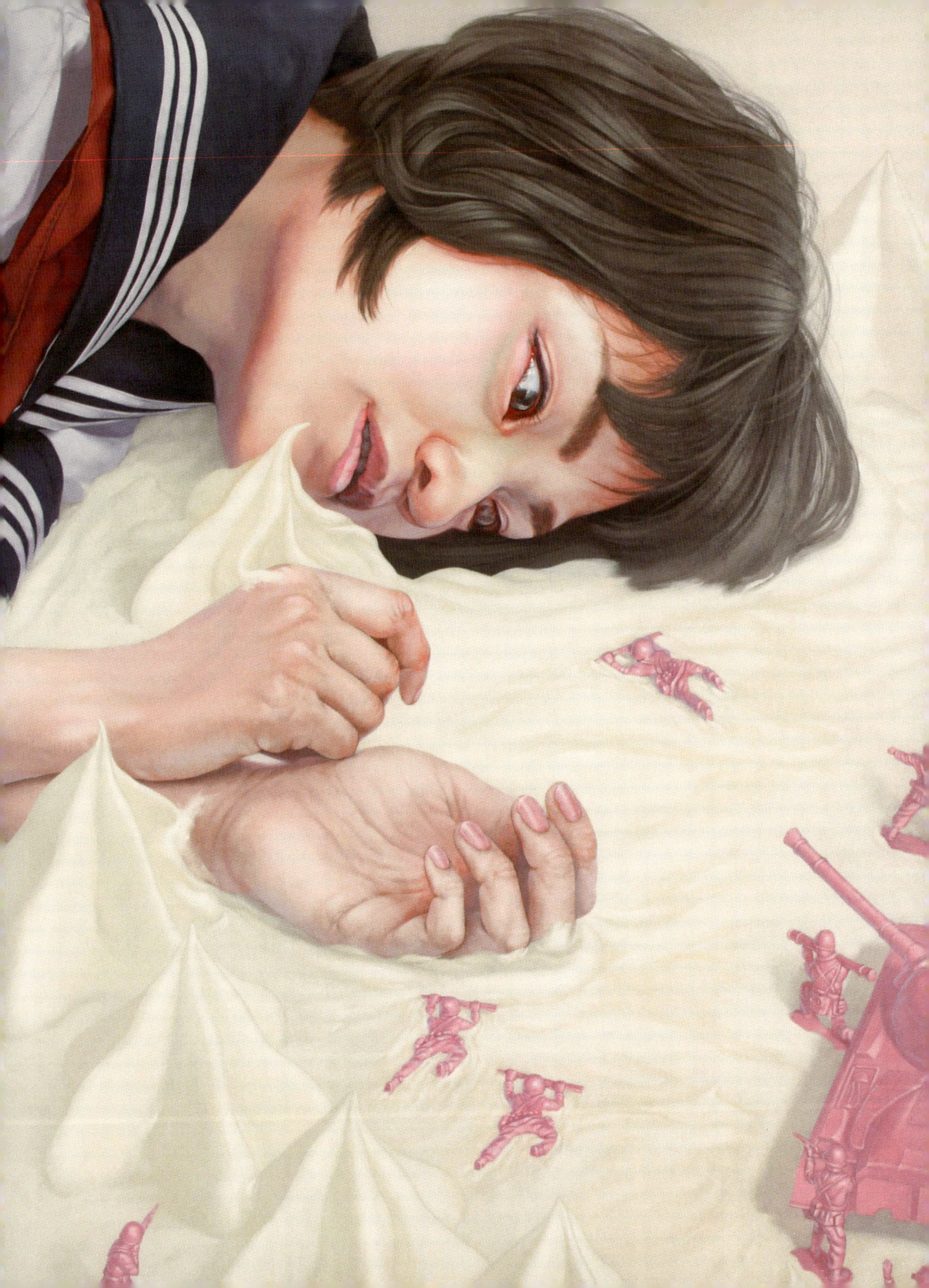

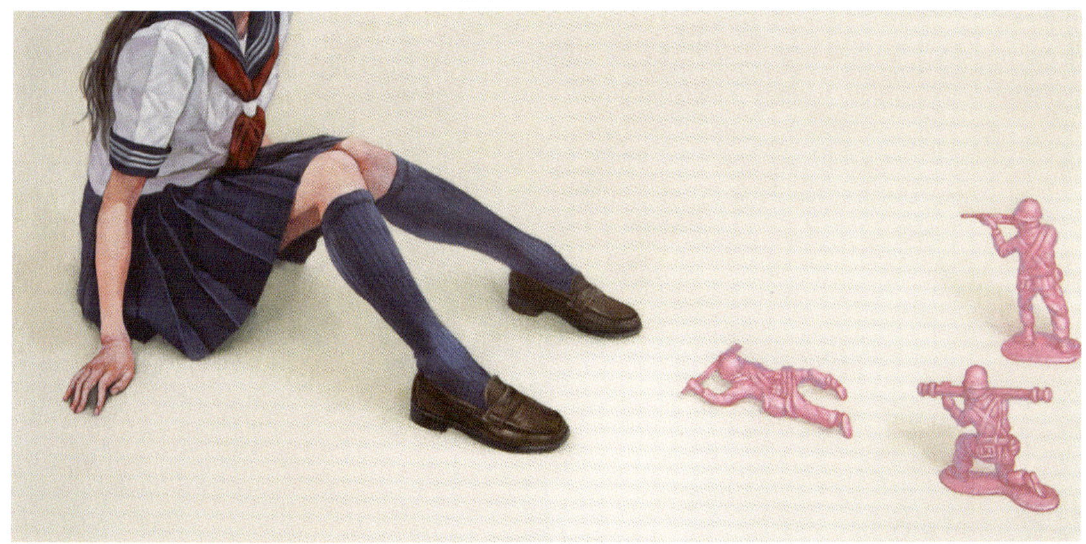

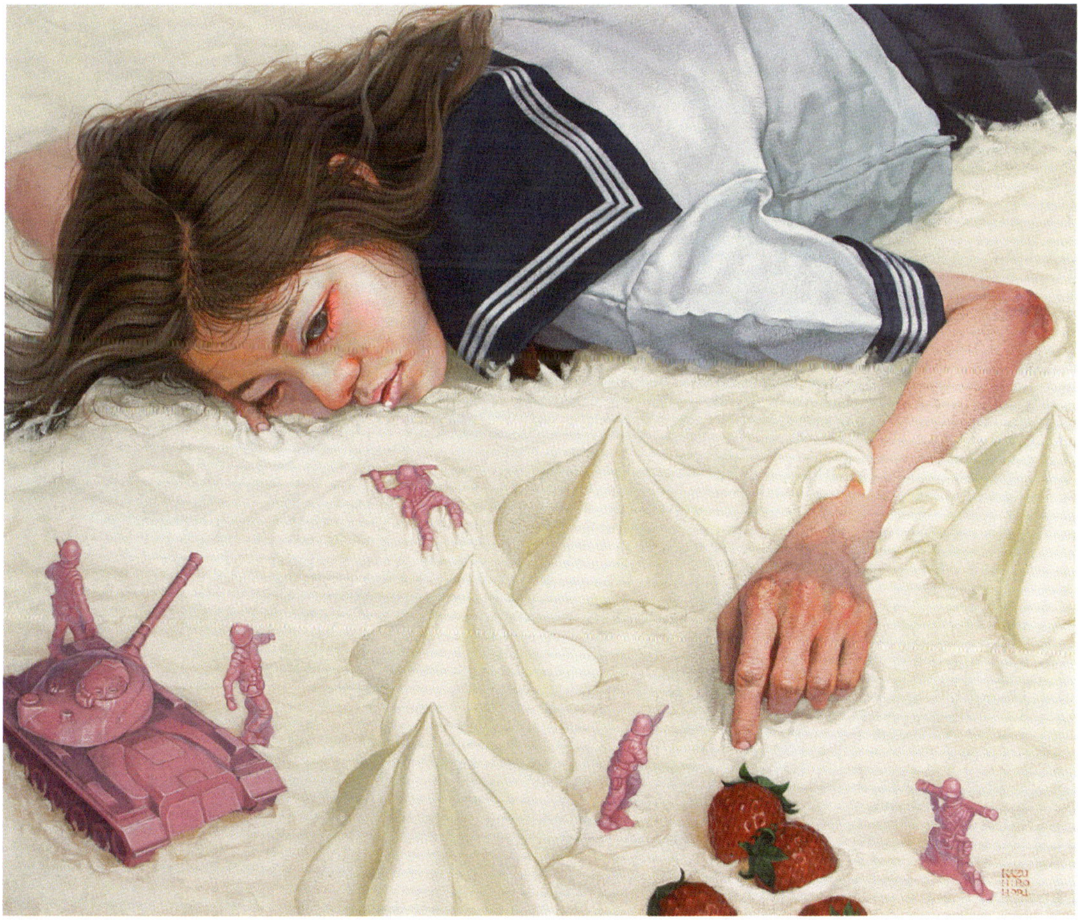

left: Game // *right, top:* Target, *bottom:* Game

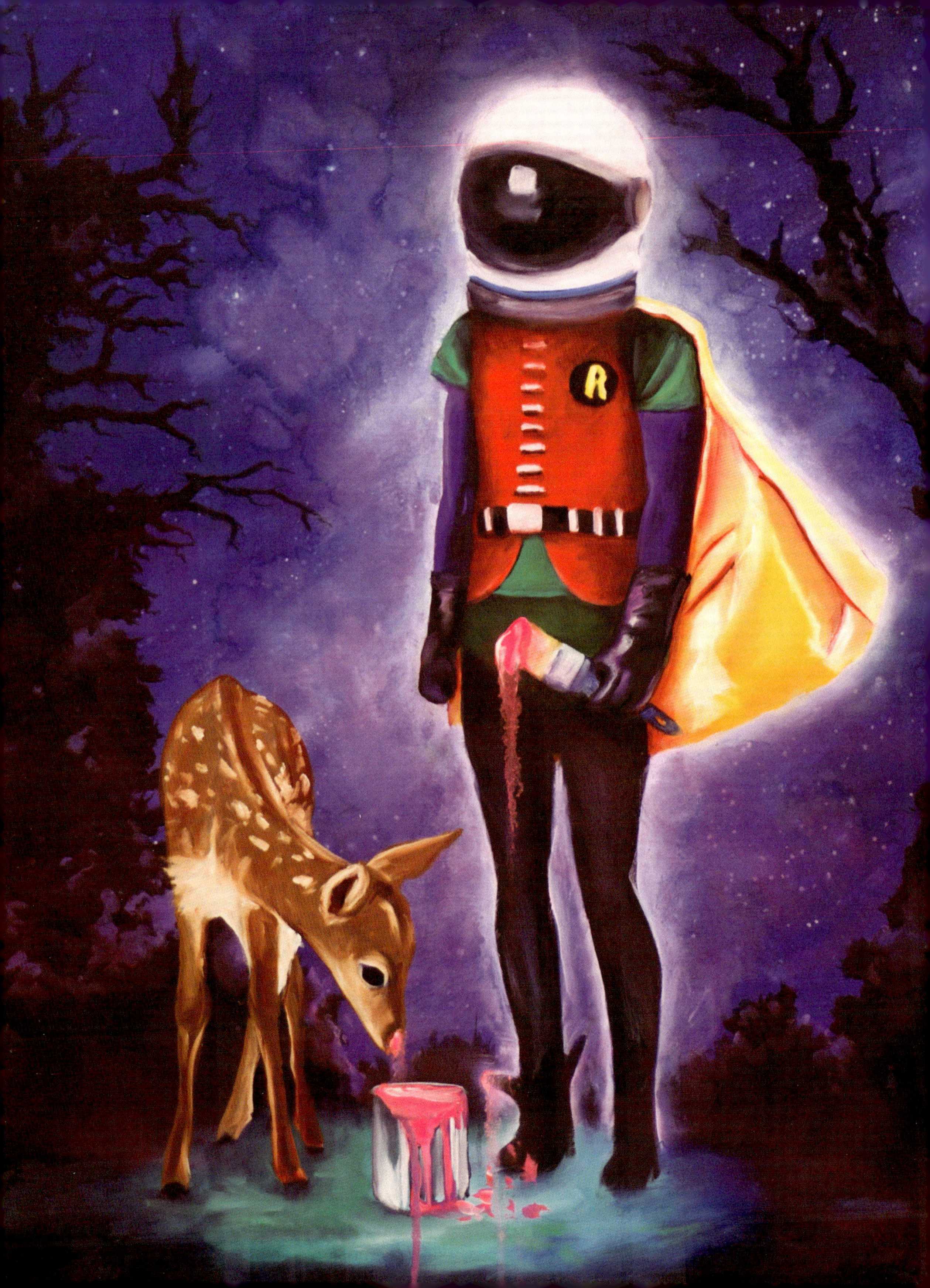
R

www.superfuturekid.com
instagram: @superfuturekid

Super Future Kid

Super Future Kid work is largely based on themes that strongly relate to certain ideas of childhood and youth, a time that still has a great influence on her personality and artistic identity.

She is deeply fascinated with the perception and perspective on the world from the view of an adolescent mind, and particularly in related ideas of mystery and strangeness, games and playfulness. Those ideas include the realms of spirituality, the occult, myths and curiosities as well as themes of character identity such as the play of dressing up and costumes and lastly the idea of the freedom of the youthful spirit itself.

The medium of Painting serves her as a very sensual tool in this respect. "Paint is a very primal substance that constantly evokes my curiosity. I am also fascinated by its power to create a whole world of its own, an entirely non-verbal space. Most of all do I see the act of painting as an ongoing extension of my own childhood, it allows me to explore ideas that are deeply rooted within myself and therefore help me to continuously map out and shape my identity as an artist and in the end as a human being".

Super Future Kid was born in East Germany in 1981 and attended the Chelsea Collage of Art and Design London and the Academy of Art Berlin Weissensee where she graduated in 2008. Since then, she has participated in exhibitions nationally and internationally in cities including London, New York, Los Angeles, Dallas and Berlin. At present she is living and working in London.

El trabajo de Super Future Kid se basa en temas fuertemente relacionados con ciertas ideas de la infancia y la juventud, una época que todavía tiene una gran influencia en su personalidad y su identidad artística.

Ella está profundamente fascinada con la percepción y la perspectiva del mundo desde el punto de vista de una mente adolescente, y particularmente con las ideas relativas al misterio y extrañeza, a juegos y jovialidad. Estas incluyen la espiritualidad, el ocultismo, los mitos y las curiosidades, así como los temas de identidad de carácter, el juego de vestirse, los disfraces y, por último, la idea de la libertad del espíritu juvenil en sí mismo.

La pintura le sirve como una herramienta sensual. "La pintura es una sustancia muy primordial que evoca constantemente mi curiosidad. También me fascina por su poder de crear un mundo entero propio, un espacio completamente no verbal. Sobre todo, veo el acto de pintar como una prolongación de mi propia infancia, me permite explorar ideas profundamente arraigadas dentro de mí y me ayuda a dibujar y configurar continuamente mi identidad como artista y como ser humano".

Super Future Kid nació en el este de Alemania en 1981 y fue al Chelsea College de Arte y Diseño de Londres y a la Academia de Arte de Berlin Weissensee, donde se graduó en 2008. Desde entonces, ha participado en exposiciones nacionales e internacionales en ciudades como Londres, Nueva York, Los Ángeles, Dallas y Berlín. Actualmente vive y trabaja en Londres.

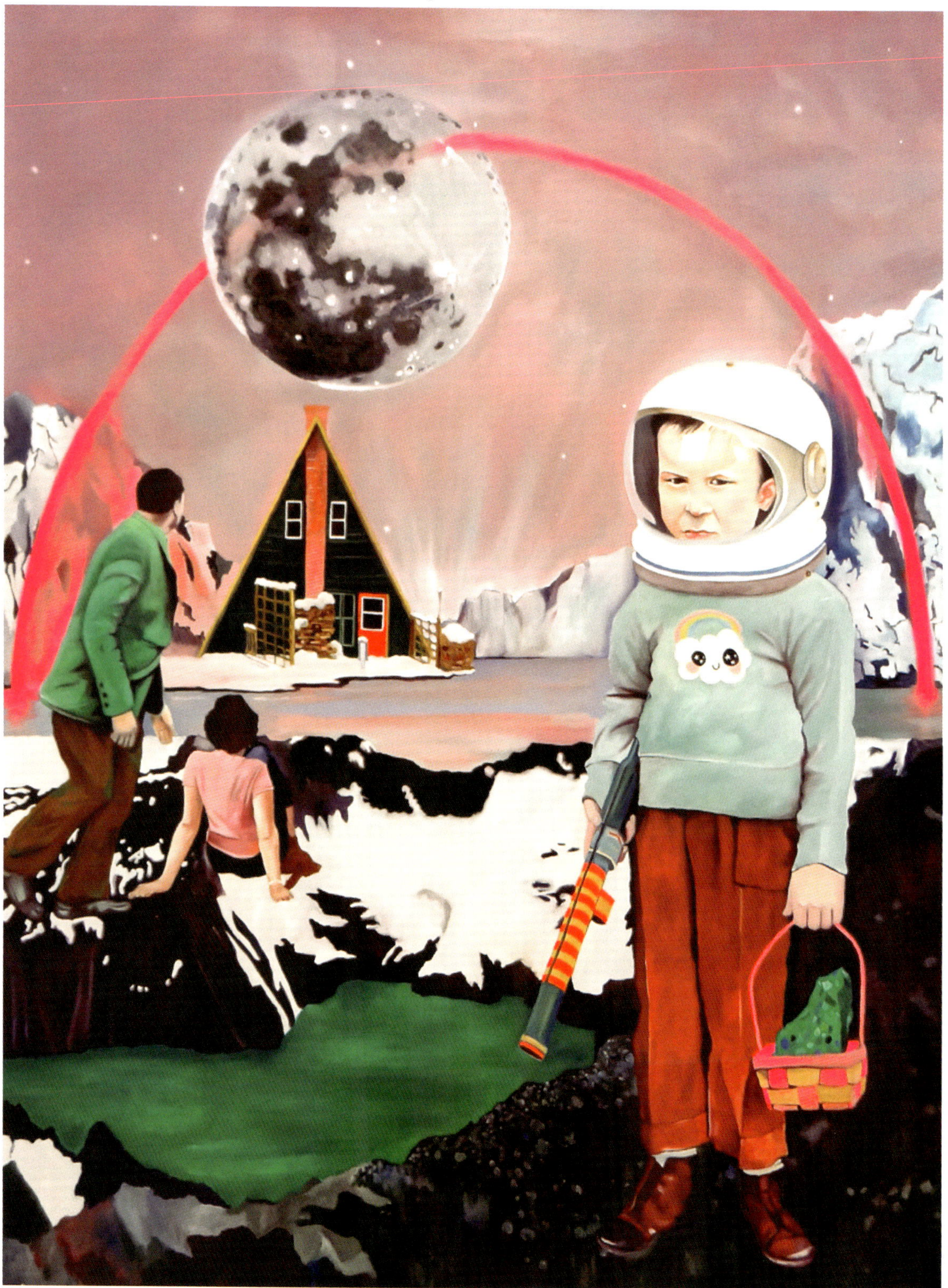

left: Space Traveler // *right:* Pug Spooks

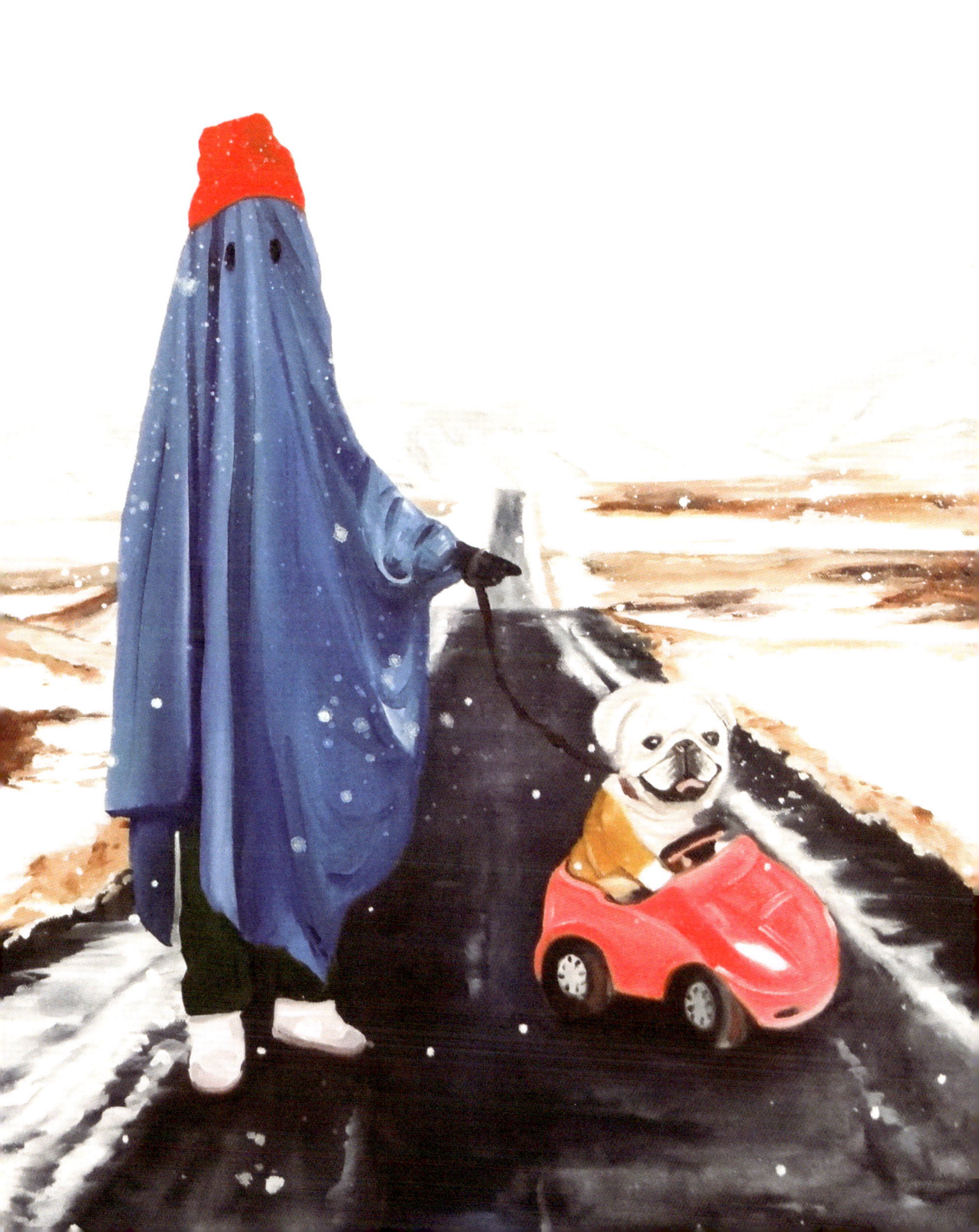

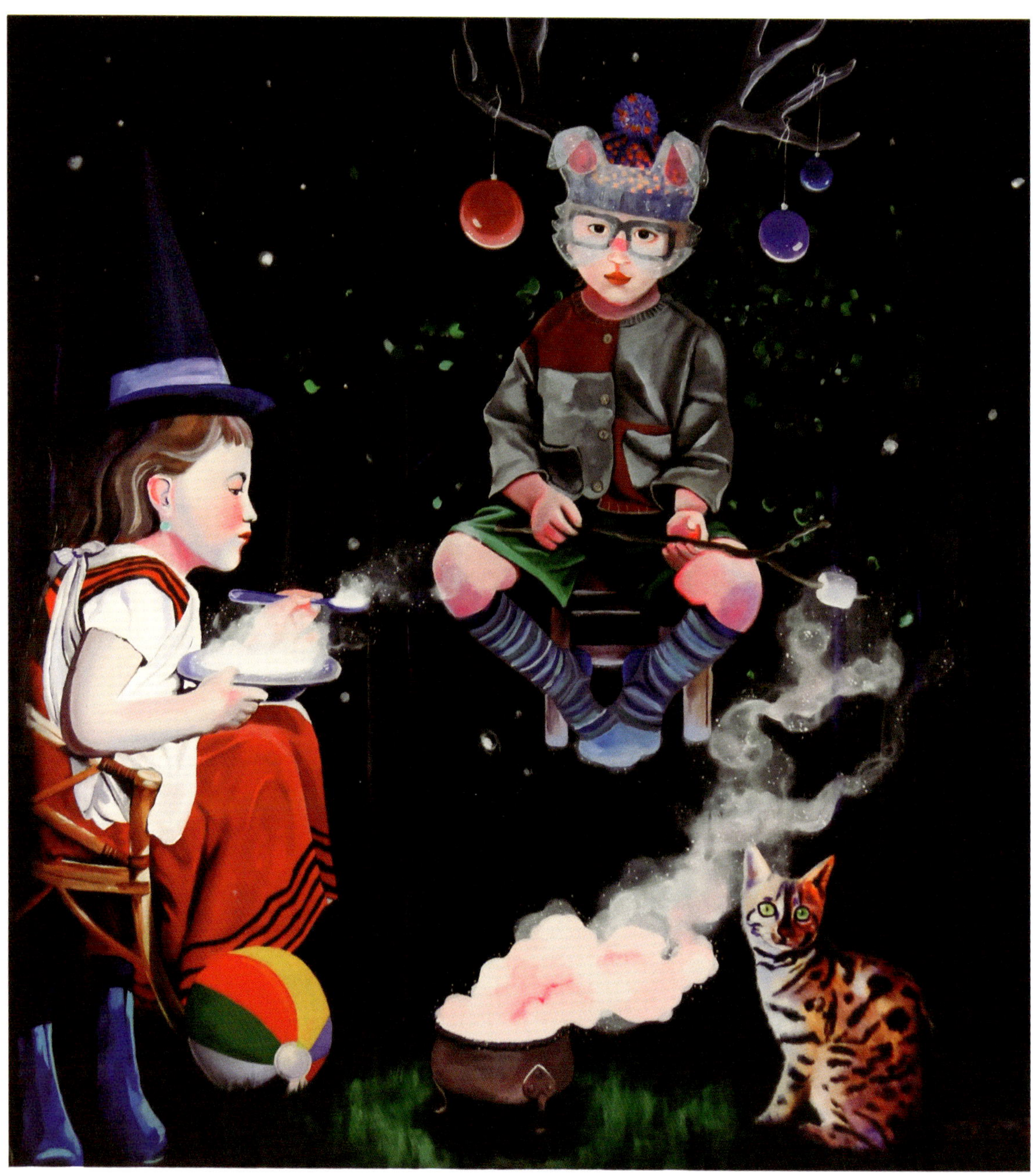

Hocus Pocus

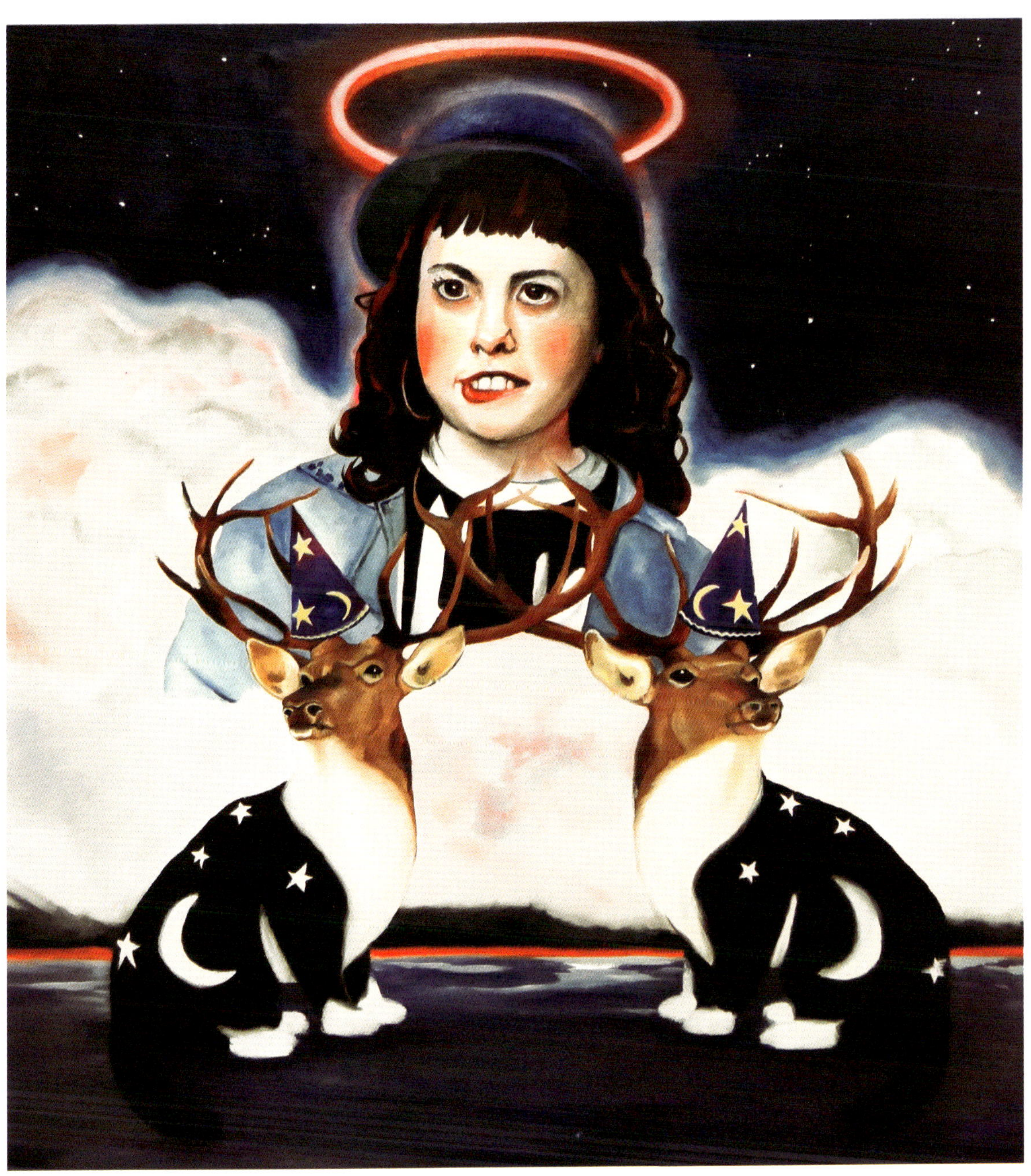

Cosmic Flake // ***next page:*** Electric candy

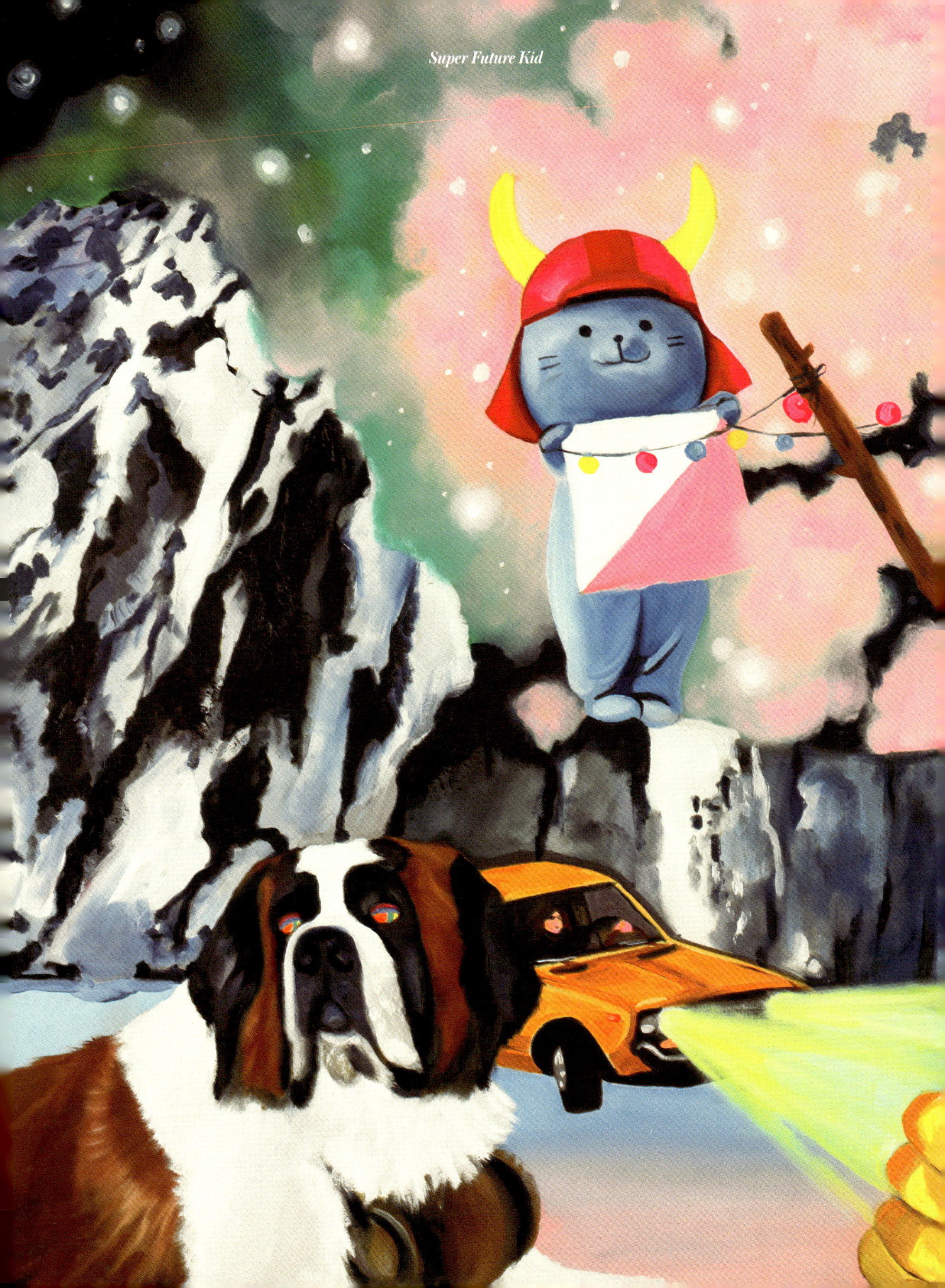
Super Future Kid

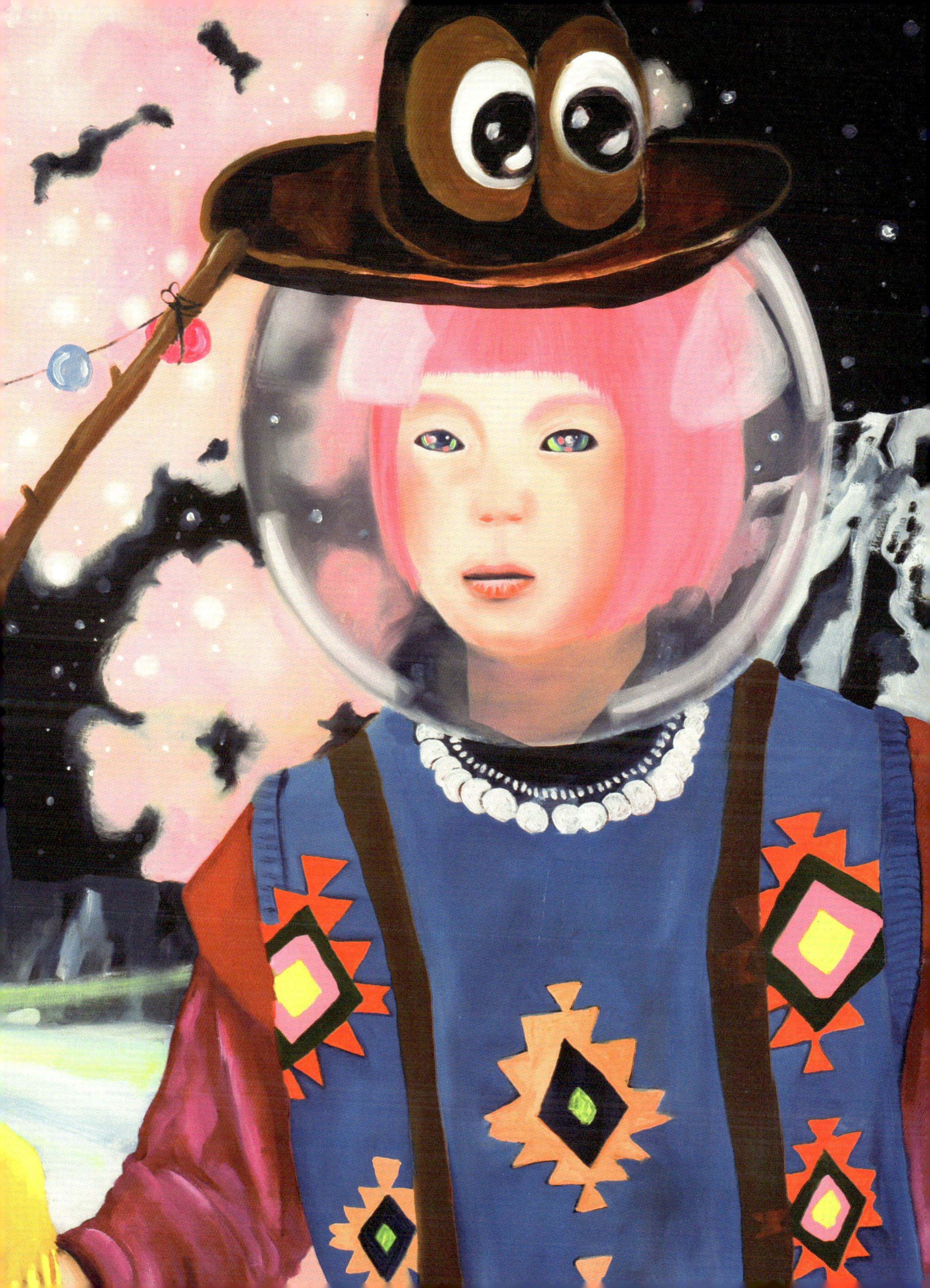

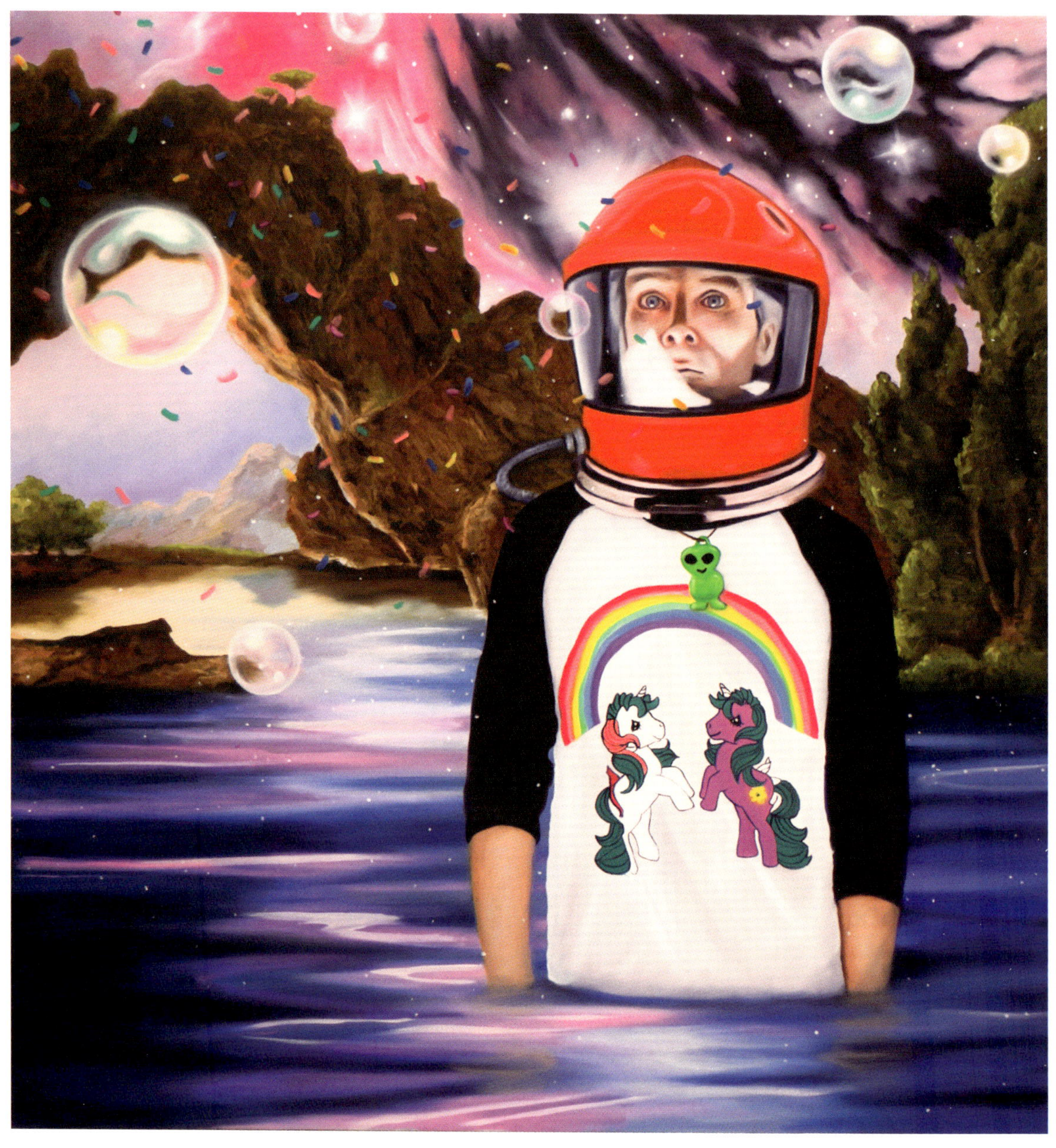

left: The other end of the spectrum // *right:* Universal hunter

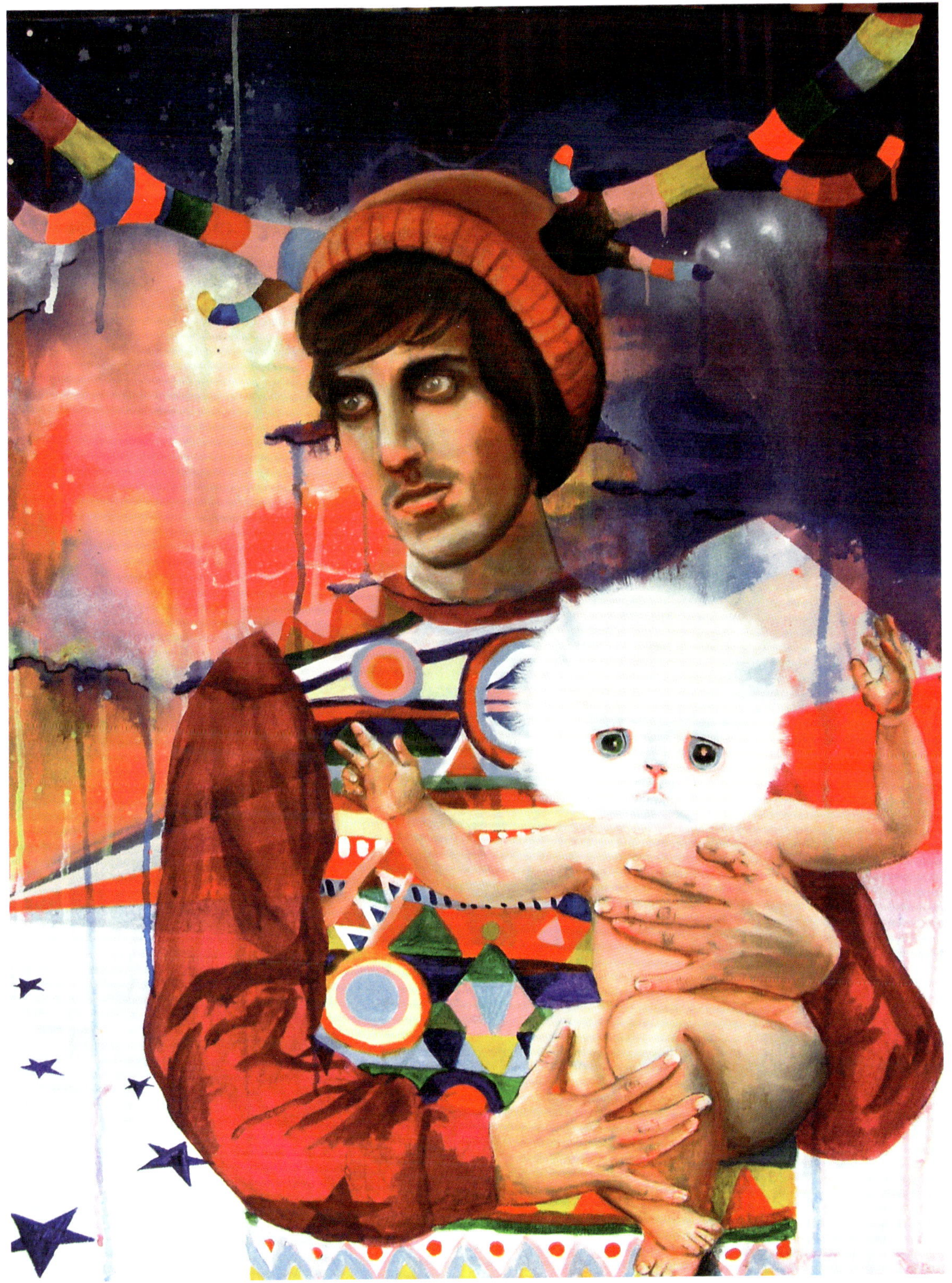

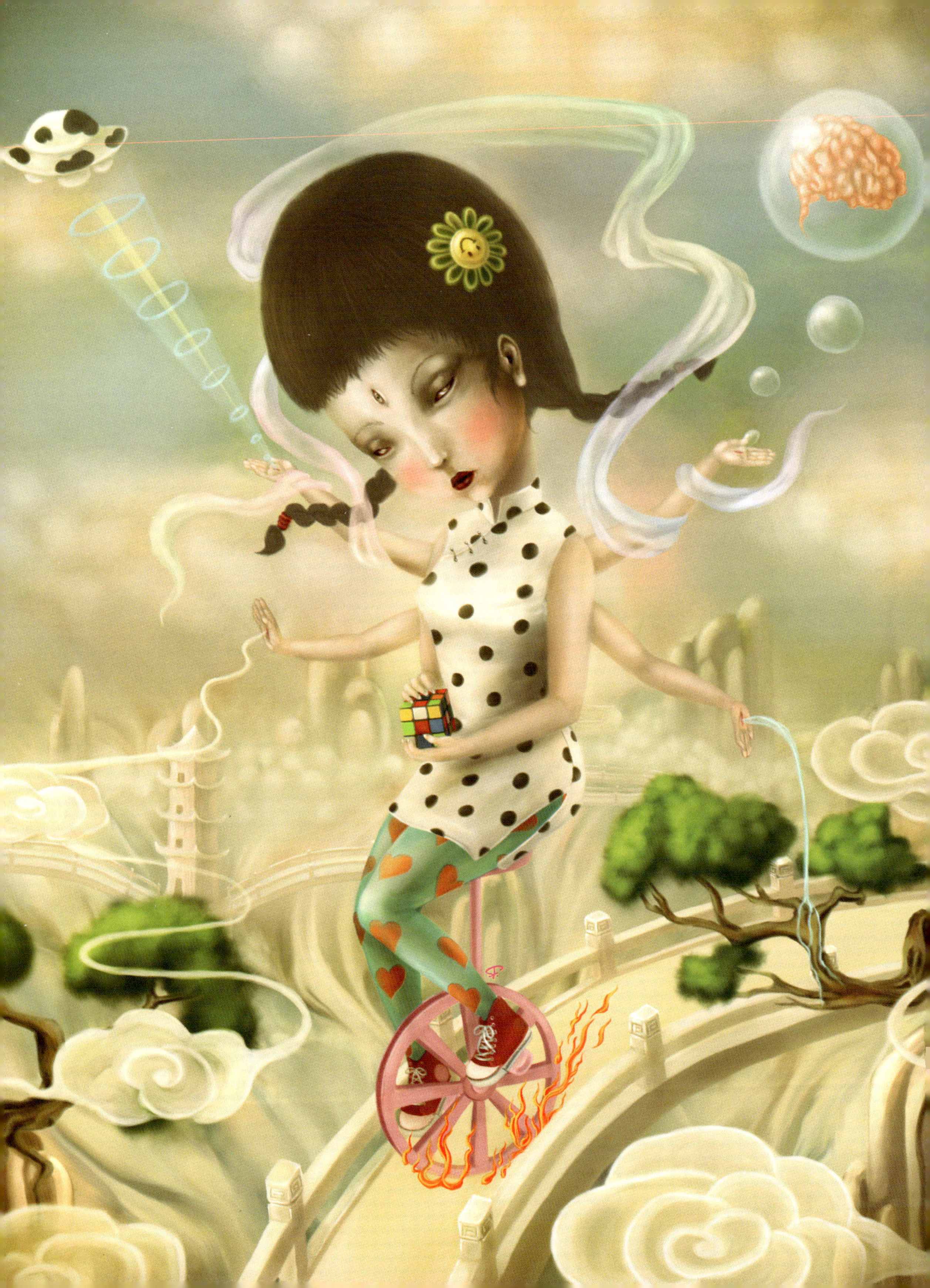

www.sonyafu.com
sonyafu.tumblr.com

Sonya Fu

Fu Man Yi (a.k.a. Sonya FU, b.1982) is a visual artist from Hong Kong. Growing up in the former British Colony where East meets West, Fu is influenced by both Oriental and Western culture. Starting from 2010, Fu has exhibited in many art galleries and international art fairs around the world. Fu's work has been featured in many art publications including *Curvy*, *Beautiful Bizarre Magazine* and the *Semi-Permanent* art books. In 2011, Fu was endorsed by *Semi-Permanent* Hong Kong as a notable and emerging artist. In the same year, Fu was awarded with *Perspective Magazine's* '40 Under 40' which celebrates top young creative talent throughout Asia.

Fu's chosen medium - digital painting - encompasses an intricate technique which Fu paints with very detailed and delicate brushwork. Being heavily inspired by her dreams and spirituality, Fu blends her subject matters with symbolic metaphors and the unseen beauties she encounters during the transitional state between wakefulness and sleep. All of this combined introduces an eerie and obscure atmosphere in Fu's visual narratives.

Fu Man Yi (también conocida como Sonya FU, nacida en 1982) es una artista visual de Hong Kong. Creció en una Colonia Británica donde Oriente se encuentra con Occidente, Fu está influenciada tanto por la cultura oriental como por la occidental. Desde 2010, Fu ha expuesto en muchas galerías de arte y ferias internacionales de arte. La obra de Fu ha aparecido en publicaciones de arte como *Curvy*, *Beautiful Bizarre Magazine* y los libros de arte *Semi-Permanent*. En 2011, Fu fue avalada por *Semi-Permanent* Hong Kong como una artista notable y emergente. En el mismo año, fue galardonada por el programa '40 Under 40' de la revista *Perspective*, que homenajea a los mejores jóvenes talentos creativos en Asia.

El medio escogido por Fu, la pintura digital, abarca una técnica compleja que Fu pinta con una pincelada muy detallada y delicada. Estando fuertemente inspirada por sus sueños y espiritualidad, Fu mezcla sus temas con metáforas simbólicas y bellezas invisibles que encuentra durante el estado de transición entre la vigilia y el sueño. Combinando todo esto, en las narrativas visuales de Fu se introduce una atmósfera misteriosa y oscura.

▸ It's a Beautiful Day, *digital painting*

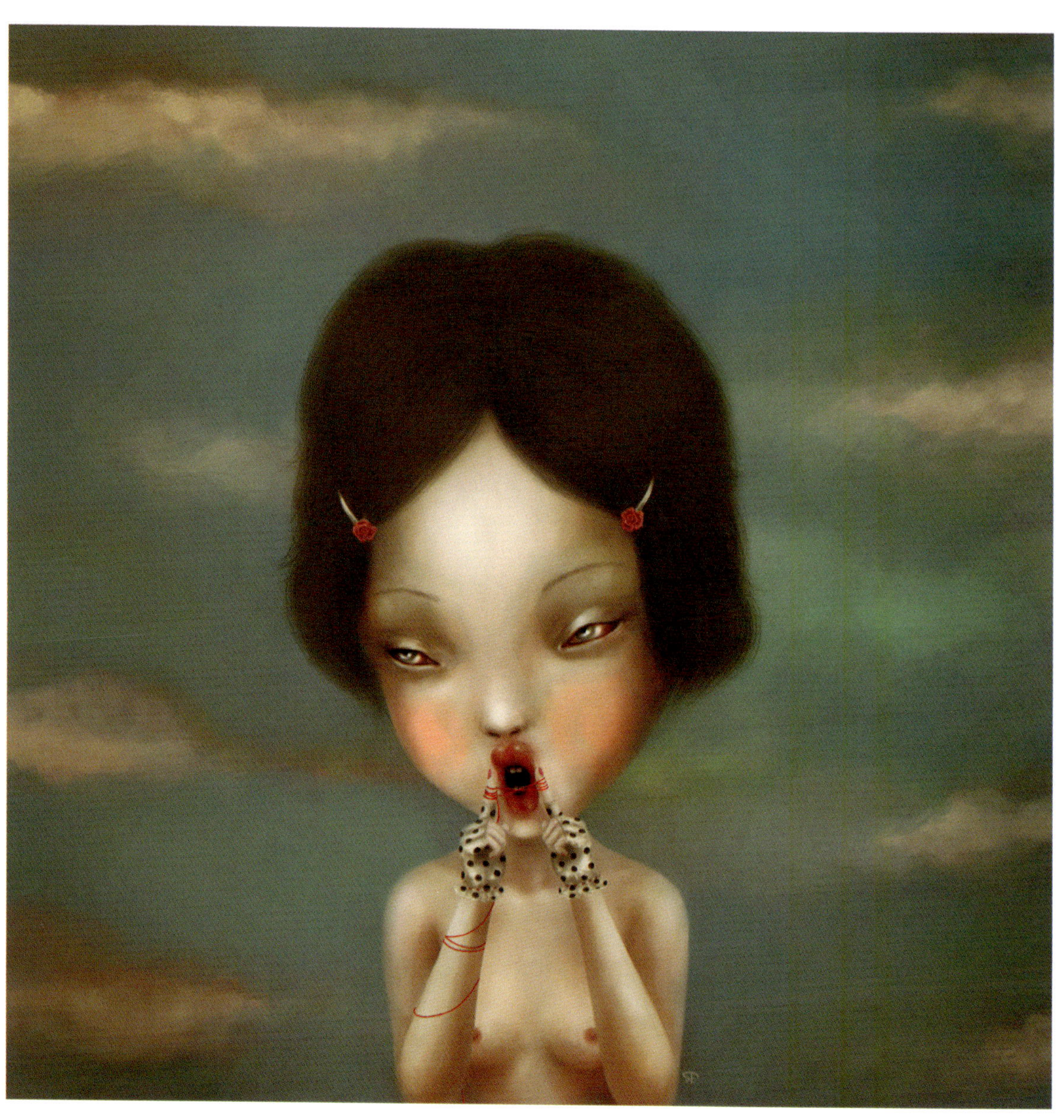

Better Left Unsaid, *digital painting*

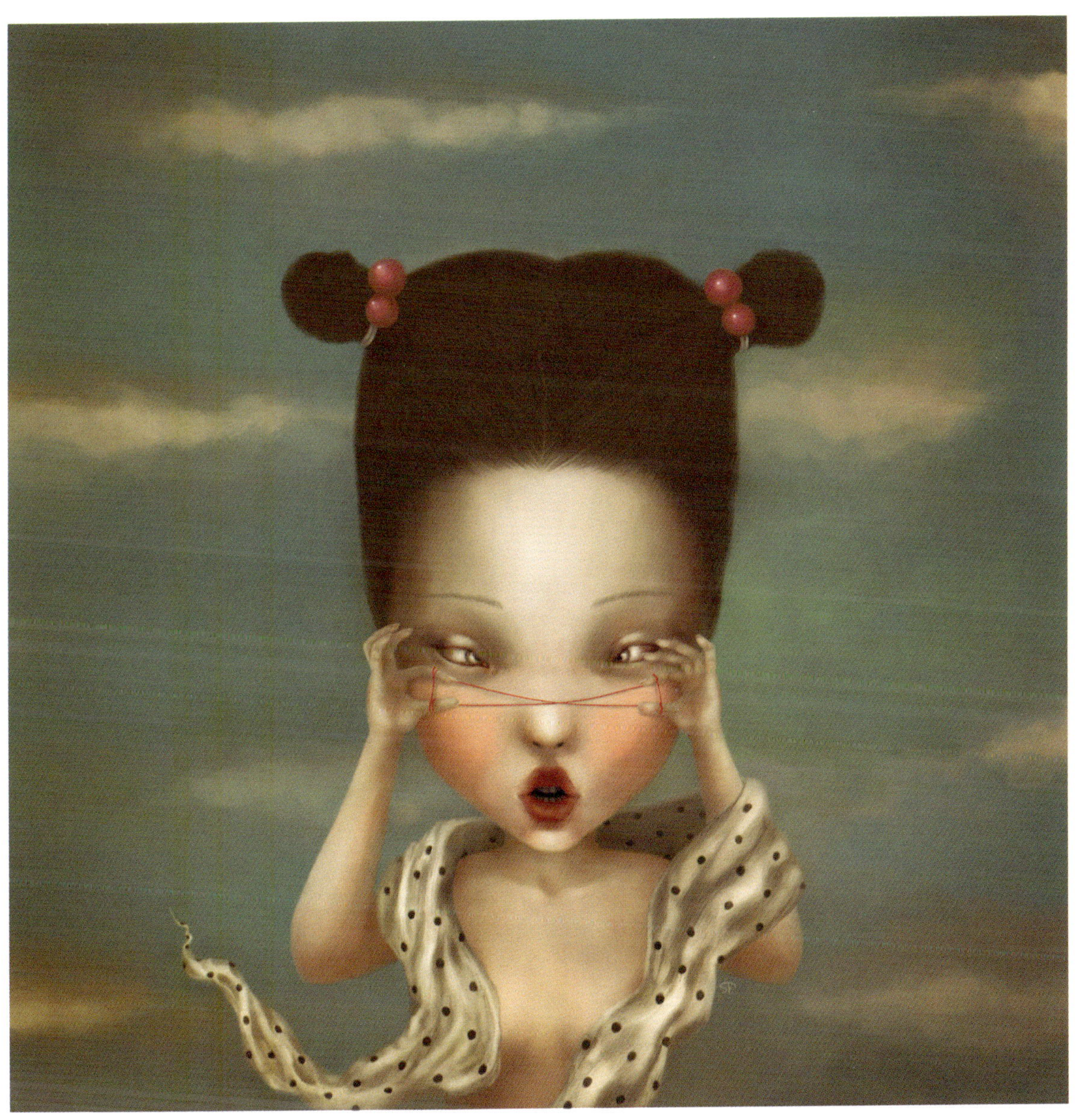

Better Left Unseen, *digital painting*

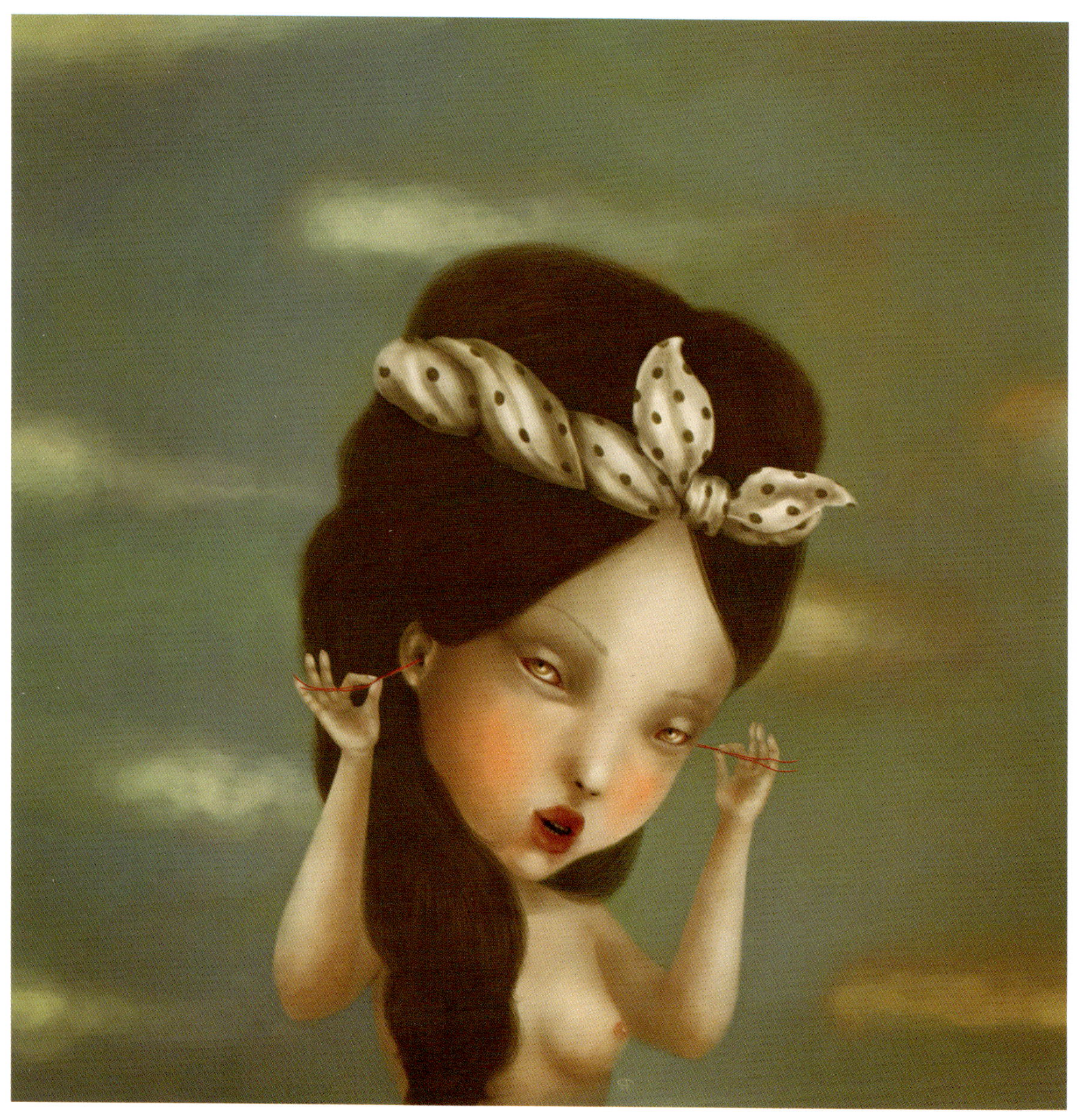

left: Better Left Unheard, *digital painting* // *right:* Sweetheart, in the end, *digital painting*

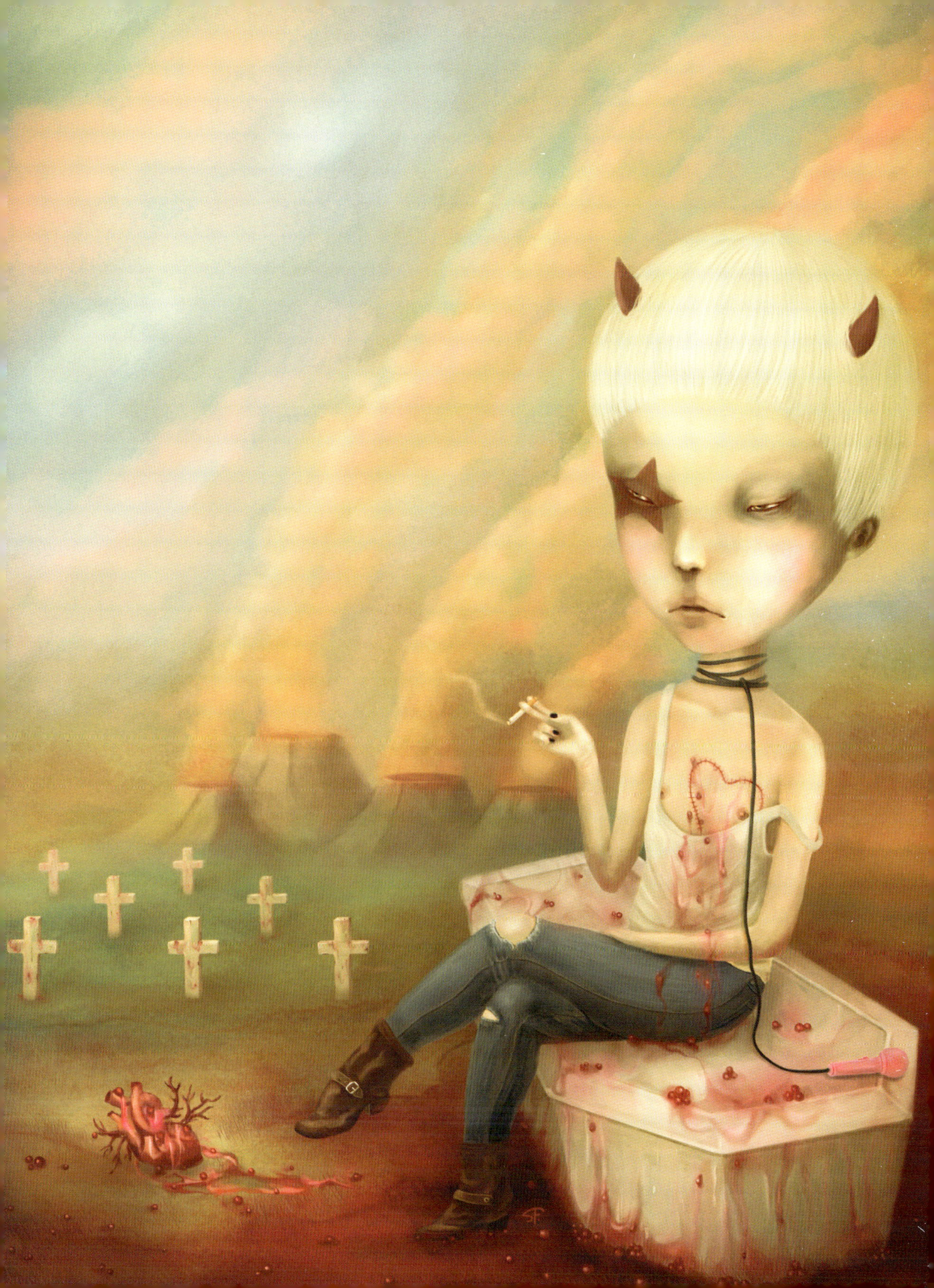

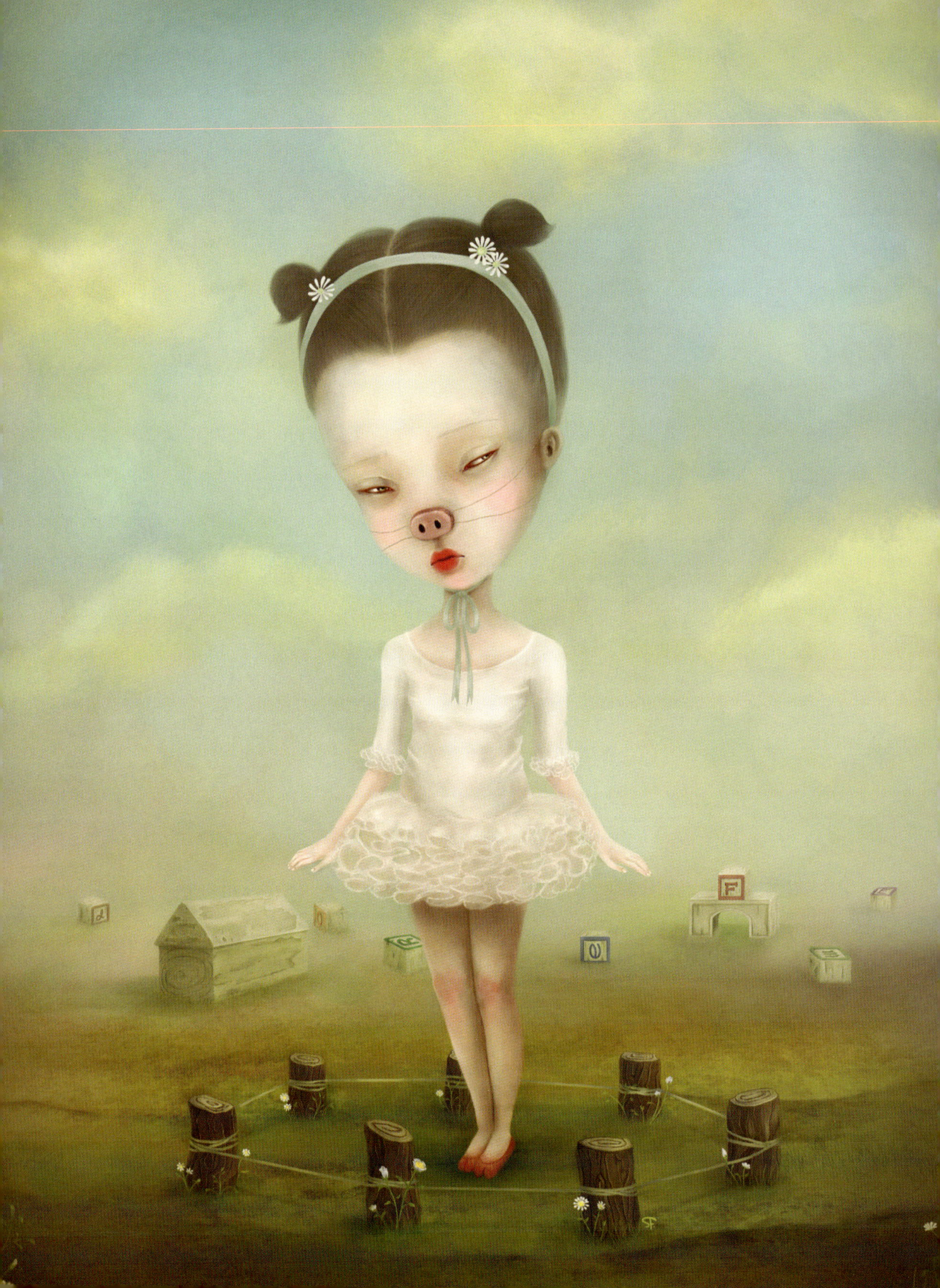
F

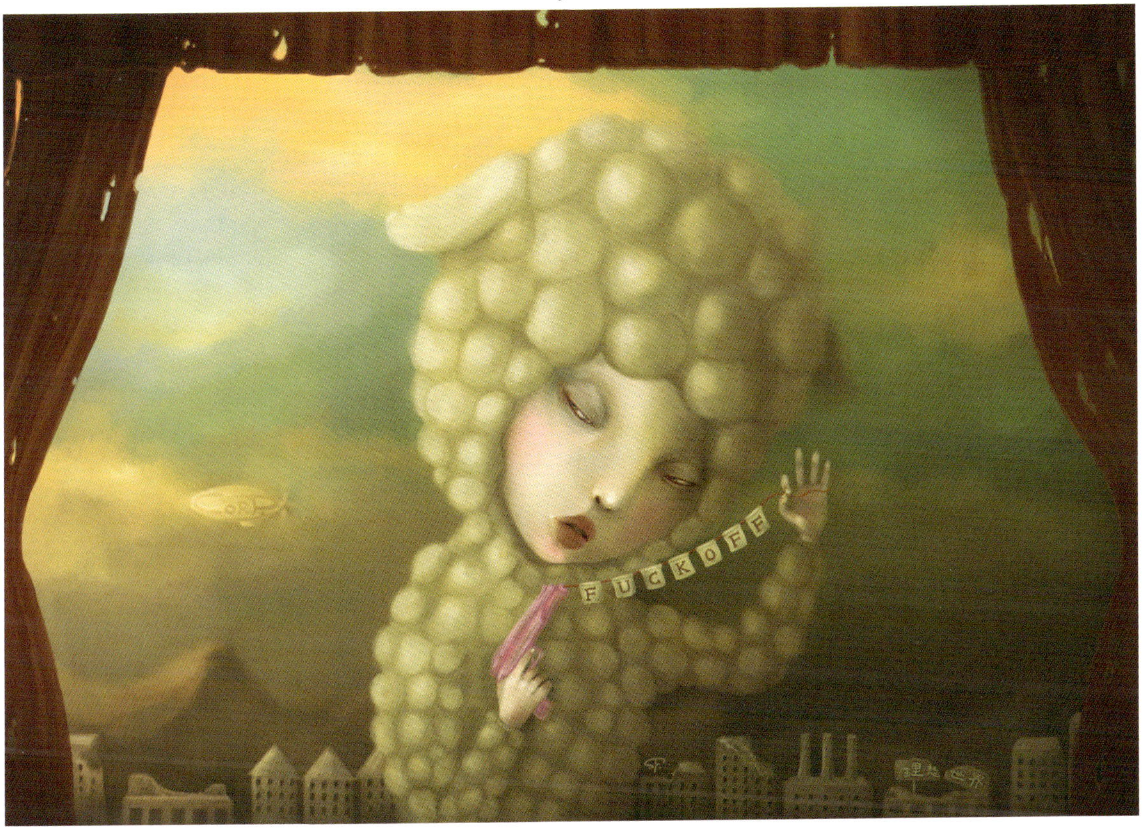

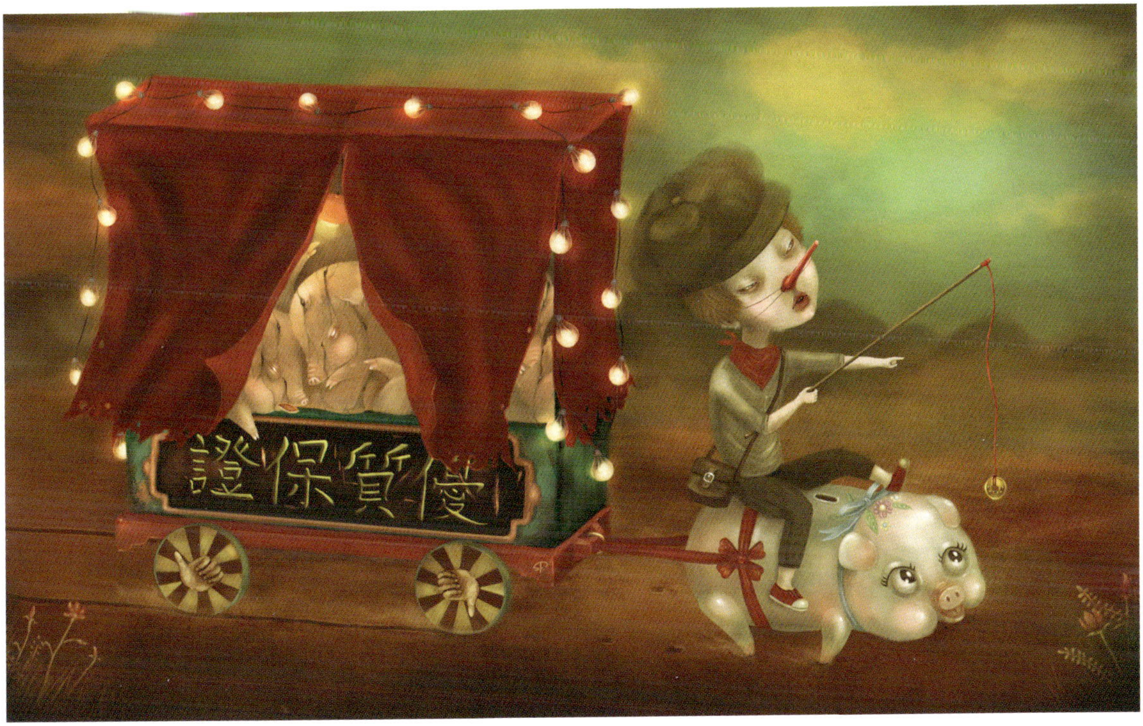

left: Play Dumb // ***right, top:*** Fxxk Off Okay?, ***bottom:*** Quality Checked, *digital paintings*

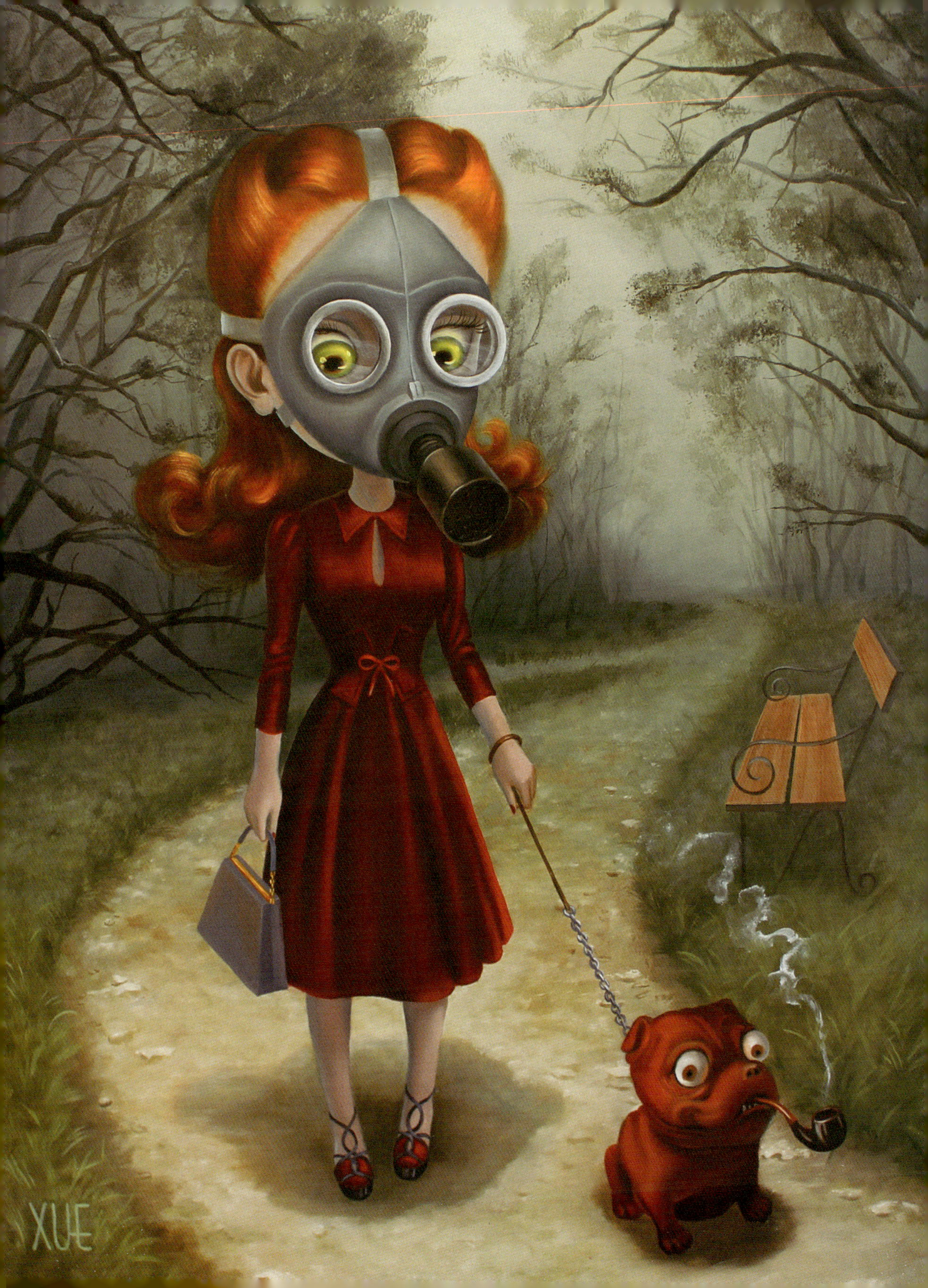
XUE

xuewang.weebly.com
Facebook fan page: XUE WANG Art's Page

Xue Wang

Having established herself in the international art market, Xue Wang is currently involved in producing her spellbinding imagery with Washington Green Fine Art & Castle Galleries in the UK. Her work has been exhibited in galleries as far afield in the UK, Australia and California USA.

Xue was born in China in 1980 and relocated to London to finish her studies in fashion design. After completing her degrees she worked as a fashion designer.Painting and drawing, playing around with ideas, juxtaposing images and allowing her imagination free reign have all helped guide her development. The self-reflective intimacy of art, which has always been latent in her, forced Xue's transition from fashion to painting. Her academic painting technique using glazes and fine detailing is essentially self-taught.

Xue's creative impulse "is driven by a fascination with childhood paraphernalia: dolls, toys, fairy tales, stage sets, fun fairs, found objects mixed with whimsy". In the artist's hands the cute and creepy meld. Classic Hollywood iconography is given a gothic twist; princesses stare out from dark towers in gloomy silence while spooky-eyed dolls cavort together. There is an edgy state of unease to it all.

"Any search for particular meaning in my idiosyncratic work may not yield much" she observes. And yet there is an enigma to her phantasmagorical vision. Xue's work speaks to the child in us but the message is an eerie one.

Habiéndose establecido en el mercado internacional del arte, Xue Wang está actualmente involucrada en la elaboración de su hechizante imaginería con la editorial Washington Green Fine Art y las galerías Castle en el Reino Unido. Su obra ha sido expuesta en galerías de el Reino Unido, Australia y California (EE.UU).

Xue nació en China en 1980 y se trasladó a Londres para terminar sus estudios en diseño de moda. Después de terminar su carrera, trabajó como diseñadora de moda. Pintar, dibujar, jugar con ideas, yuxtaponer imágenes y permitir que su imaginación vaya por libre, han ayudado a guiar su desarrollo. La intimidad auto-reflexiva del arte, que siempre ha estado latente en ella, obligó a Xue a pasar de la moda a la pintura. Su técnica de pintura académica utilizando veladuras y detalles finos es esencialmente autodidacta.

El impulso creativo de Xue "se guia por una fascinación con la parafernalia de la infancia: muñecas, juguetes, cuentos de hadas, mezclados con fantasía". Se fusionan lo bonito y lo espeluznante. A la iconografía clásica de Hollywood se le da un giro gótico; las princesas miran desde torres oscuras en sombrío silencio mientras que las muñecas de ojos fantasmagóricos retozan juntas. En todo ello se aprecia un estado inquieto de malestar.

"En mi obra no se produce ninguna búsqueda de un significado particular", advierte Xue. Y, sin embargo, hay un enigma en su visión fantasmagórica. La obra de Xue habla al niño que tenemos dentro pero el mensaje es inquietante.

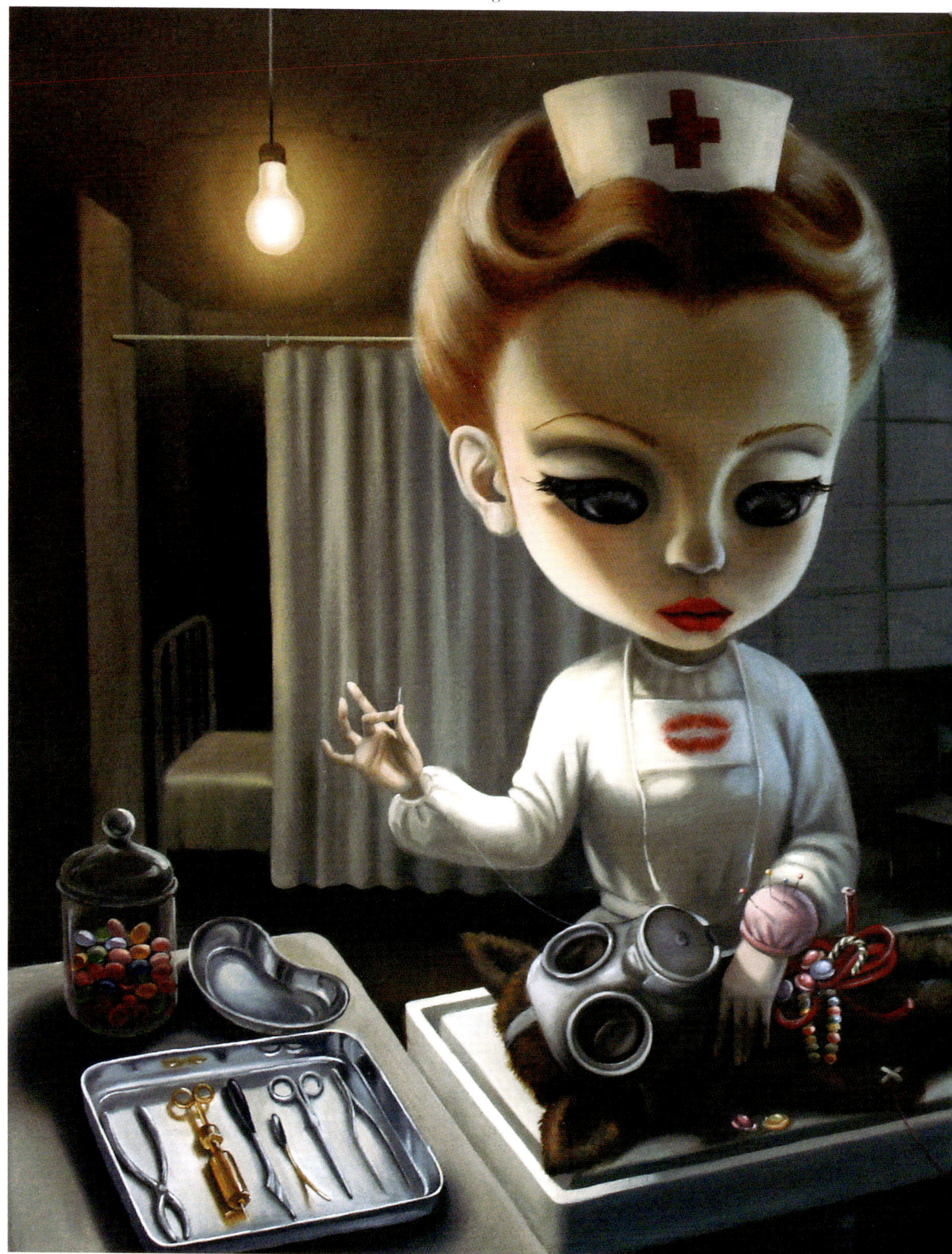

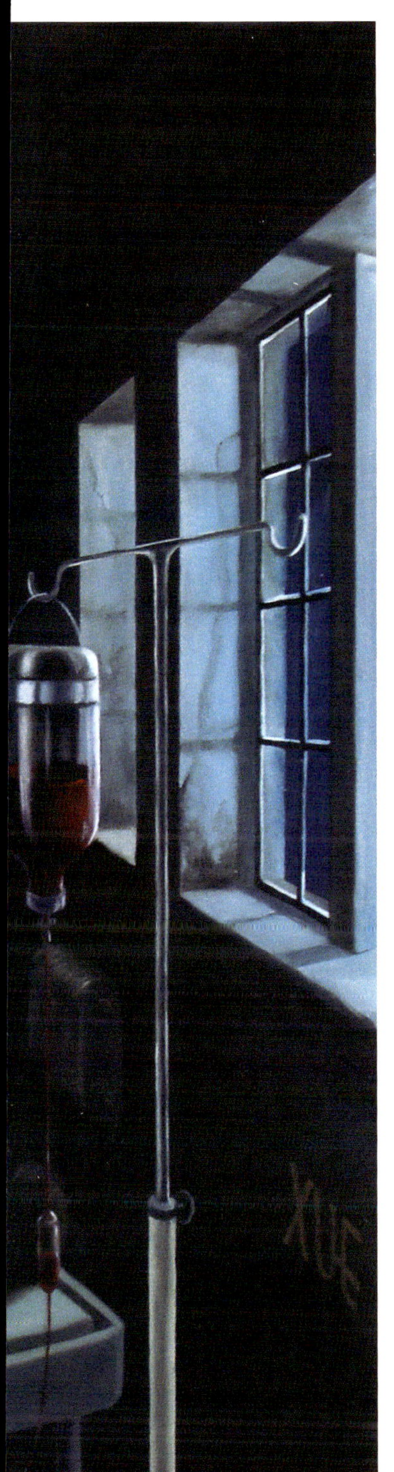

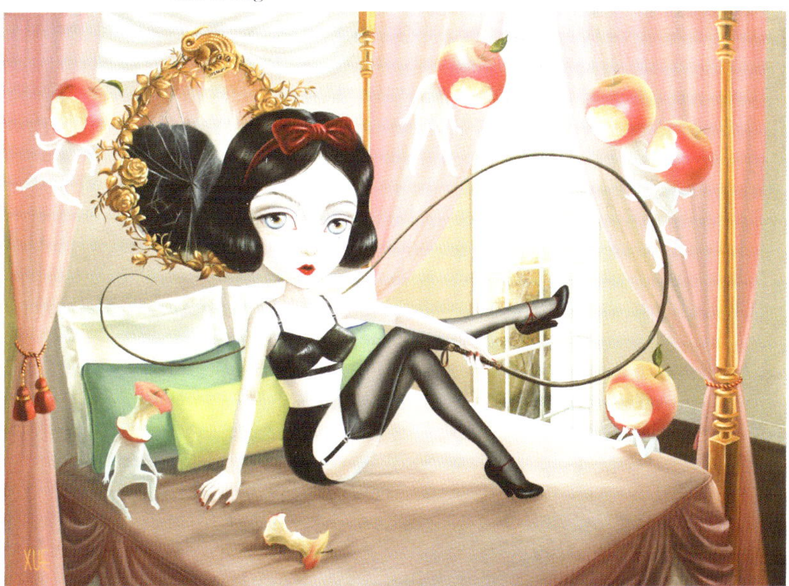

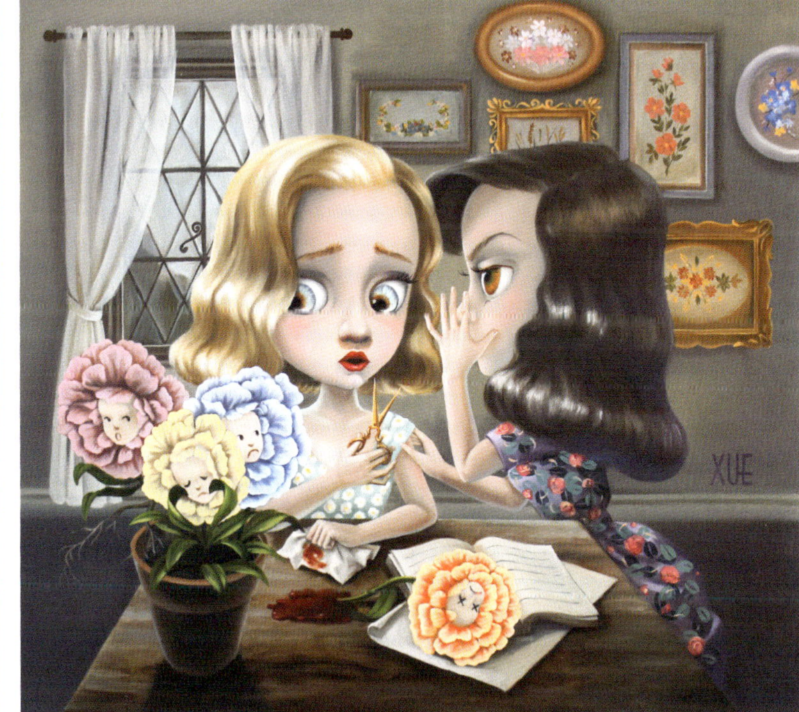

left: A Stitch in Time // *right, top:* 7 Years Good Luck, *bottom:* Abettor

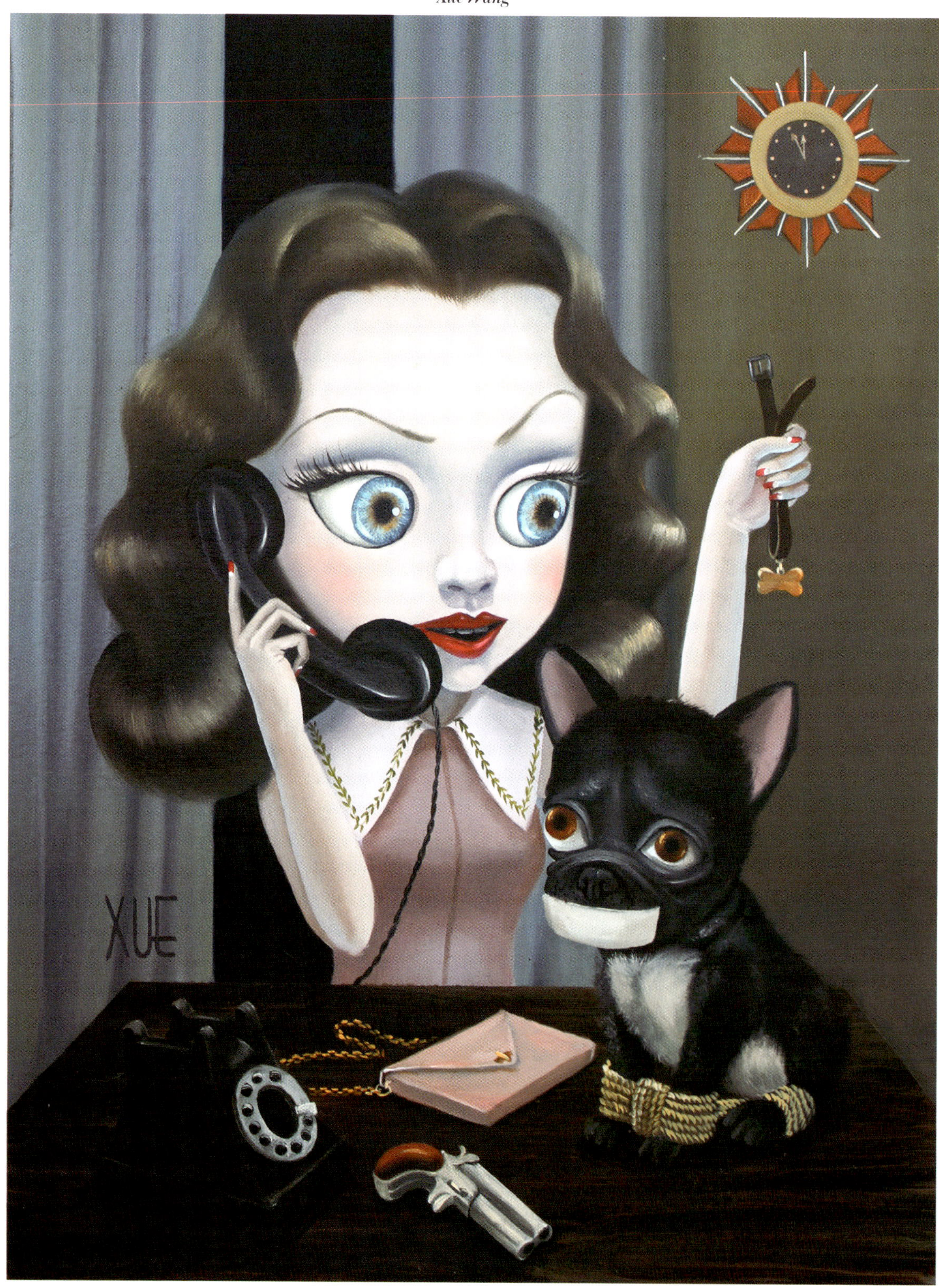

Fifteen Hundred Dollars in Used Notes

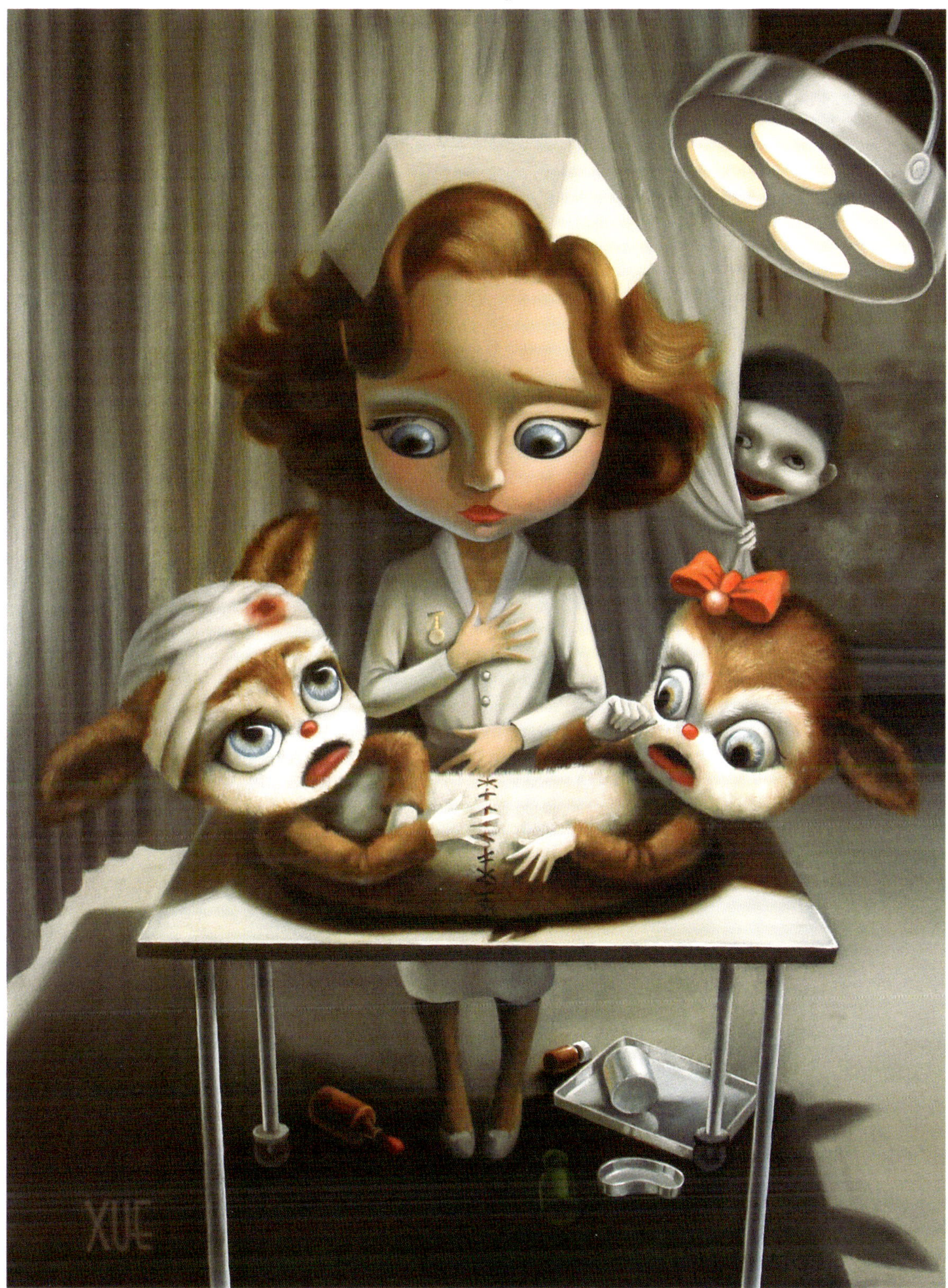

Rude Awakenings (detail)

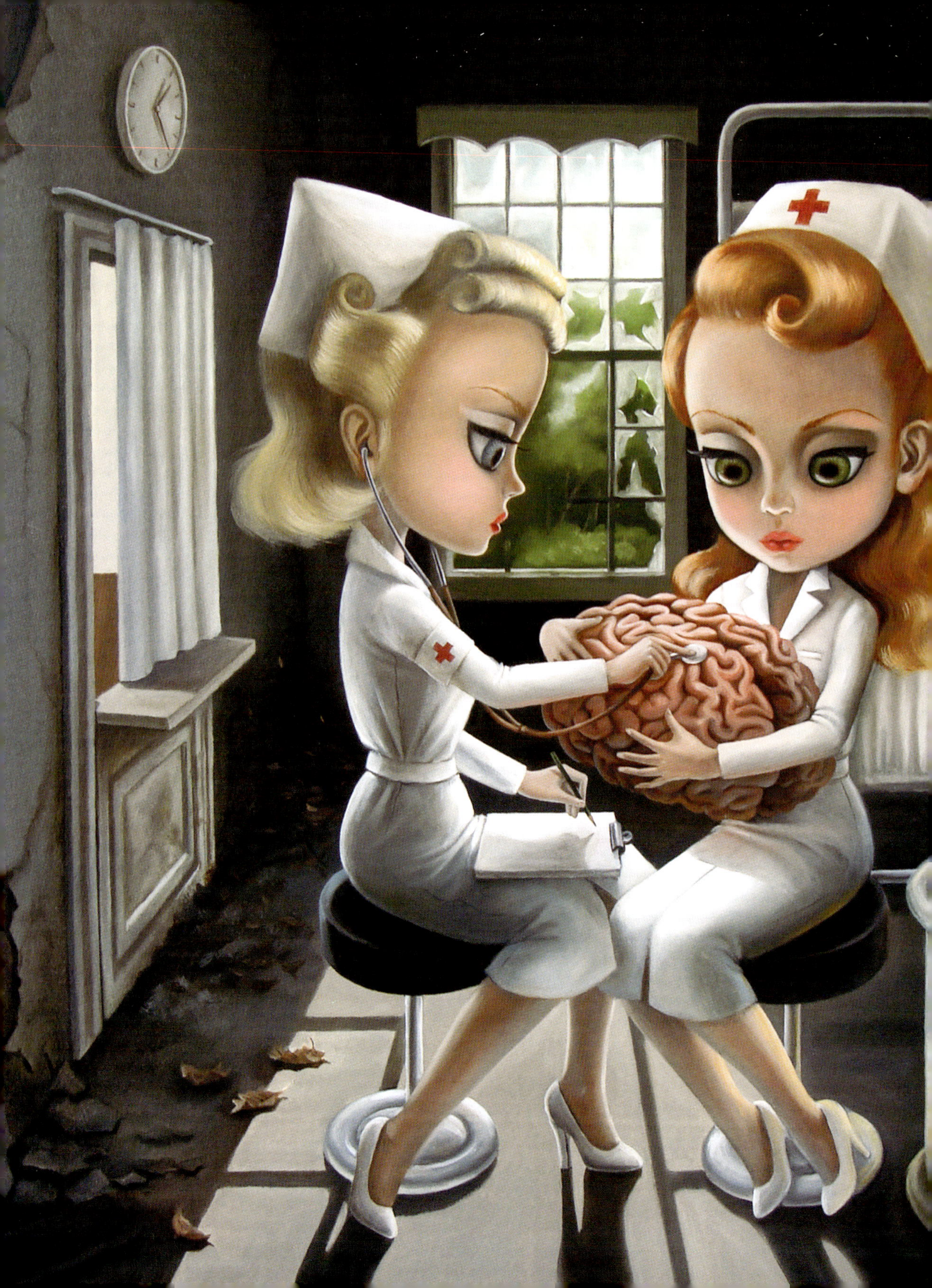

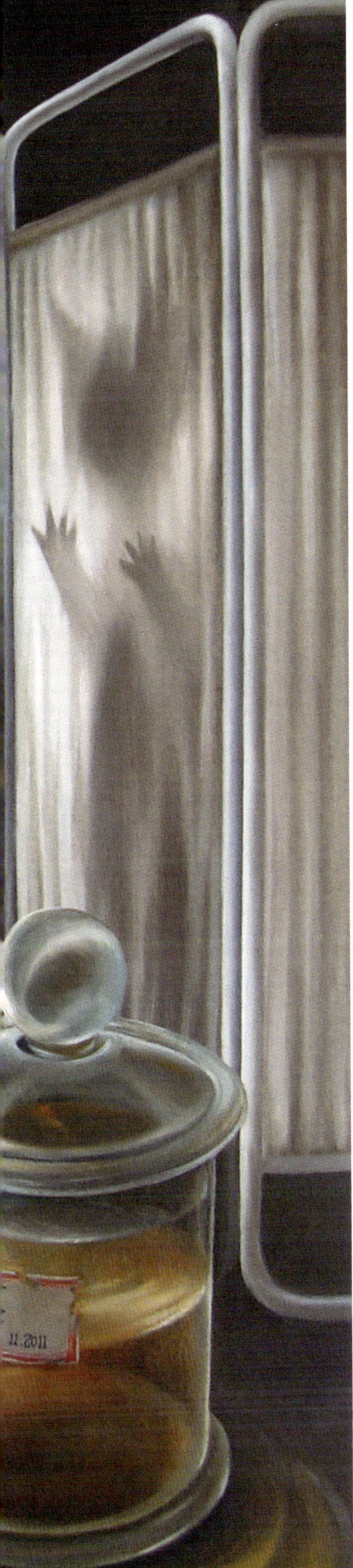

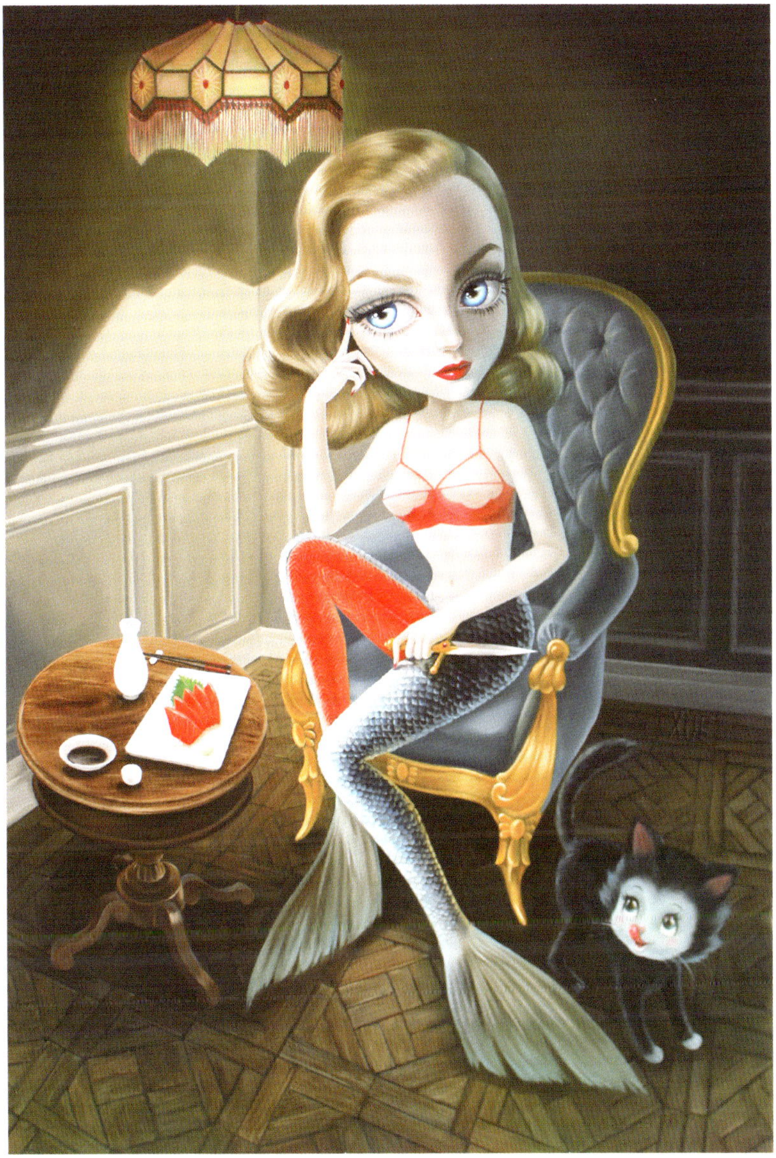

left: Intimate Thoughts // *right:* Tenfer Mercies

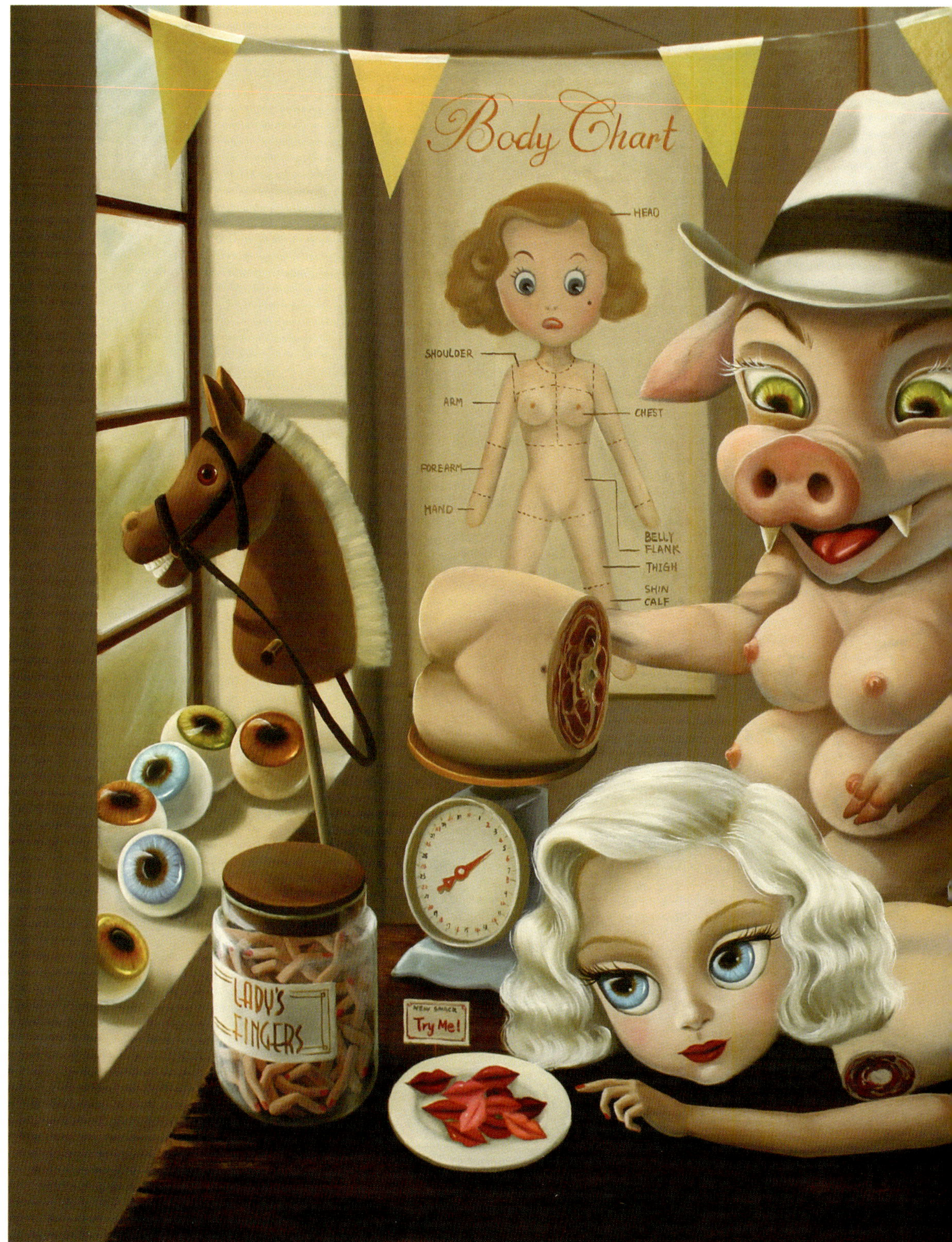
Body Chart
HEAD
SHOULDER
ARM
CHEST
FOREARM
HAND
BELLY
FLANK
THIGH
SHIN
CALF
LADY'S
FINGERS
NEW SNACK
Try Me!

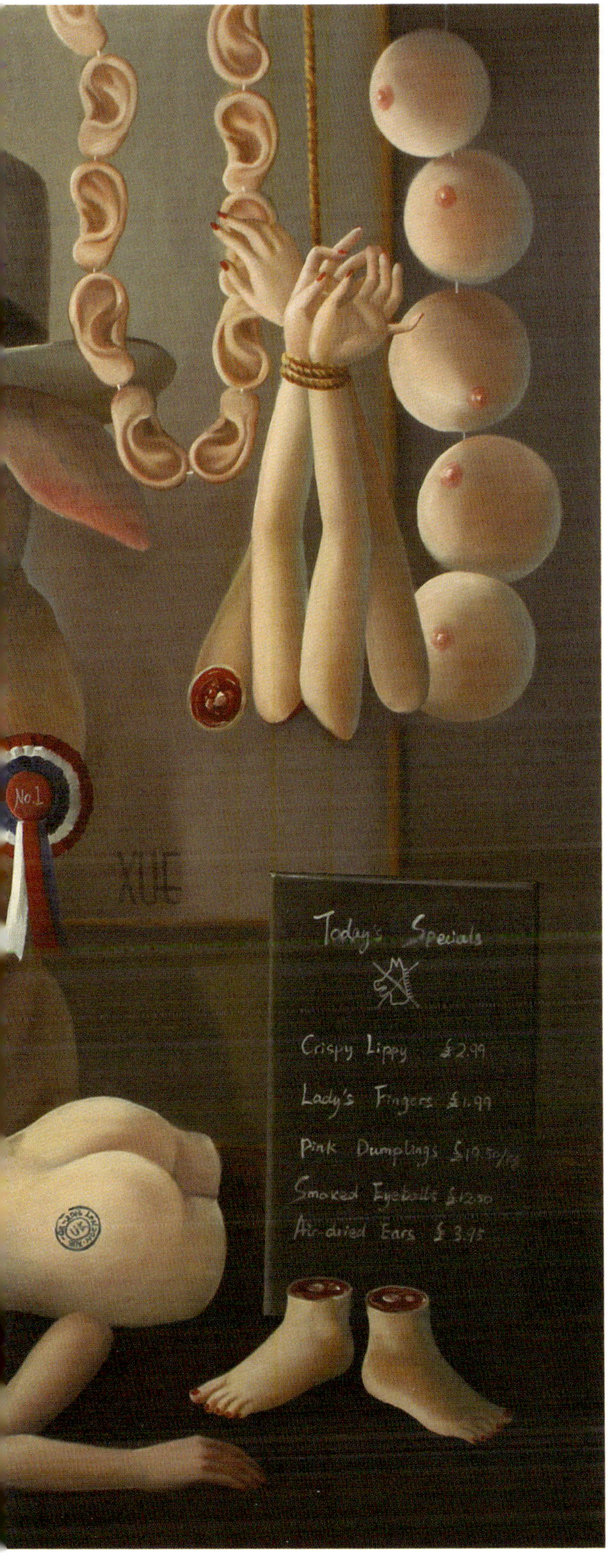

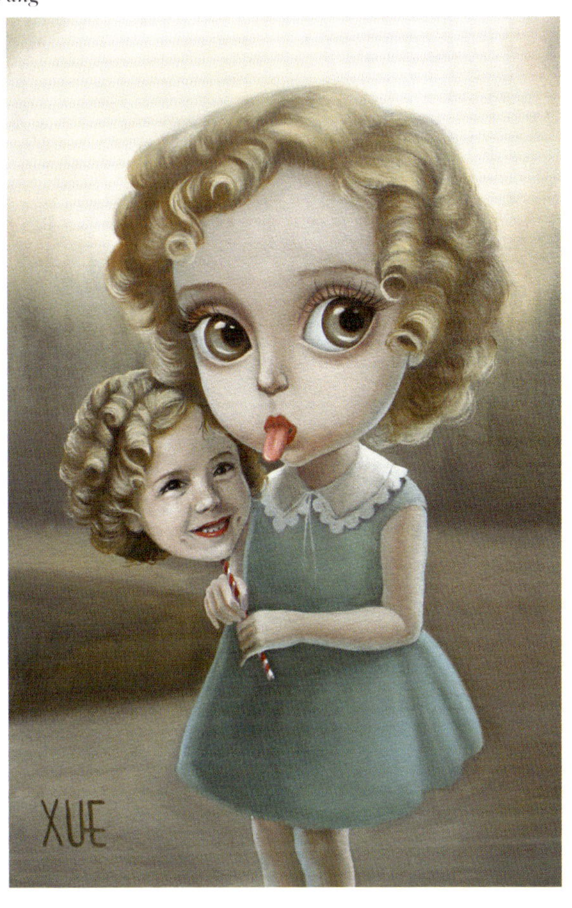

left: Prime Cuts // *right:* Lollipop

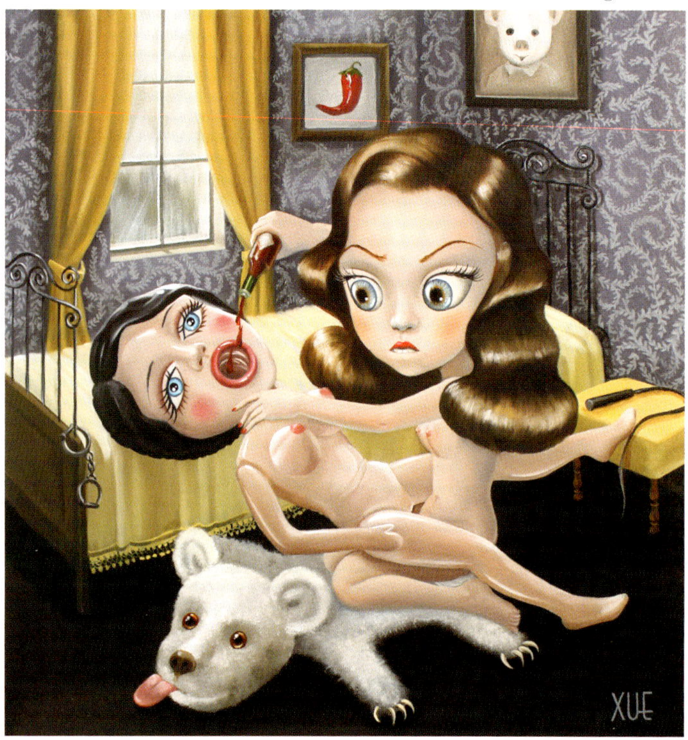

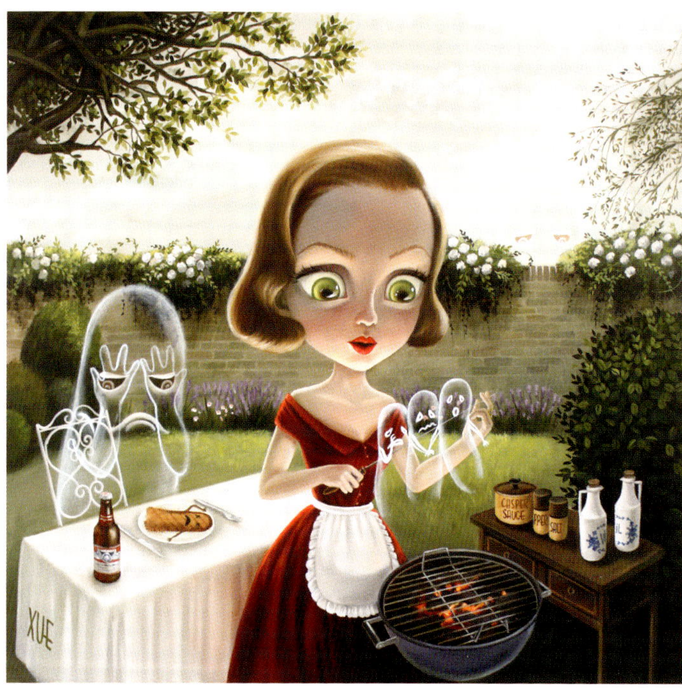

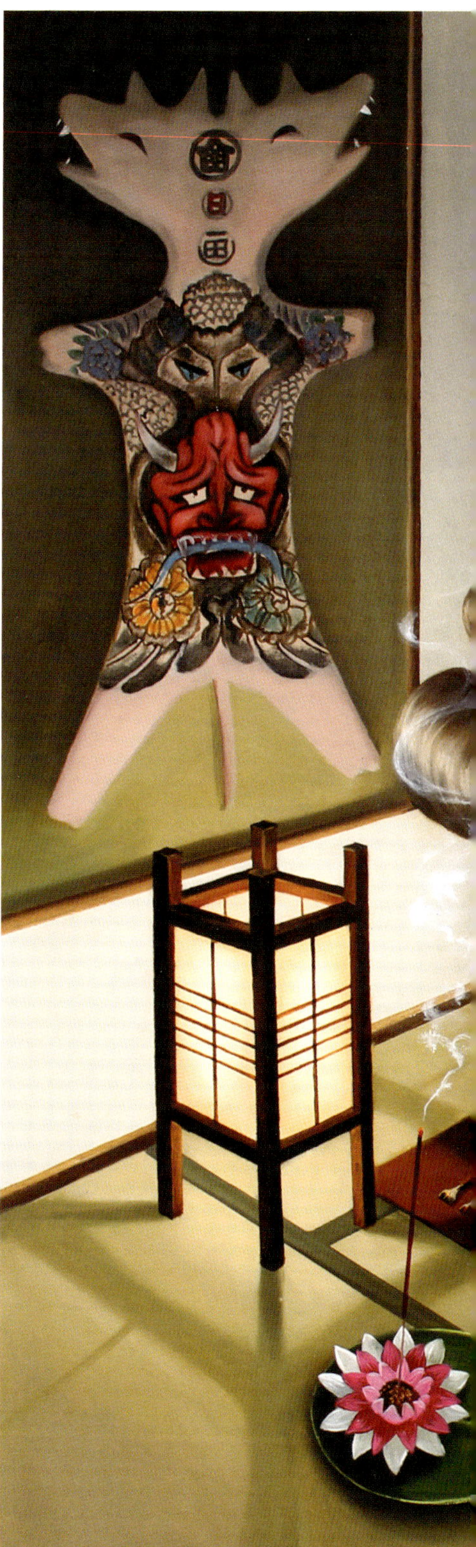

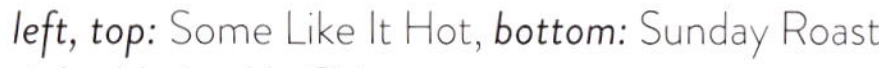
left, top: Some Like It Hot, ***bottom:*** Sunday Roast
right: Under My Skin

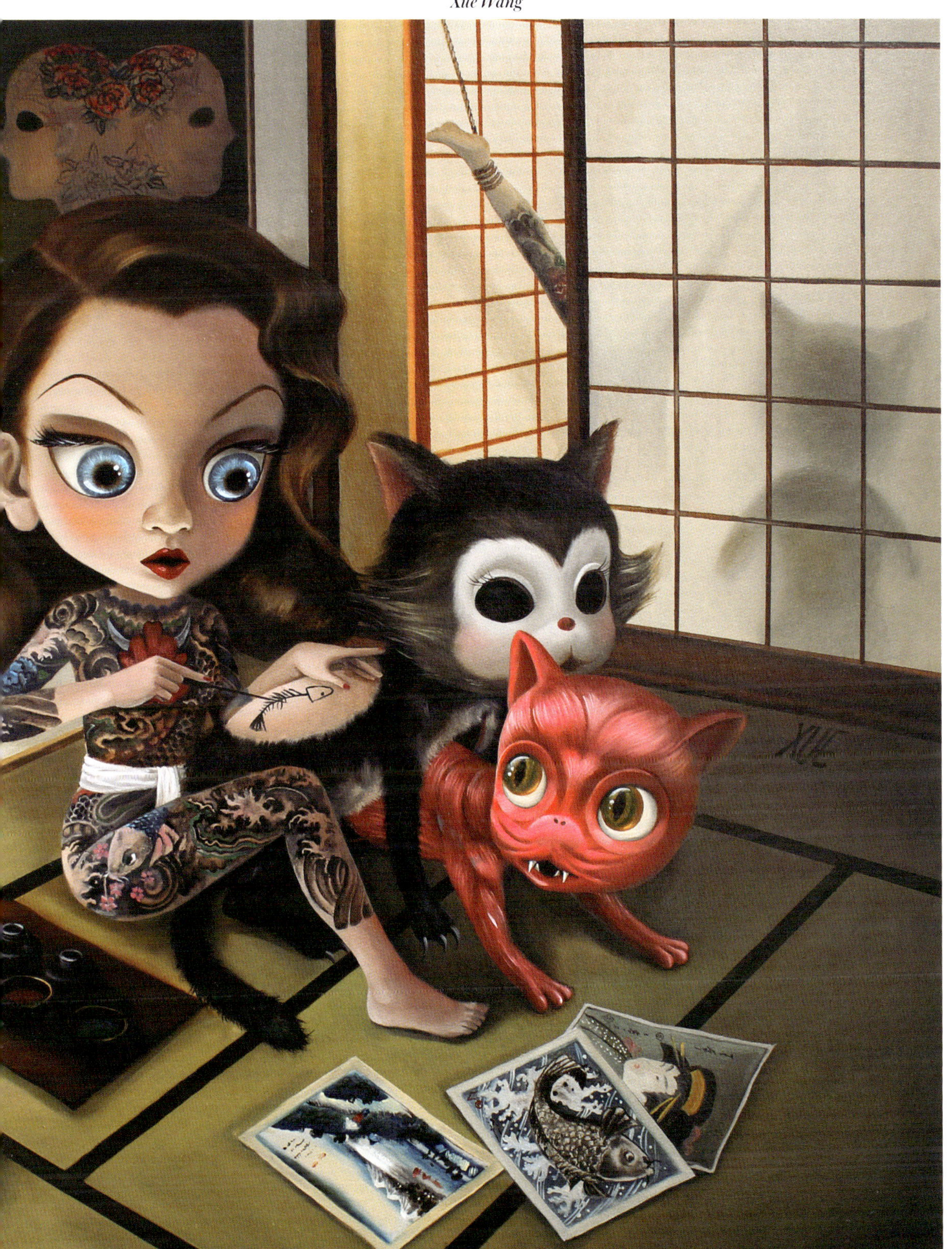

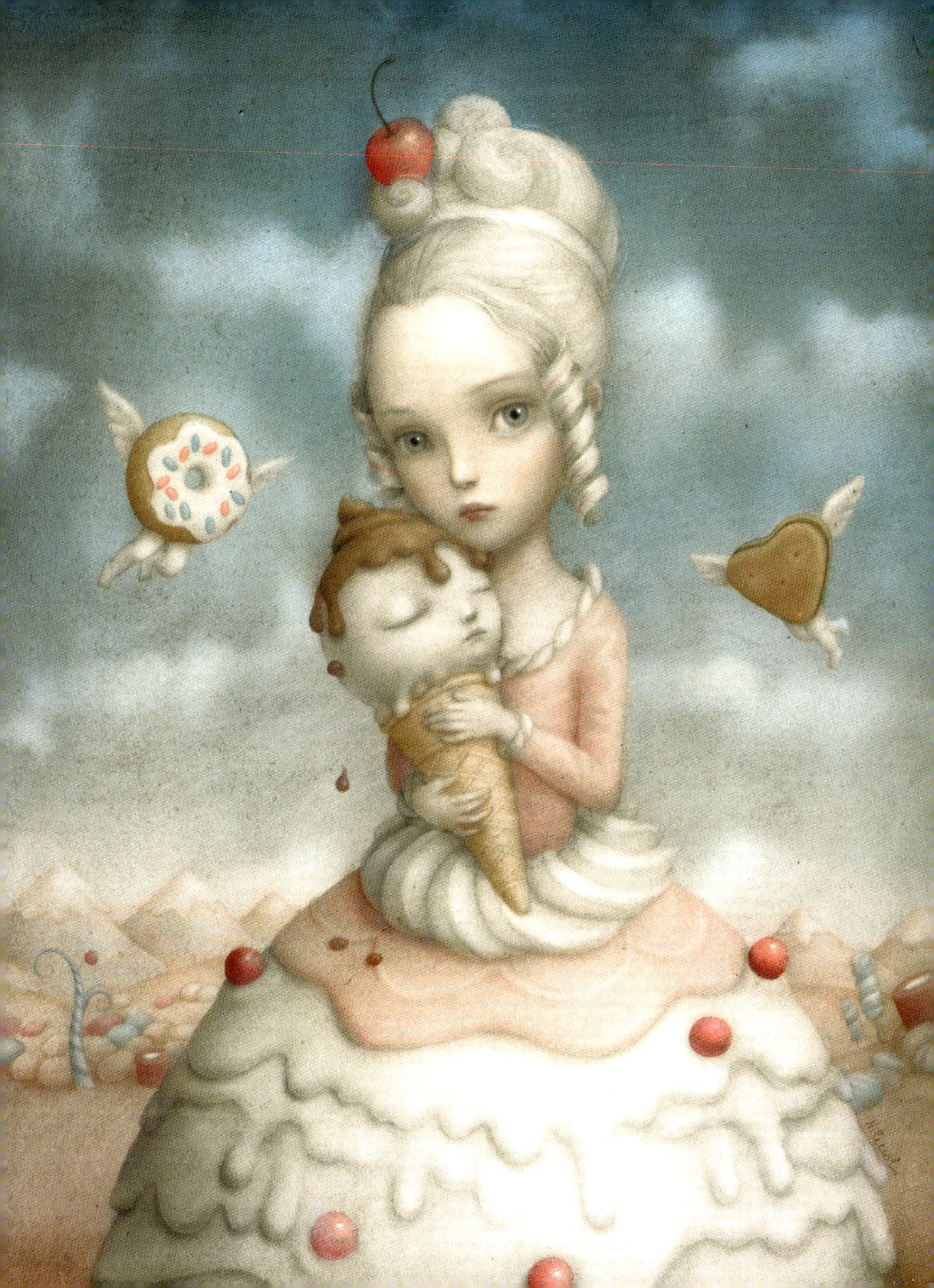

www.nicolettaceccoli.com

Nicoletta Ceccoli

Nicoletta Ceccoli born in the Republic of San Marino and she lives there. She graduated in animation from the Istituto d'Arte di Urbino.

In 1995, she started working as illustrator and, since then, she had illustrated more than 30 childen's books, picture books and created advertising illustrations for some of the main companies worldwide. Lately she also designed an animation film produced by Luc Besson in France 'Jack et la Mechanique du Coeur', directed by Stephane Berla and Mathias Malzieau.

Her art has been exhibited in galleries worldwide. Her work is whimsical tough disturbing plays with contraddictions, like the dark side of a nursery rhyme, a dream of lovely things with a hint of darkness.

Nicoletta Ceccoli nació en la República de San Marino y vive allí. Se graduó en animación en el Instituto de Arte de Urbino.

En 1995 empezó a trabajar como ilustradora y, desde entonces, ha ilustrado más de 30 libros infantiles, libros ilustrados e ilustraciones publicitarias creadas para algunas de las principales empresas del mundo. Recientemente también diseñó una película de animación producida por Luc Besson en Francia: "Jack y la mecánica del corazón", dirigida por Stephane Berla y Mathias Malzieau.

Su arte ha sido expuesto en galerías de todo el mundo. Su obra es caprichosa y dura, de forma perturbadora juega con contradicciones, como el lado oscuro de una canción infantil, un sueño de cosas encantadoras con un toque de oscuridad.

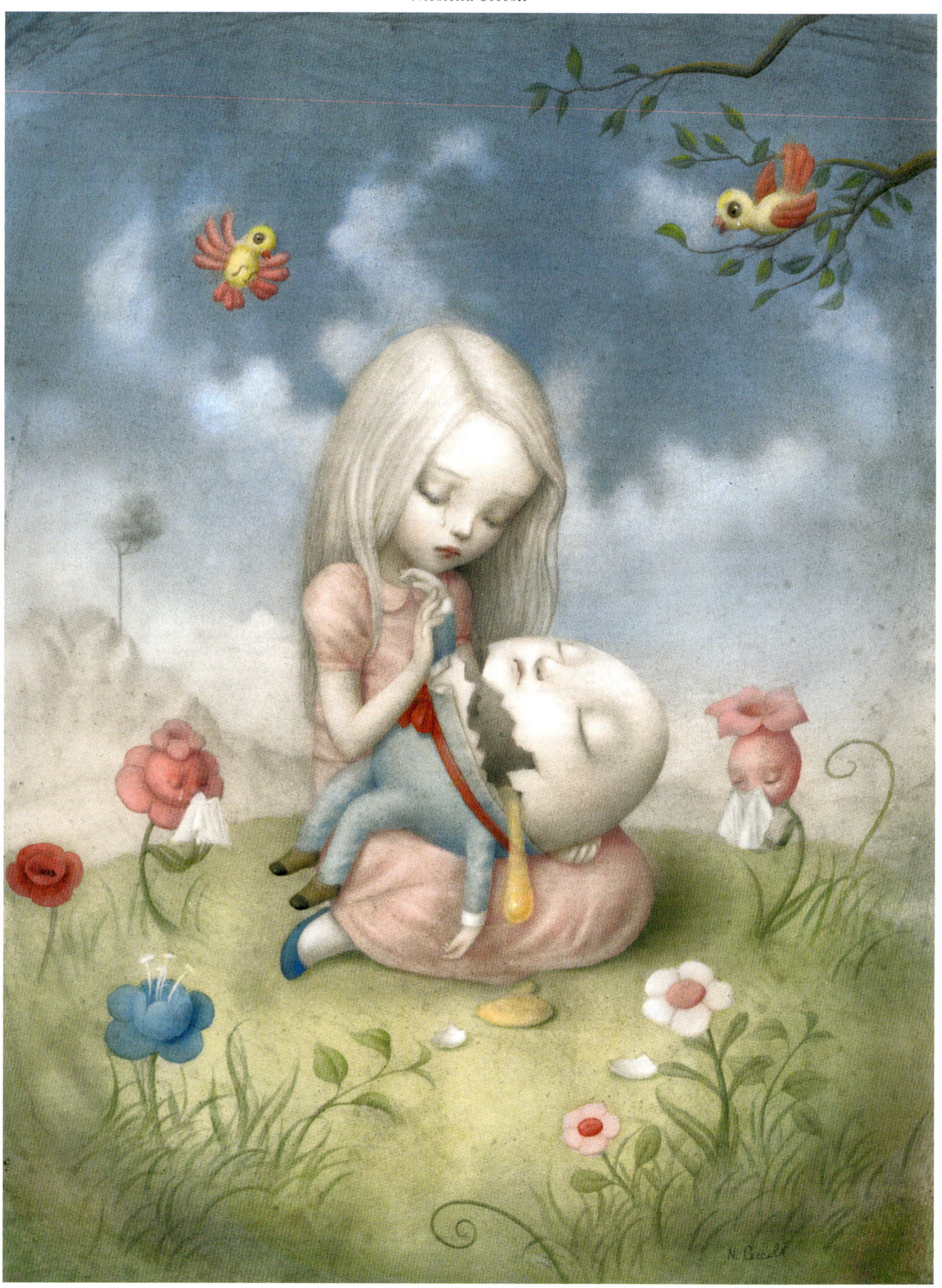

left: Too fragile // ***right:*** Just dessert

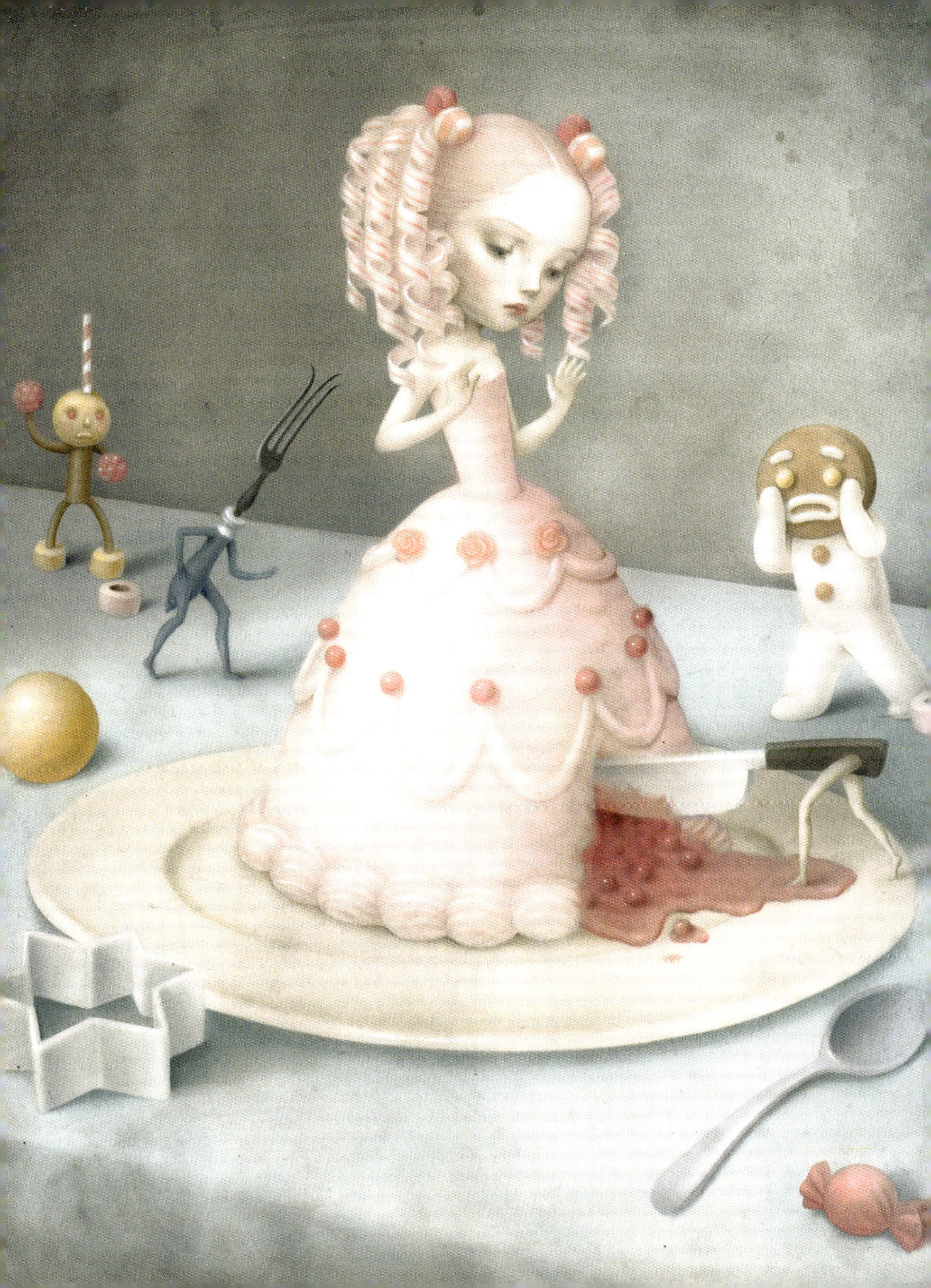

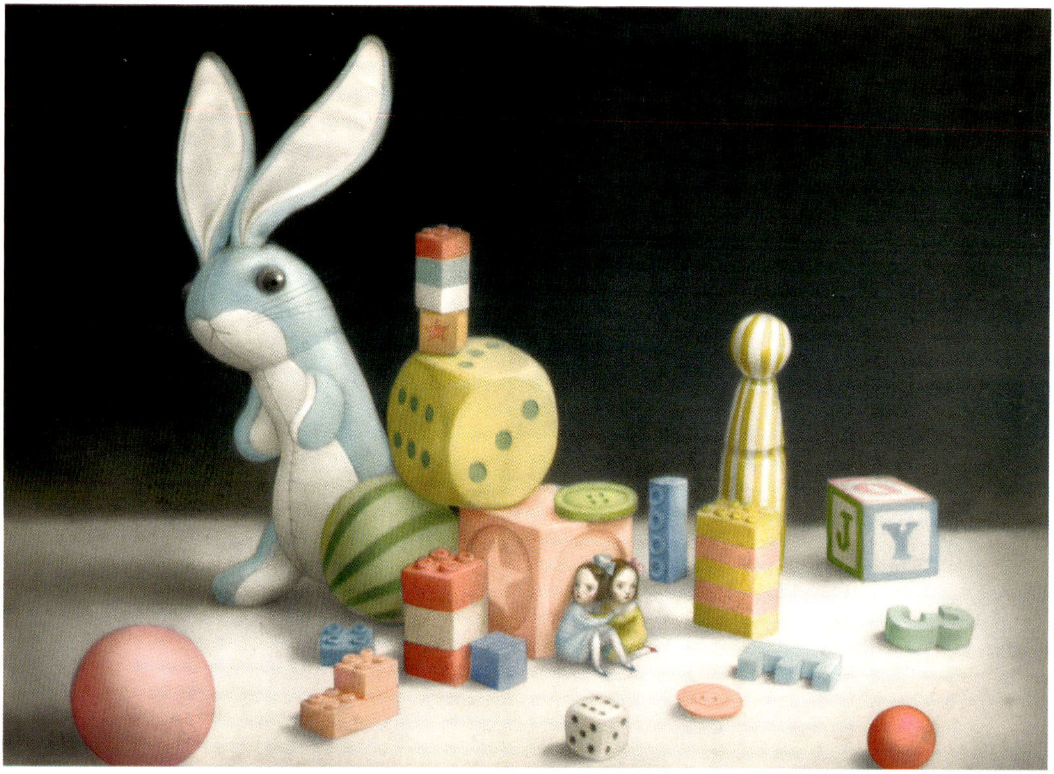

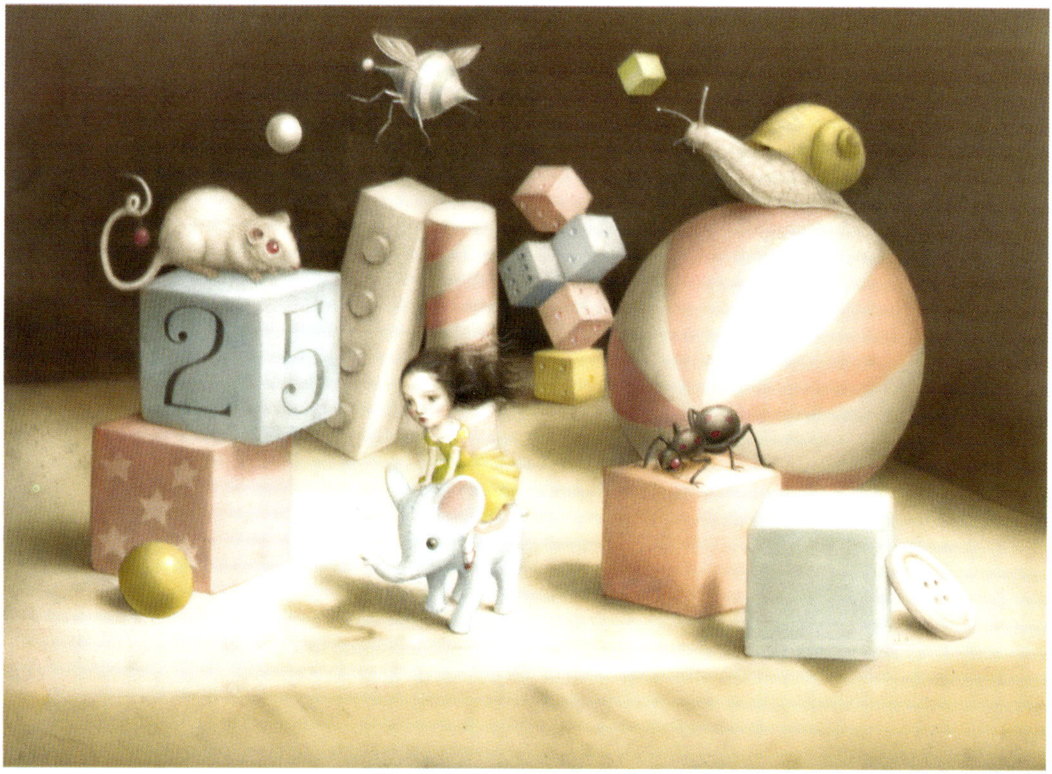

top: Nascondino, ***bottom:*** The elephant's journey

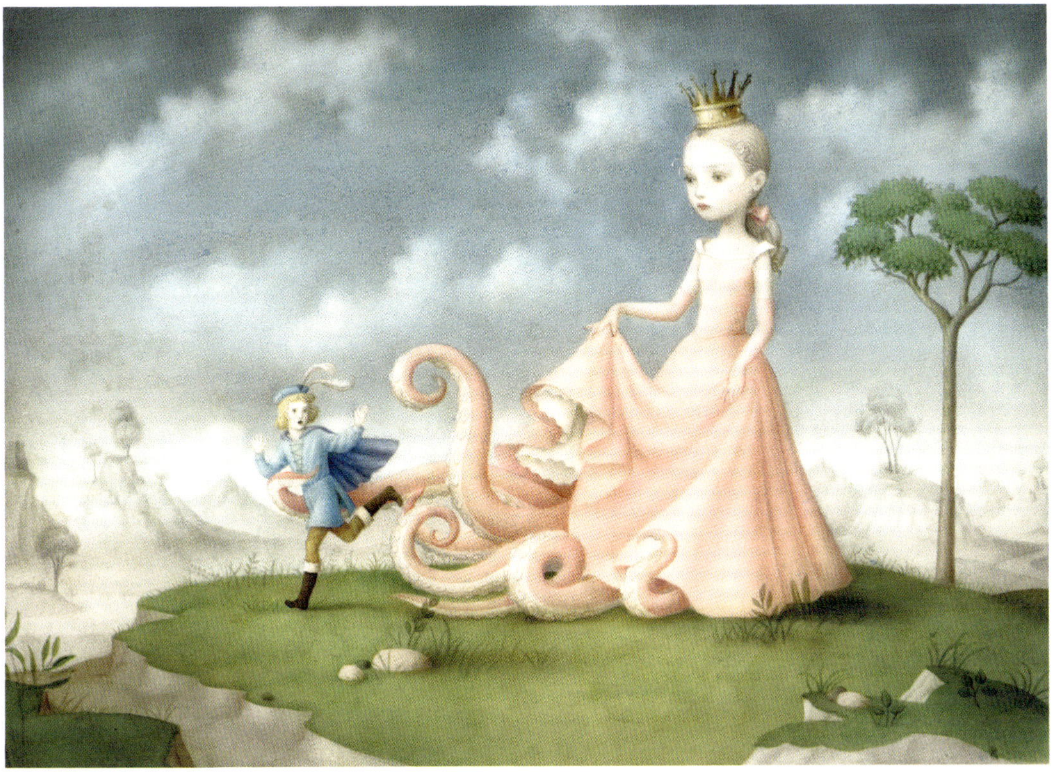

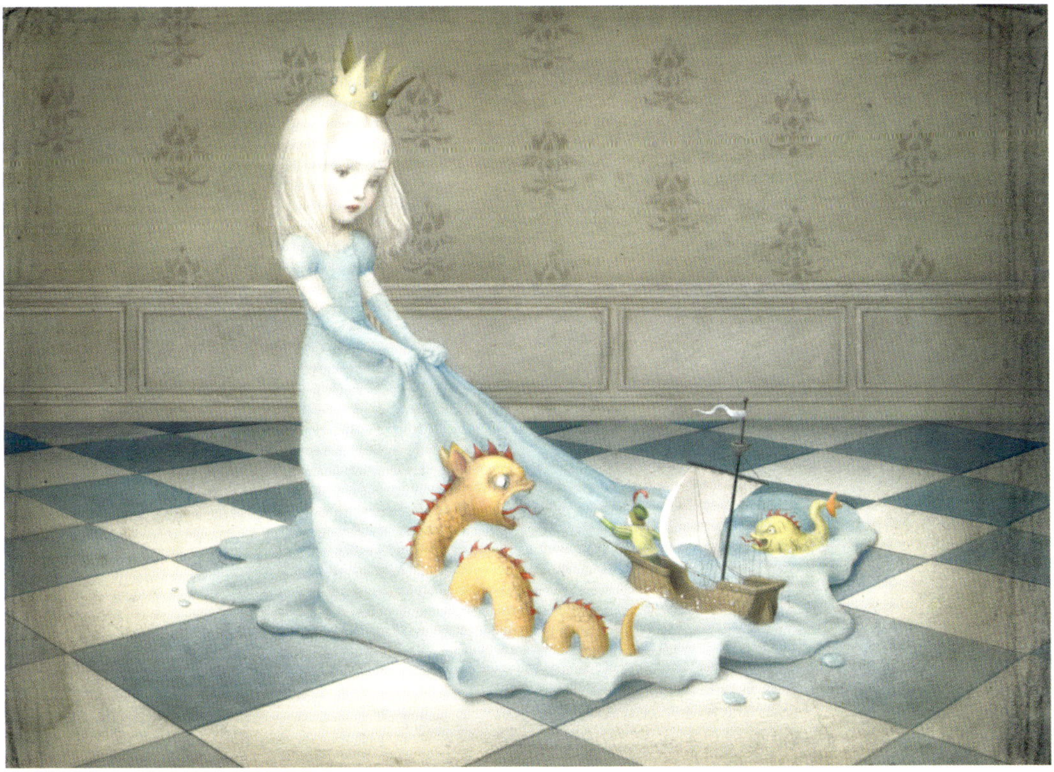

top: Dangerous Liasons, ***bottom:*** Love will tear us apart

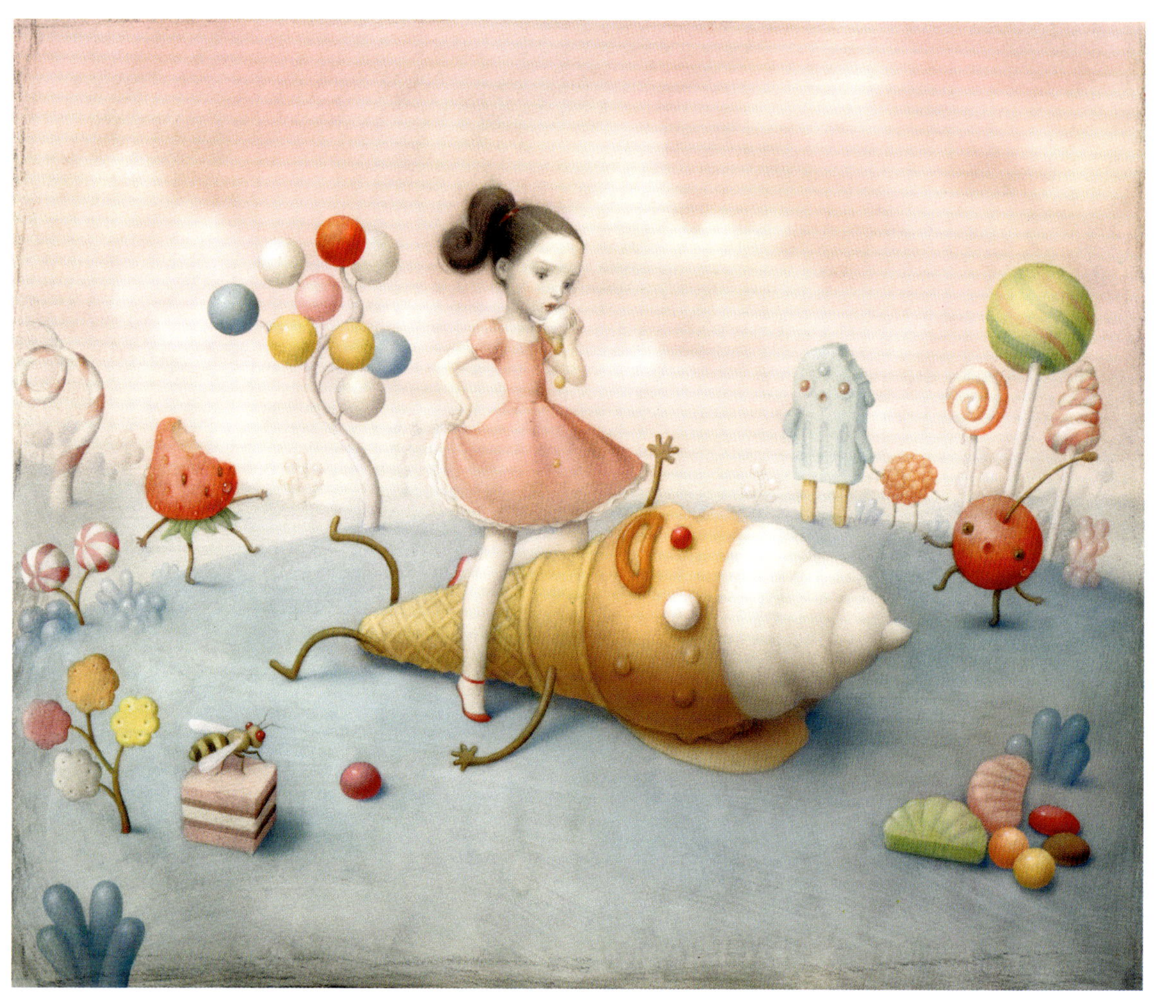

Consumed by you

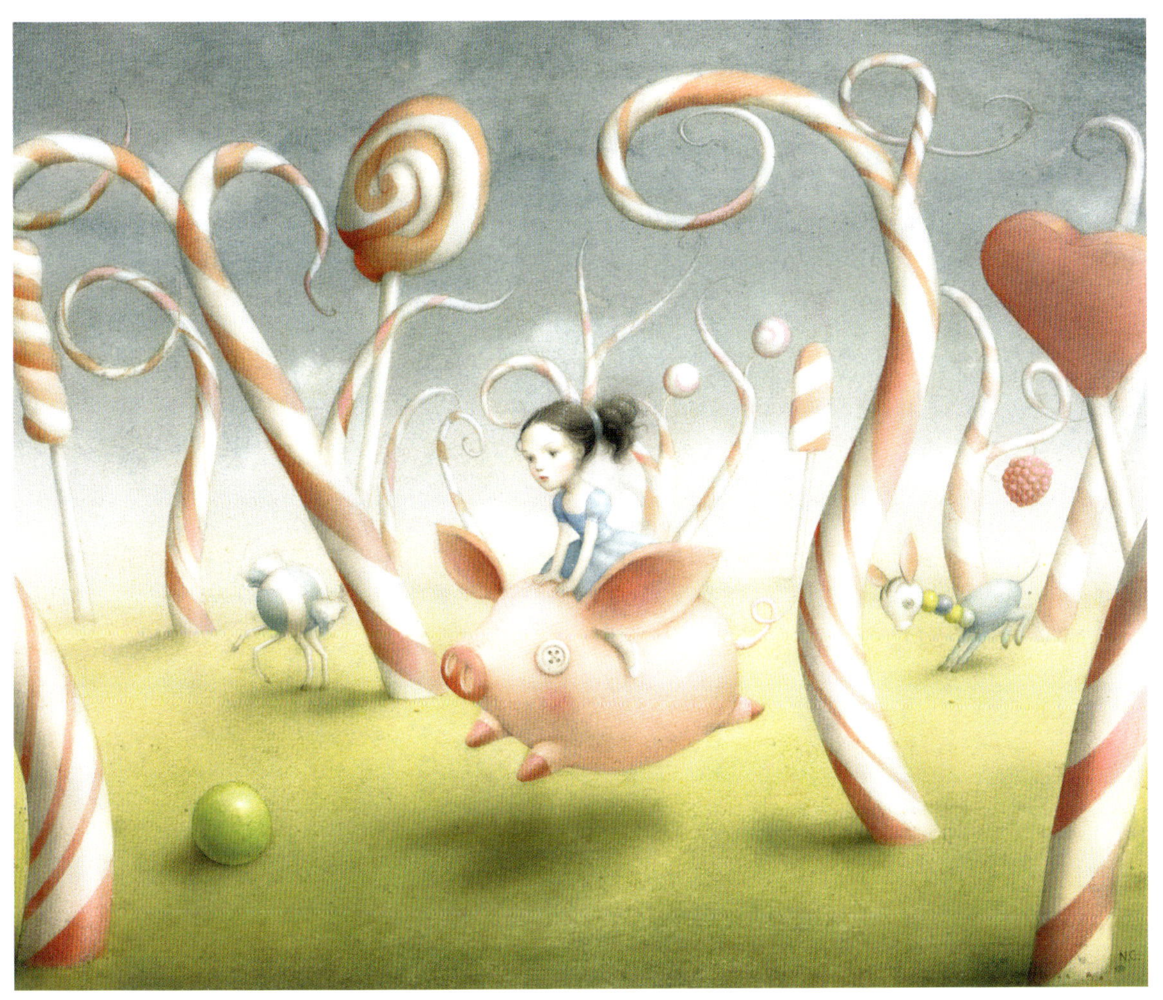

Candy forest

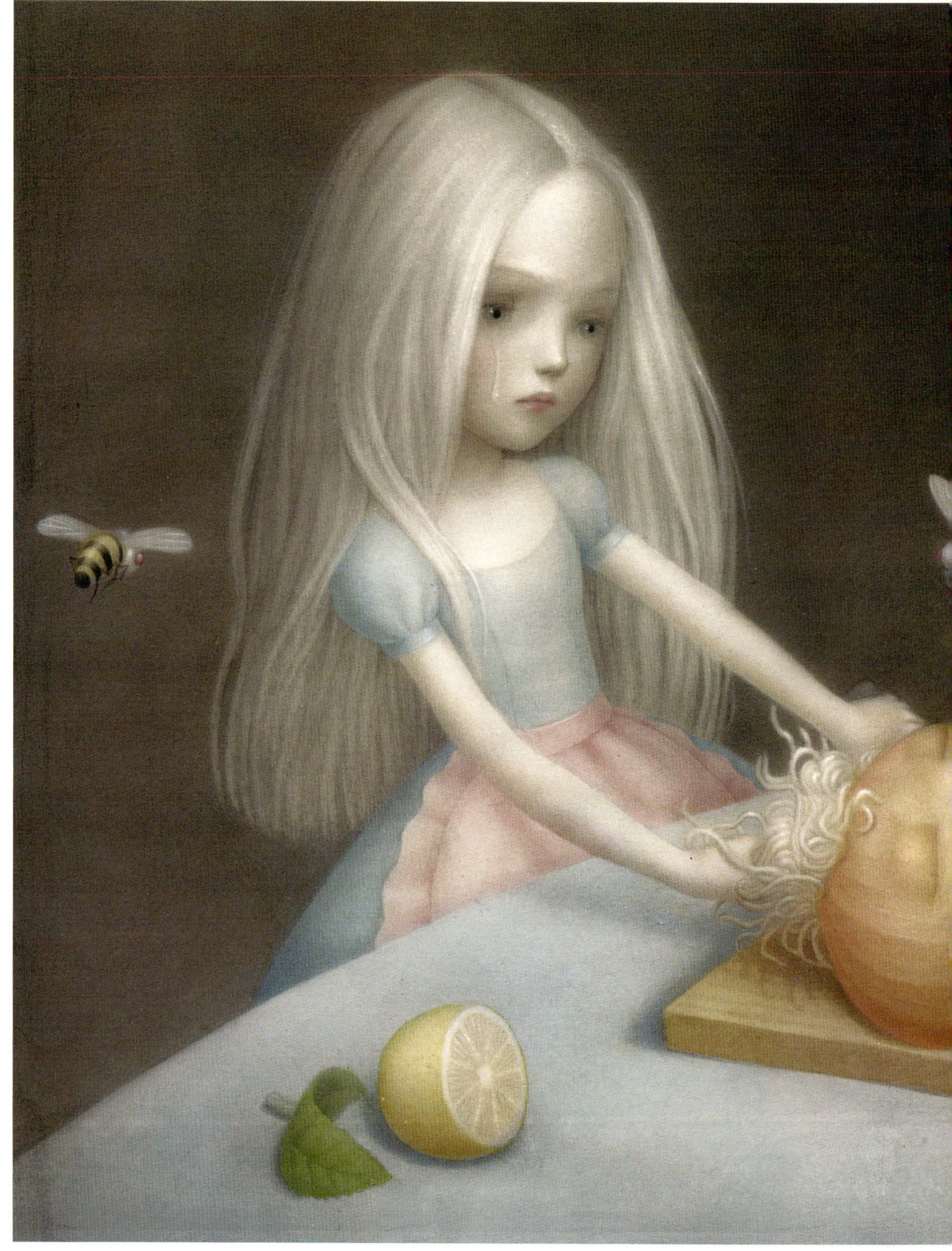

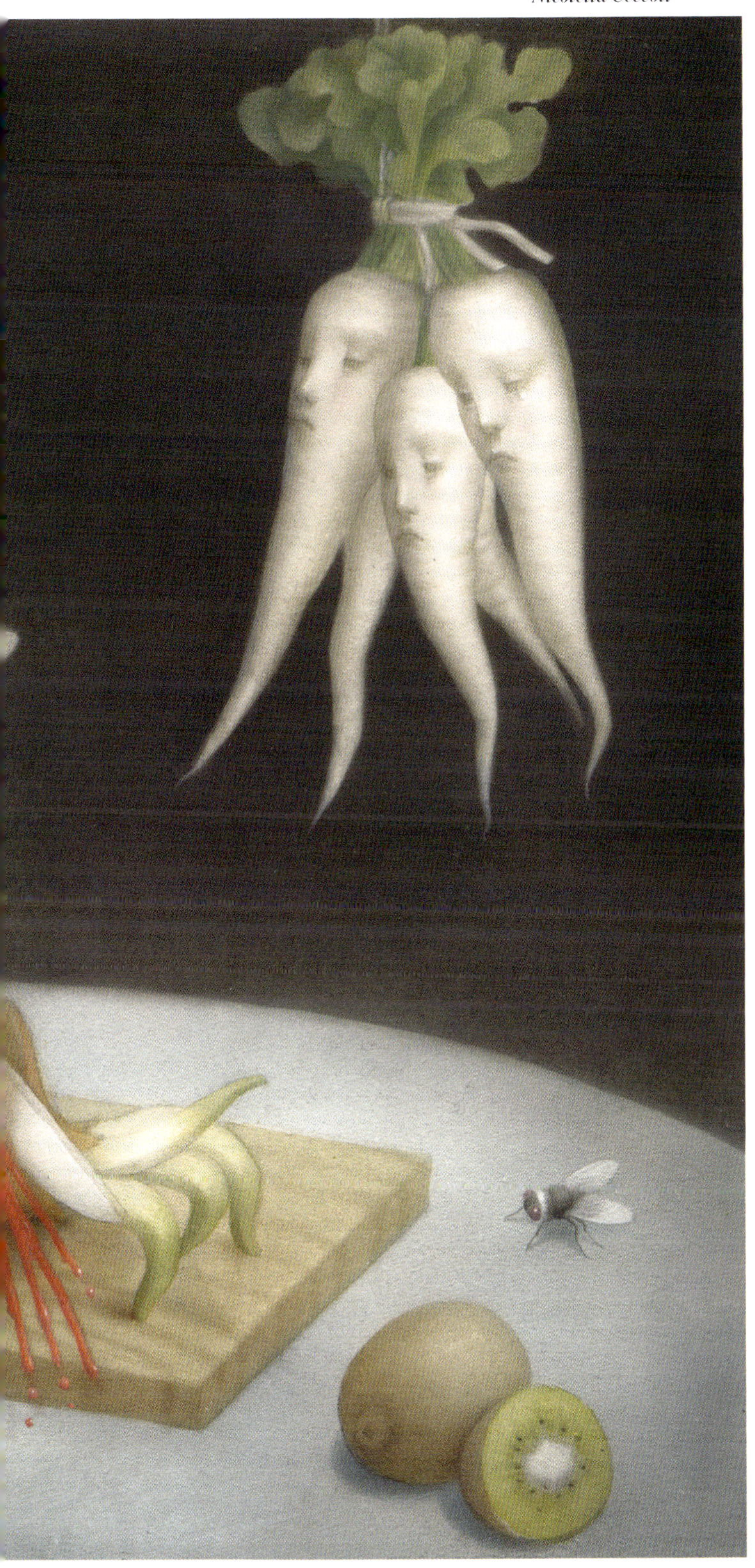

Girls don't cry

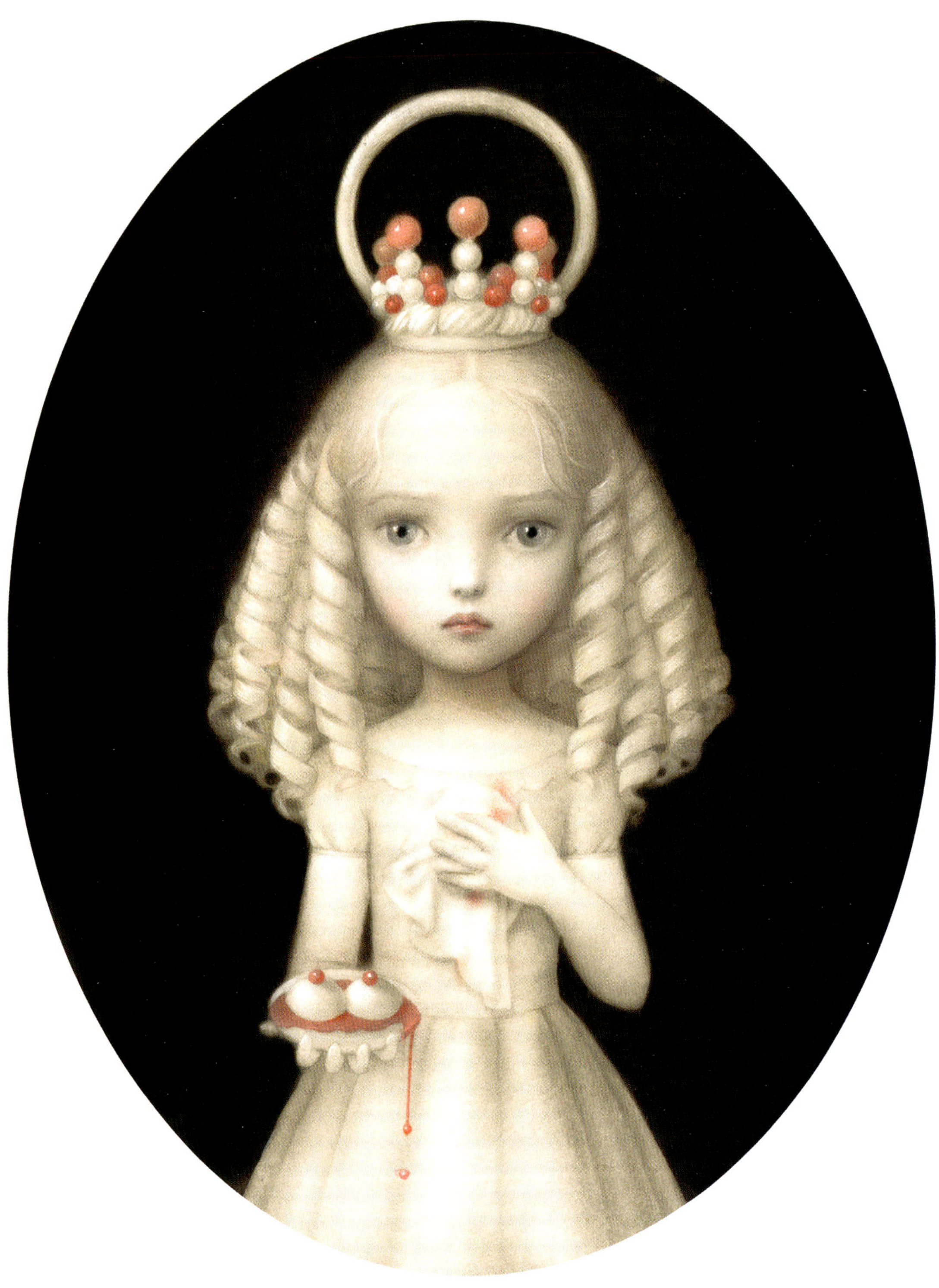

Dulcis Agata

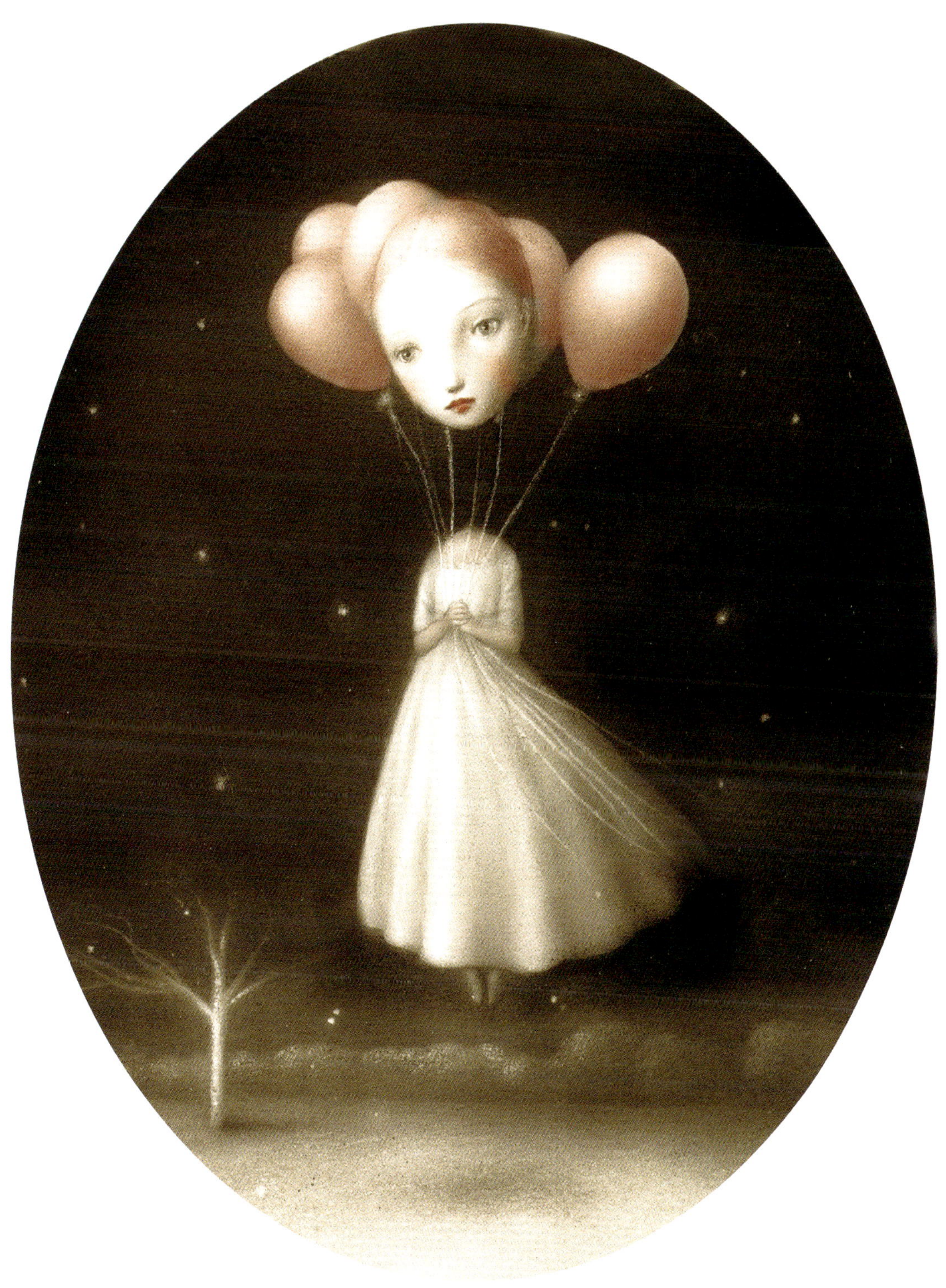

Balloon girl

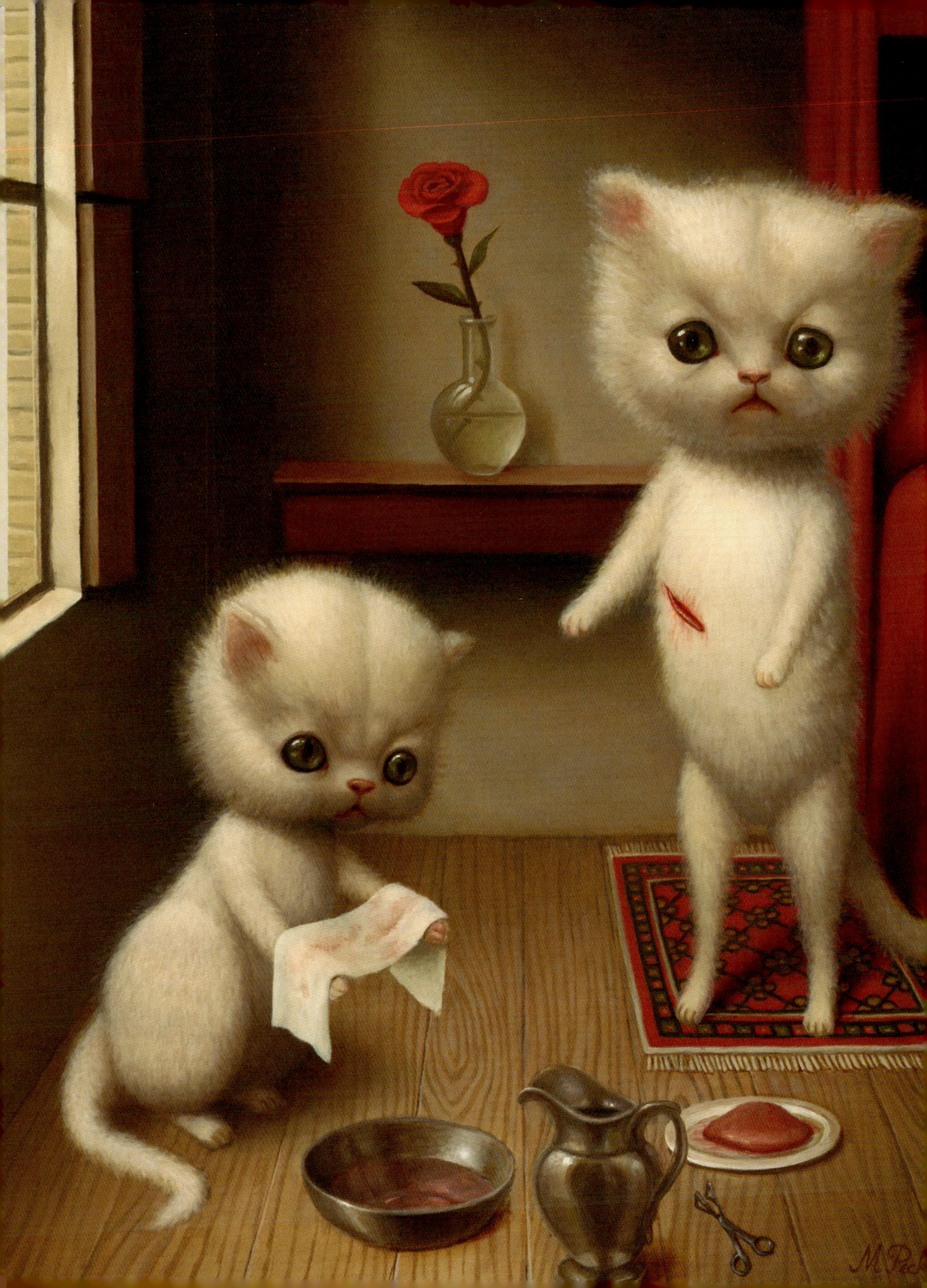

marionpeck.com

Marion Peck

Marion Peck was born on October 3, 1963 in Manila, the Philippines, while her family was on a trip around the world, and grew up in Seattle, Washington. She received a BFA from The Rhode Island School of Design in 1985. Subsequently she studied in two different MFA programs, Syracuse University in New York and Temple University in Rome. She currently lives in Portland, Oregon.

Marion Peck nació el 3 de octubre de 1963 en Manila, Filipinas, mientras su familia viajaba alrededor del mundo, y creció en Seattle (Washington). Se licenció en la Escuela de Diseño de Rhode Island en 1985. Posteriormente estudió en dos programas diferentes de Máster en la Universidad de Siracusa (Nueva York) y en la Universidad de Temple (Roma). Actualmente vive en Portland (Oregon).

▸ Kittys Sacrifice

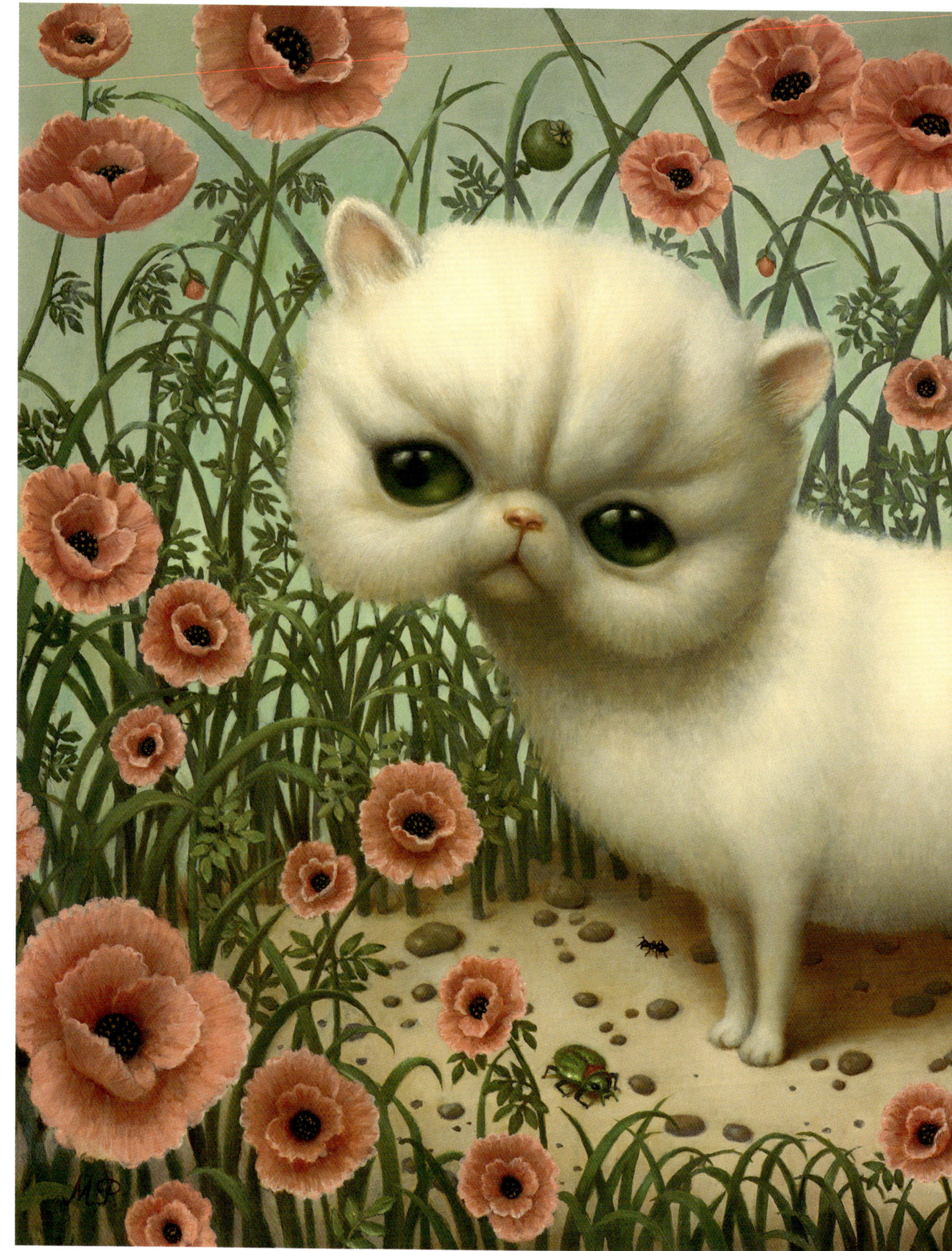

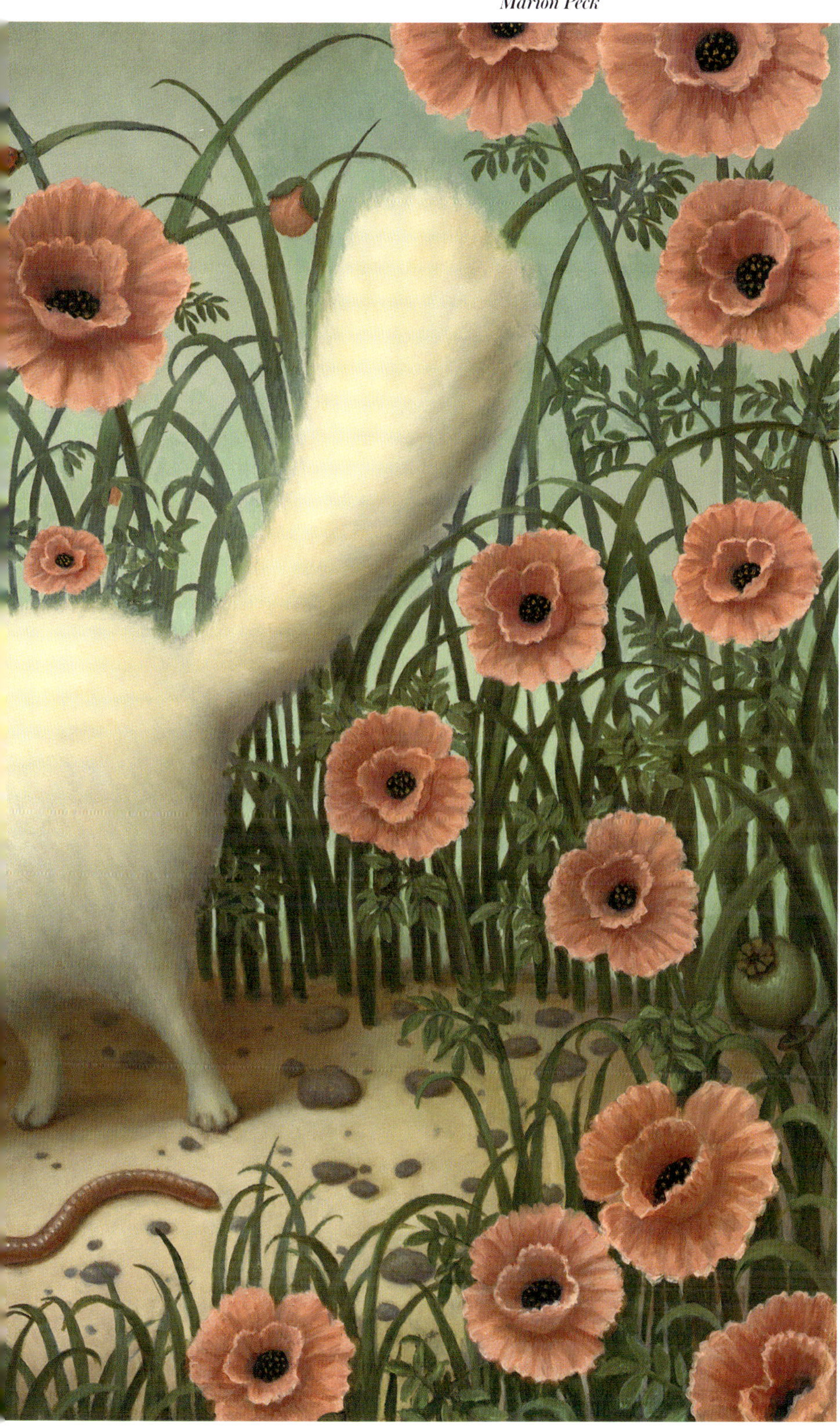

Big White Pussy

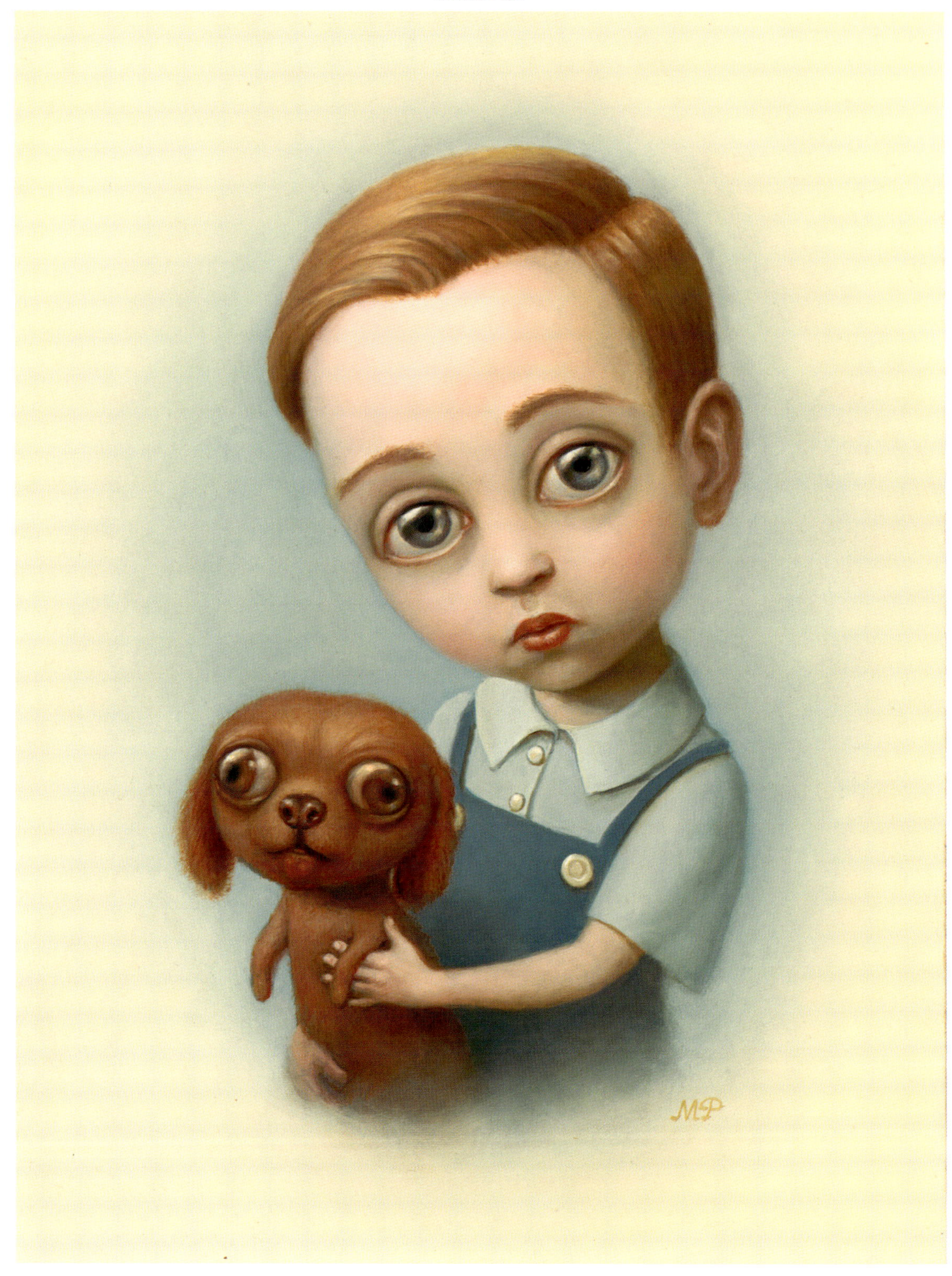

Boy with puppy

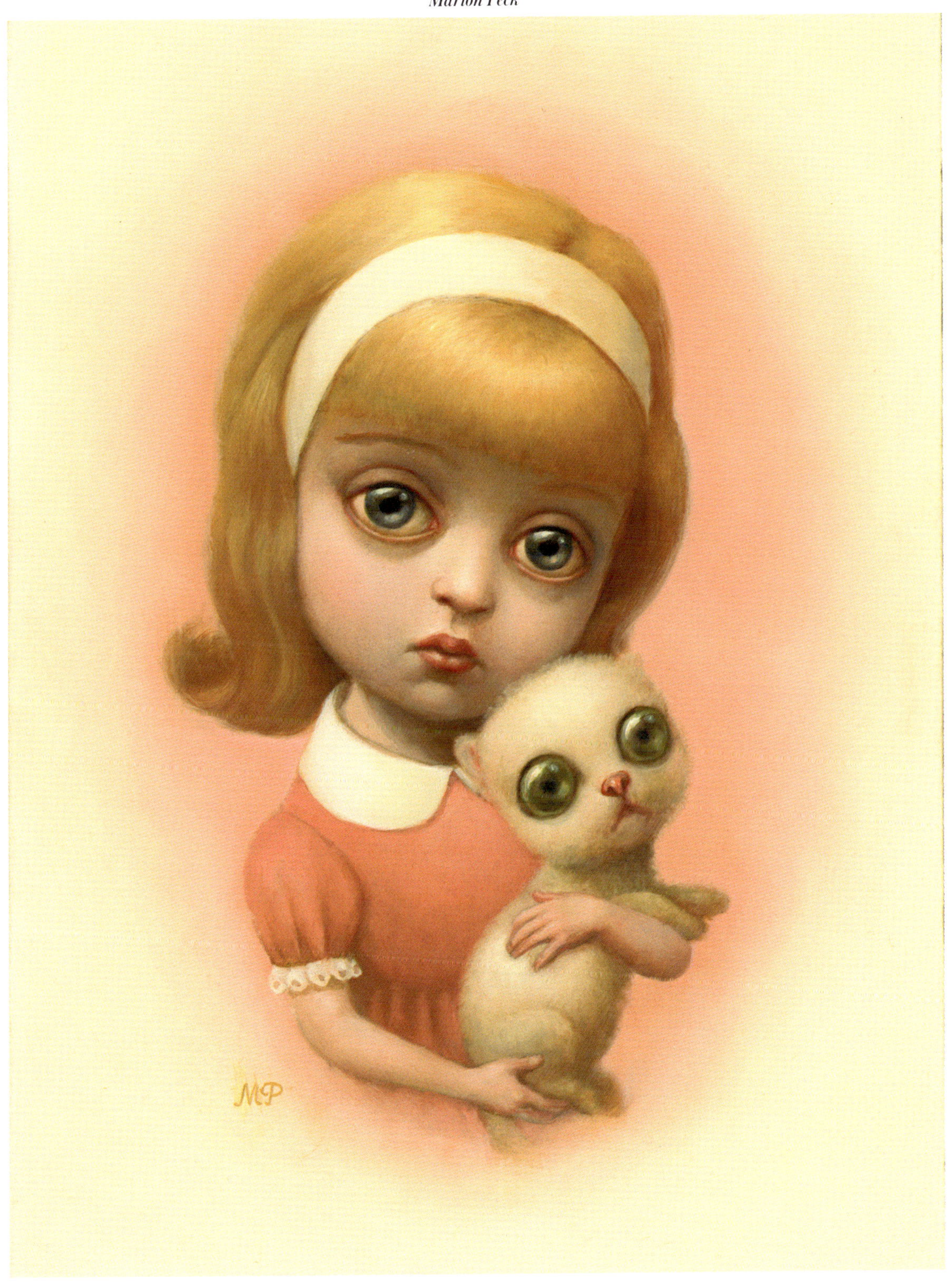

Girl with kitten

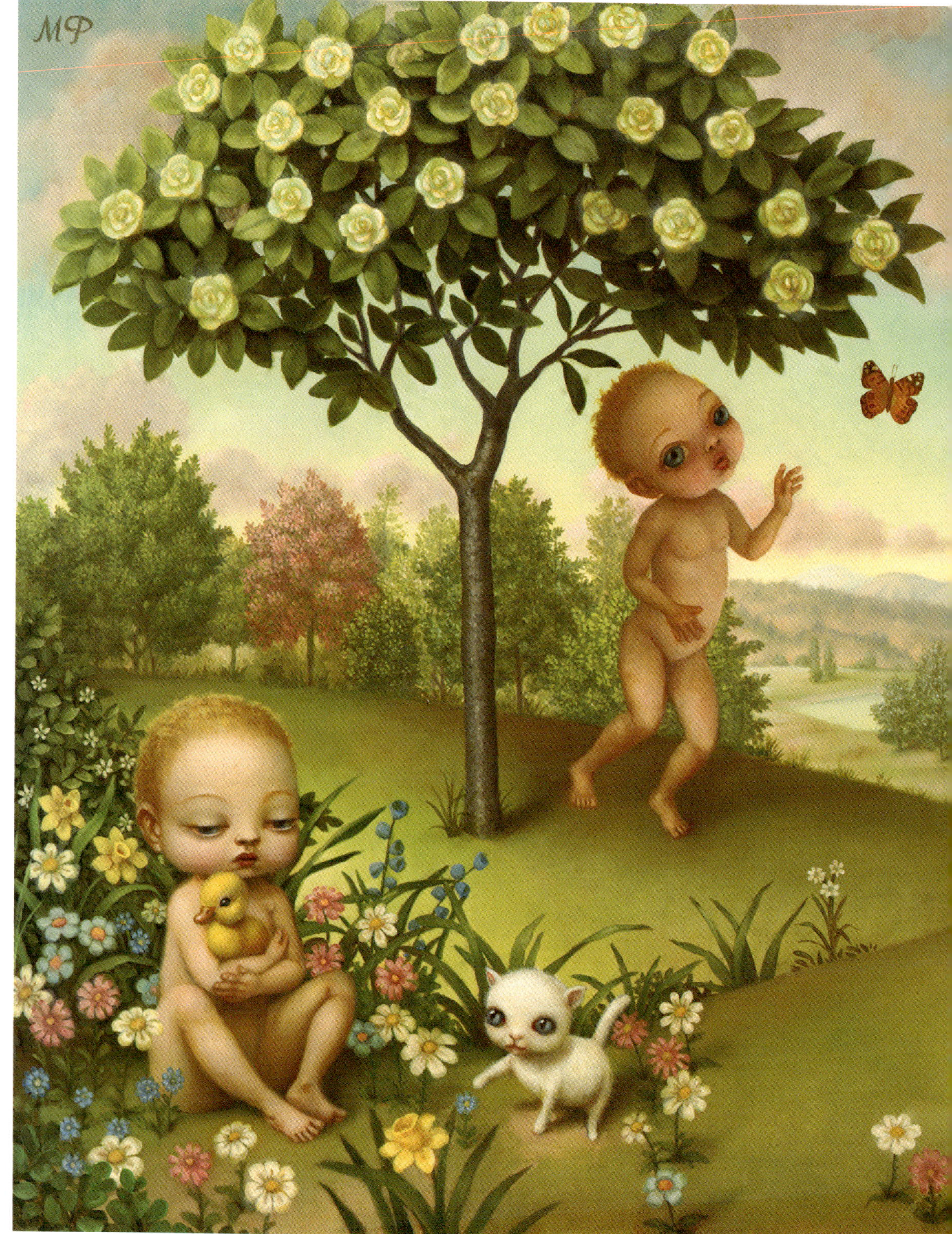
MP

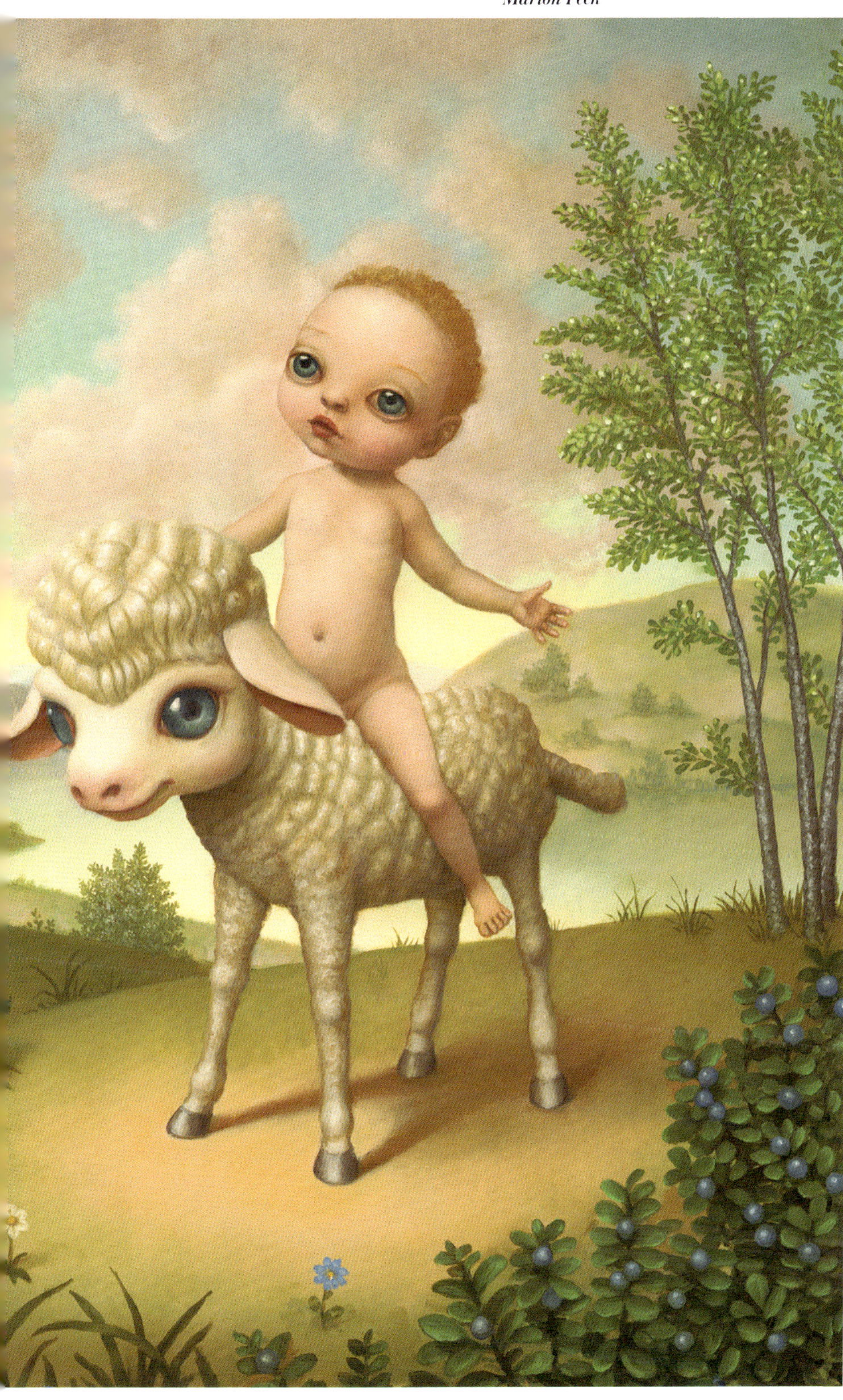

Lambland

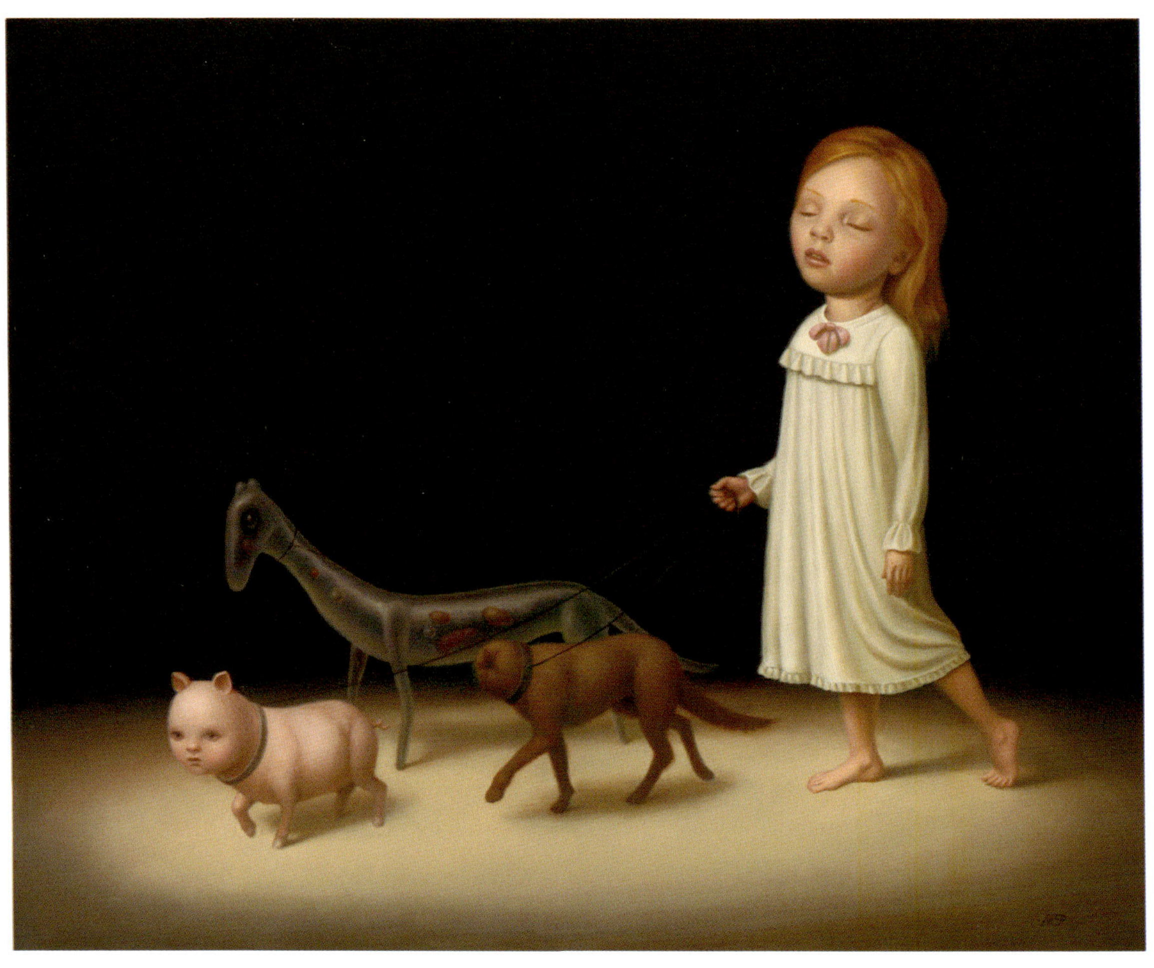

Sleepwalk

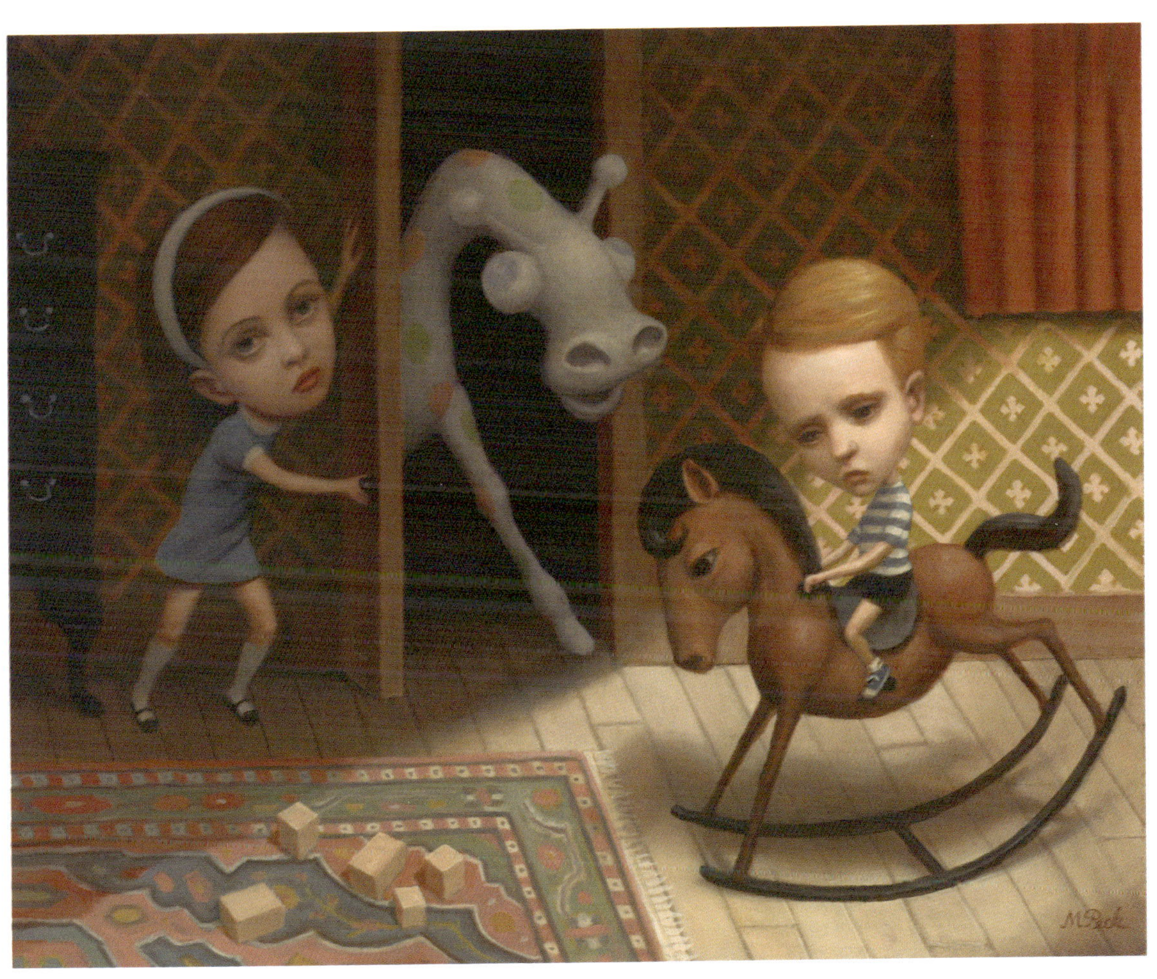

Playroom

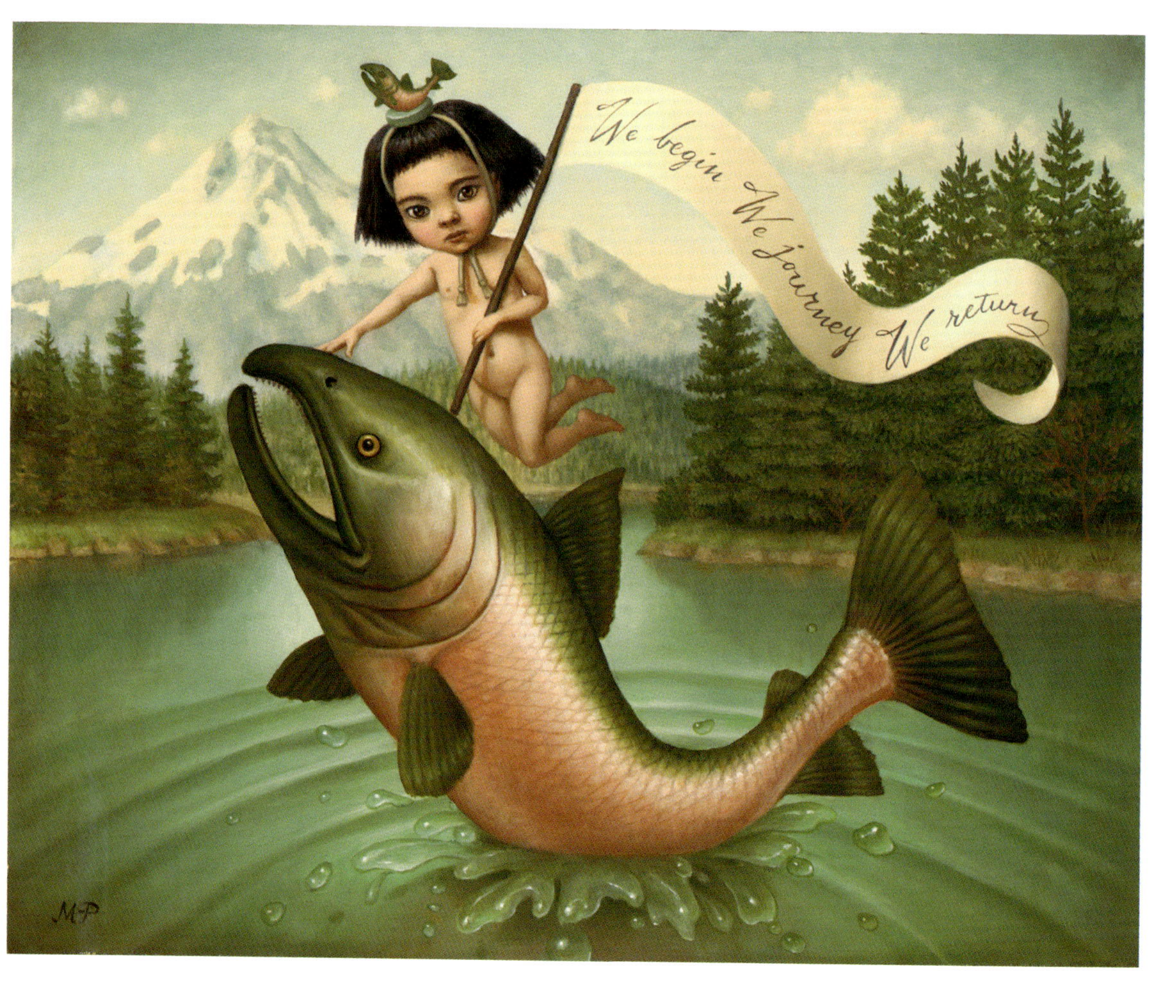

Salmon Spirit

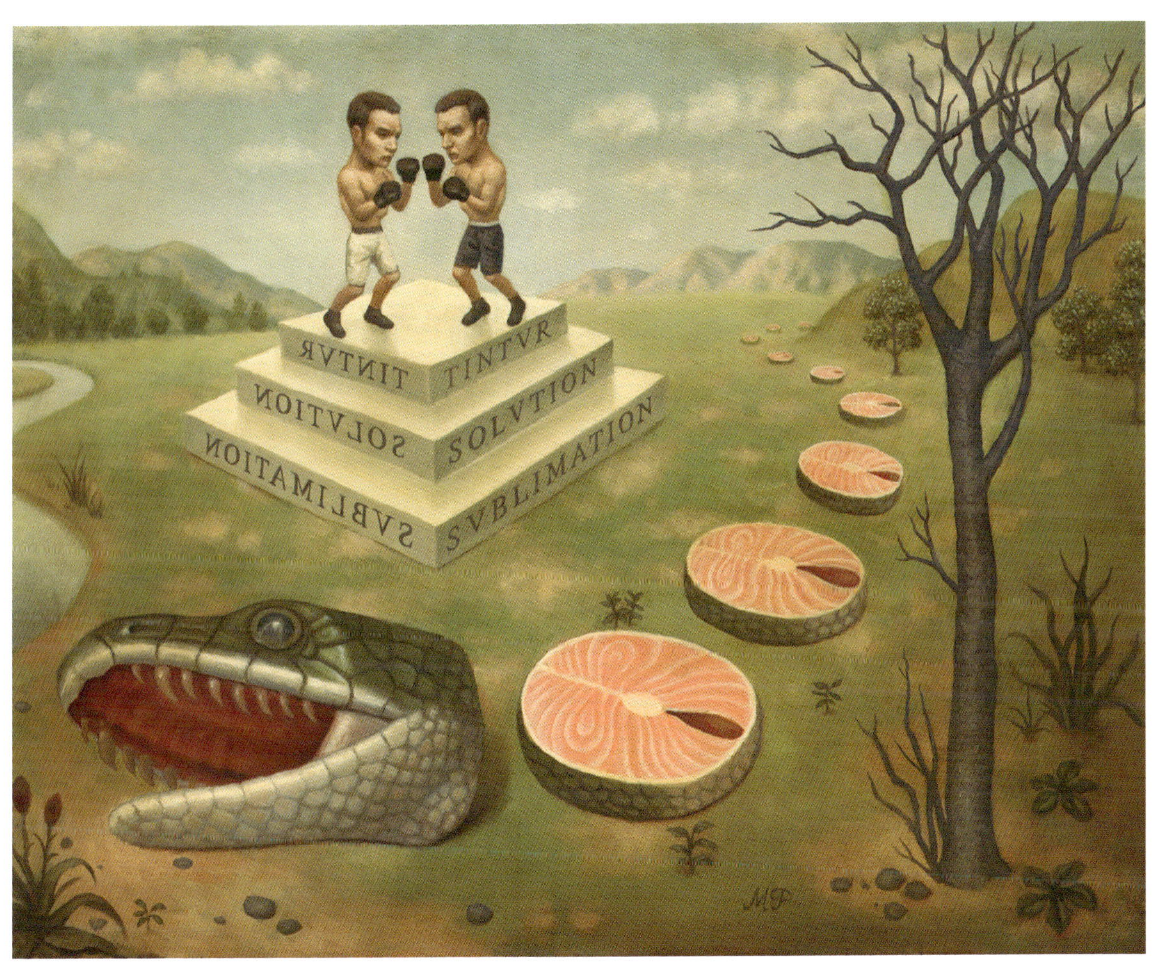

Sliced Serpent

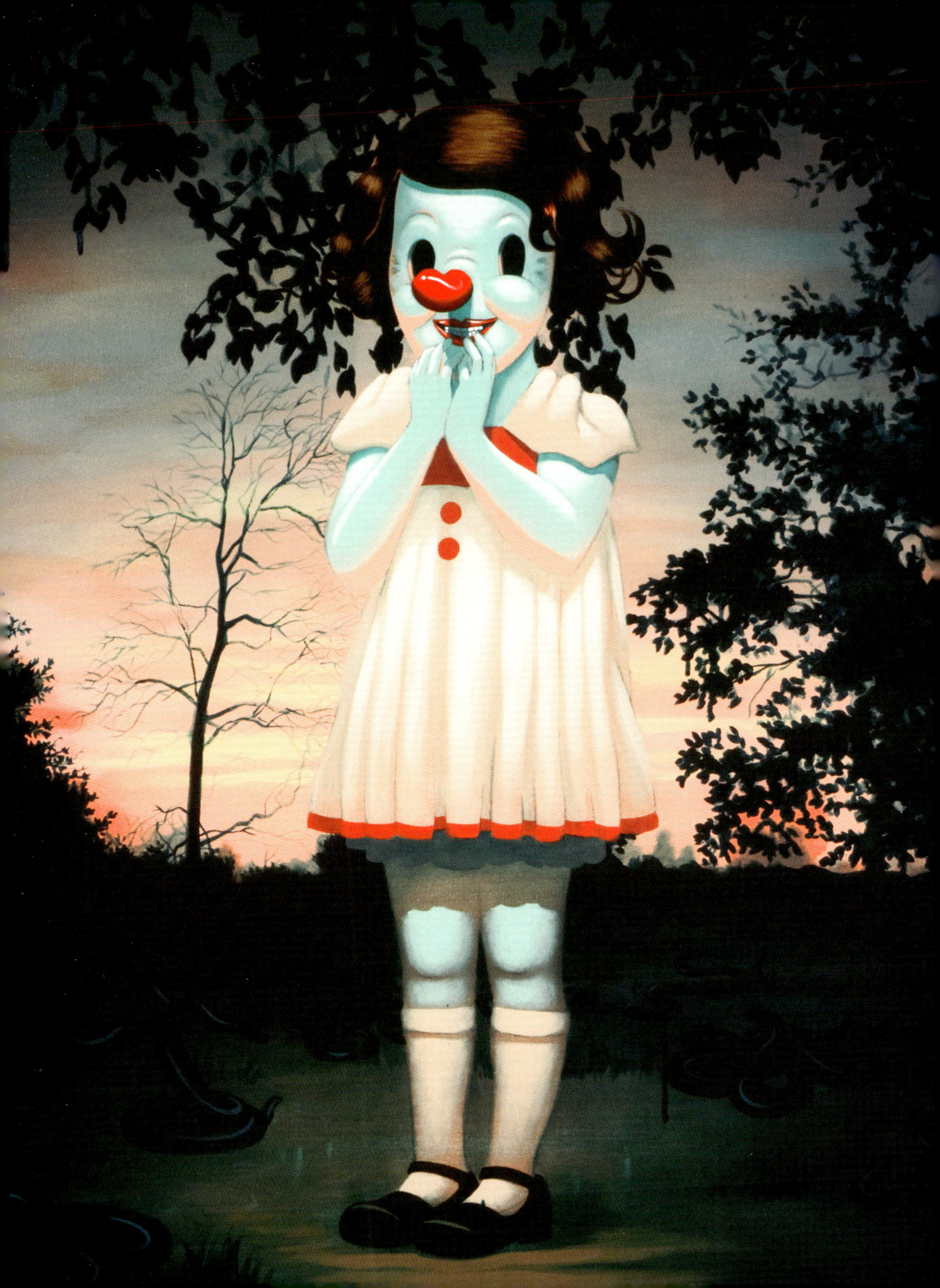

victor-castillo.com

Victor Castillo

Víctor Castillo is a Chilean painter who currently lives in Los Angeles, California. He was born in Santiago de Chile in 1973.

Víctor began to draw obsessively at the age of five, inspired by animations he saw on television, science fiction films and illustrations from records like Pink Floyd's The Wall. After a disappointing experience at art school, Víctor participated in an independent experimental artistic group in Santiago, creating sculptures, videos and mixed media. Víctor moved to Barcelona, Spain in 2004, where he established his painting style with references to comics. After visiting the Prado Museum in Madrid and seeing Goya's black paintings, he adopted aspects of classical painting in his work. He worked with the legendary Iguapop Gallery with which he began to display his work internationally, until the gallery's closure in 2010.

Víctor is currently represented by Isabel Croxtatto Gallery in Chile, Merry Karnowsky Gallery in Los Angeles, Heliumcowboy Artspace in Hamburg, Germany and Jonathan Levine Gallery in New York City, among other places around the world. His work has been exhibited in museums and galleries in Chile, Spain, the United States, Germany, France, the UK, Italy, Belgium, Denmark, China, Argentina, Brazil and Colombia, as well as appearing in numerous publications.

Víctor Castillo es un pintor chileno que reside actualmente en Los Ángeles, California. Nació en Santiago de Chile en 1973.

Víctor comenzó a dibujar obsesivamente a la edad de cinco años, inspirado en las animaciones que vio en la televisión, las películas de ciencia ficción y las ilustraciones de discos como Pink Floyd "The Wall". Después de una experiencia desilusionante con la escuela de arte, Víctor participó en un colectivo artístico experimental independiente en Santiago, creando instalaciones escultóricas videos y medios mixtos. Víctor se trasladó a Barcelona, España en 2004, donde estableció su estilo de pintura con referencias a los cómics. Después de visitar el Museo del Prado en Madrid y ver las pinturas negras de Goya, adoptó aspectos de la pintura clásica en su trabajo. Trabajo con la legendaria Galería Iguapop hasta su cierre en 2010, con quienes comenzó a mostrar su trabajo a nivel internacional.

Actualmente Víctor es representado por Isabel Croxtatto Gallery en Chile, Merry Karnowsky Gallery en Los Angeles, Heliumcowboy Artspace en Hamburgo, Alemania y Jonathan Levine Gallery en la ciudad de Nueva York, entre otros espacios en todo el mundo. Su trabajo ha sido expuesto en museos y galerías en Chile, España, Estados Unidos, Alemania, Francia, Inglaterra, Italia, Bélgica, Dinamarca, China, Argentina, Brasil y Colombia, así como en numerosas publicaciones.

▸ In Dark Trees (detail), acrylic on canvas

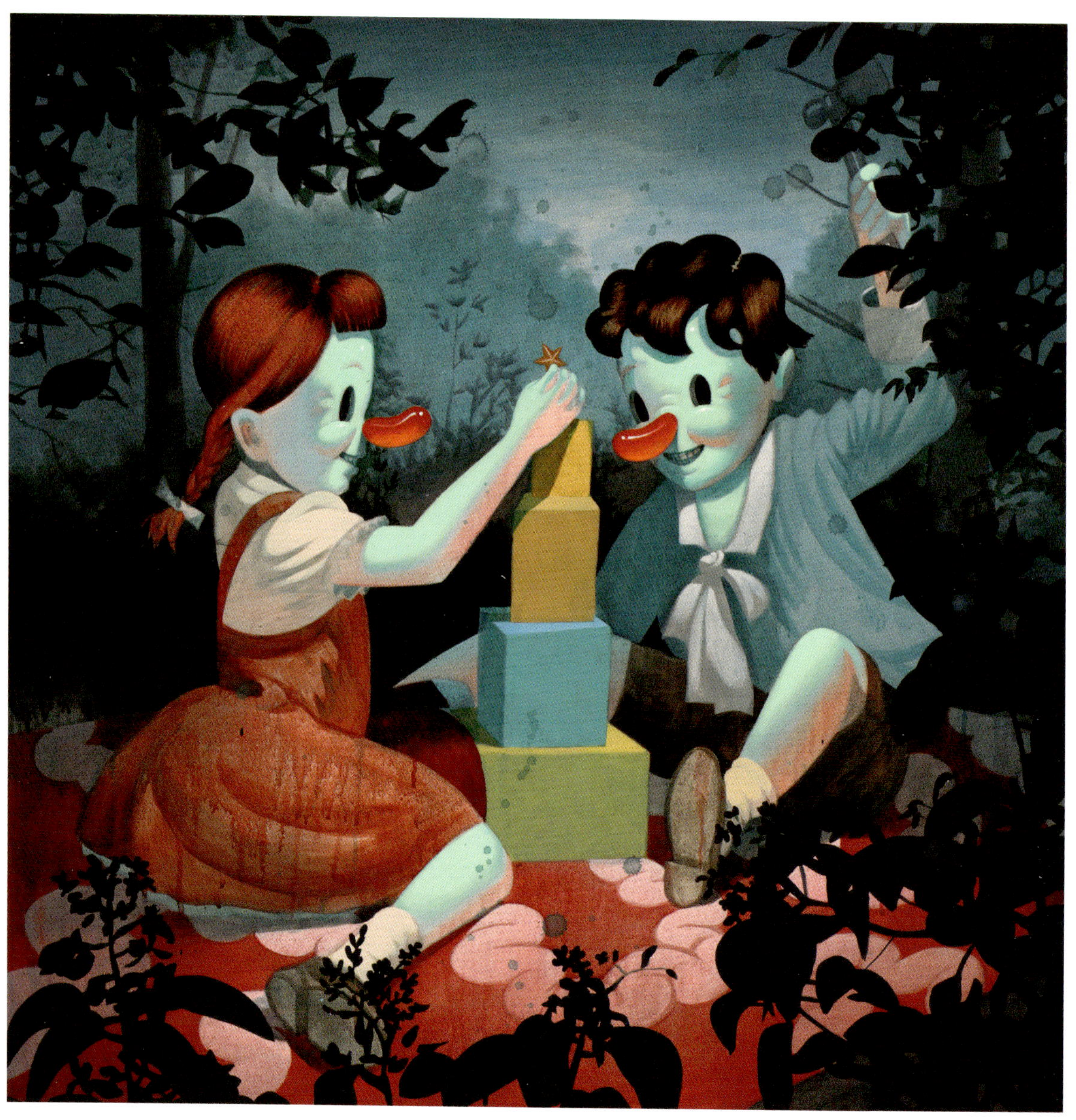

Breaking the law, acrylic on canvas

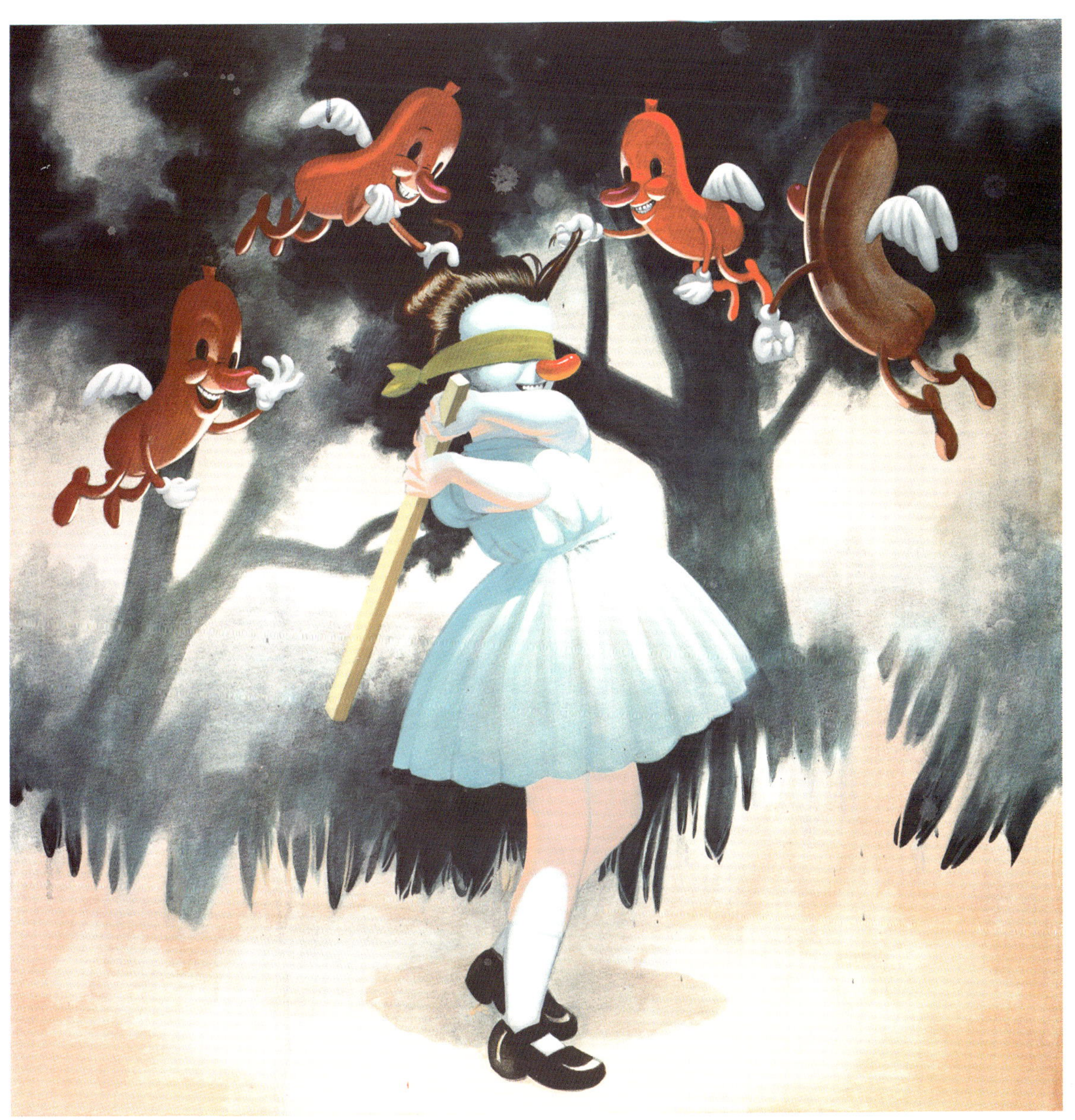

Dancing in the Mist, acrylic on canvas

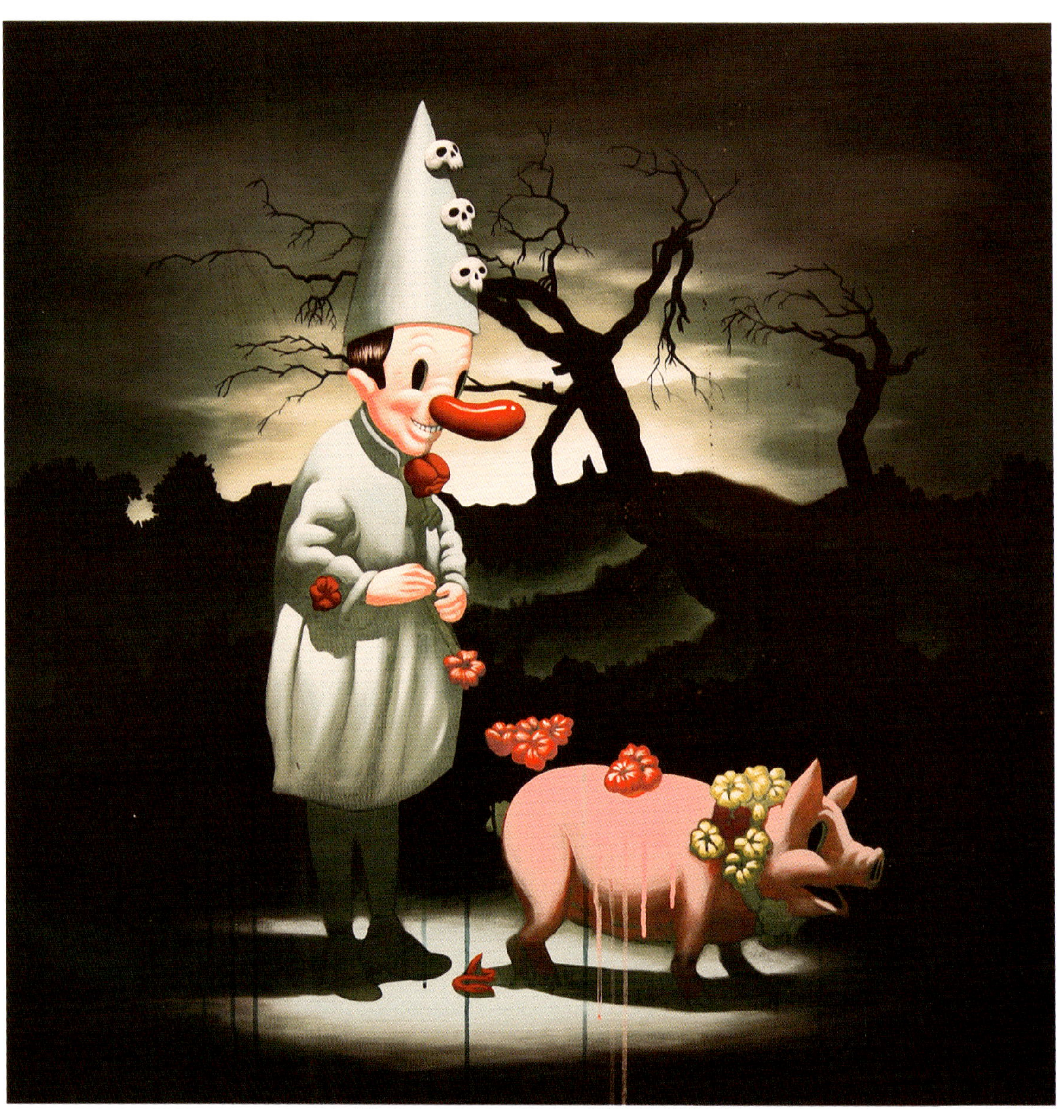

Hour the pig, acrylic on canvas

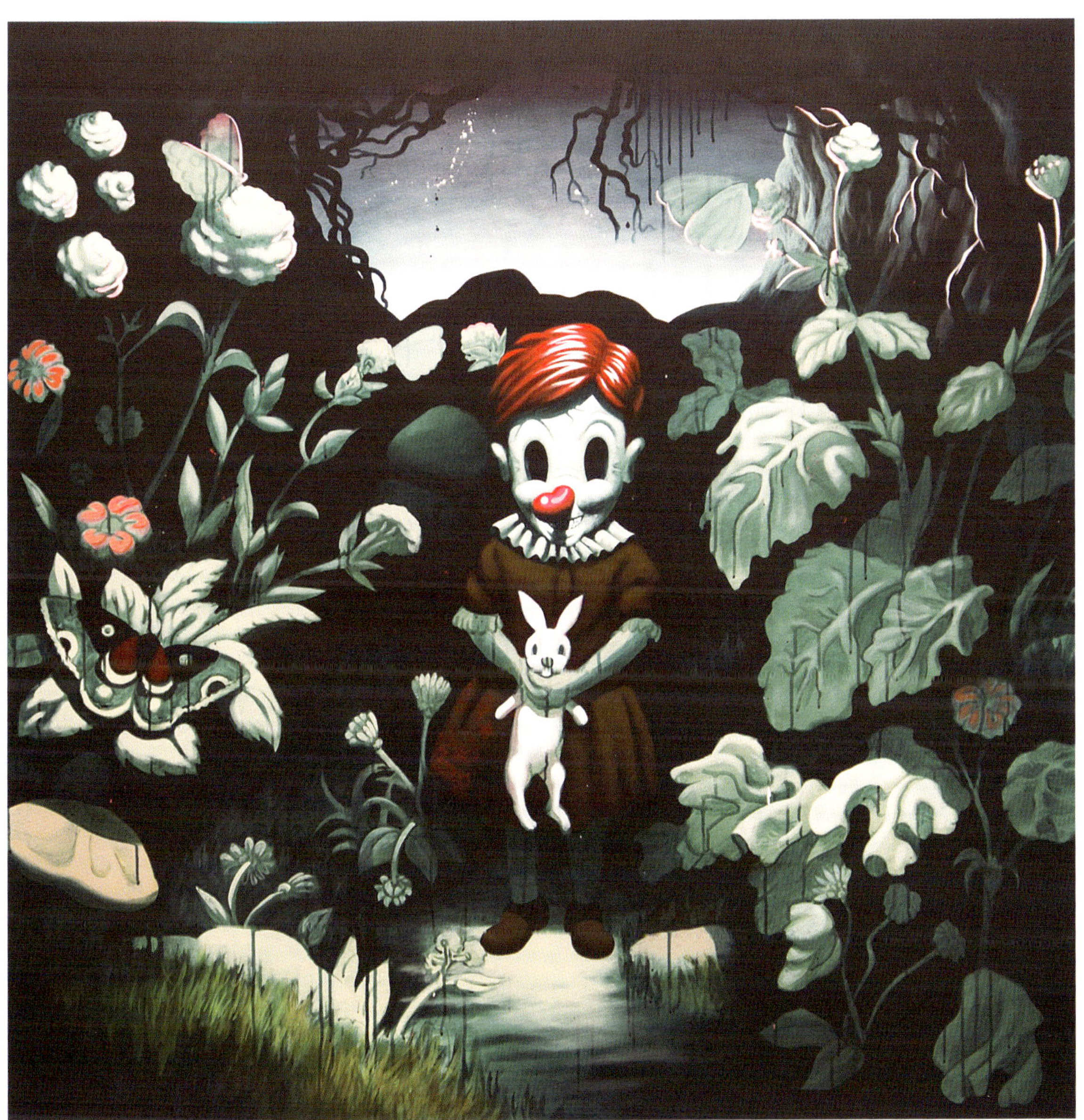

Love is a fit, acrylic on canvas

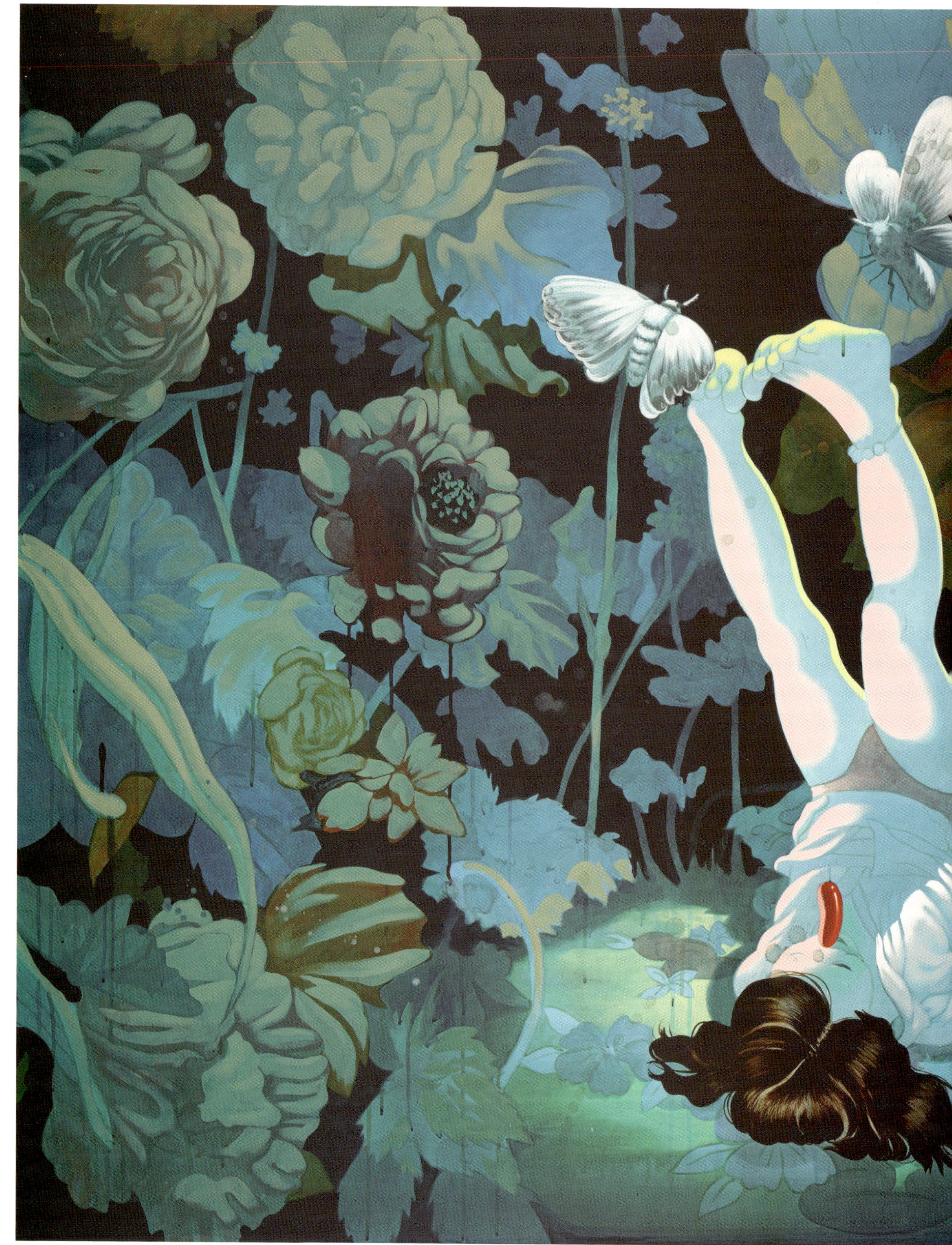

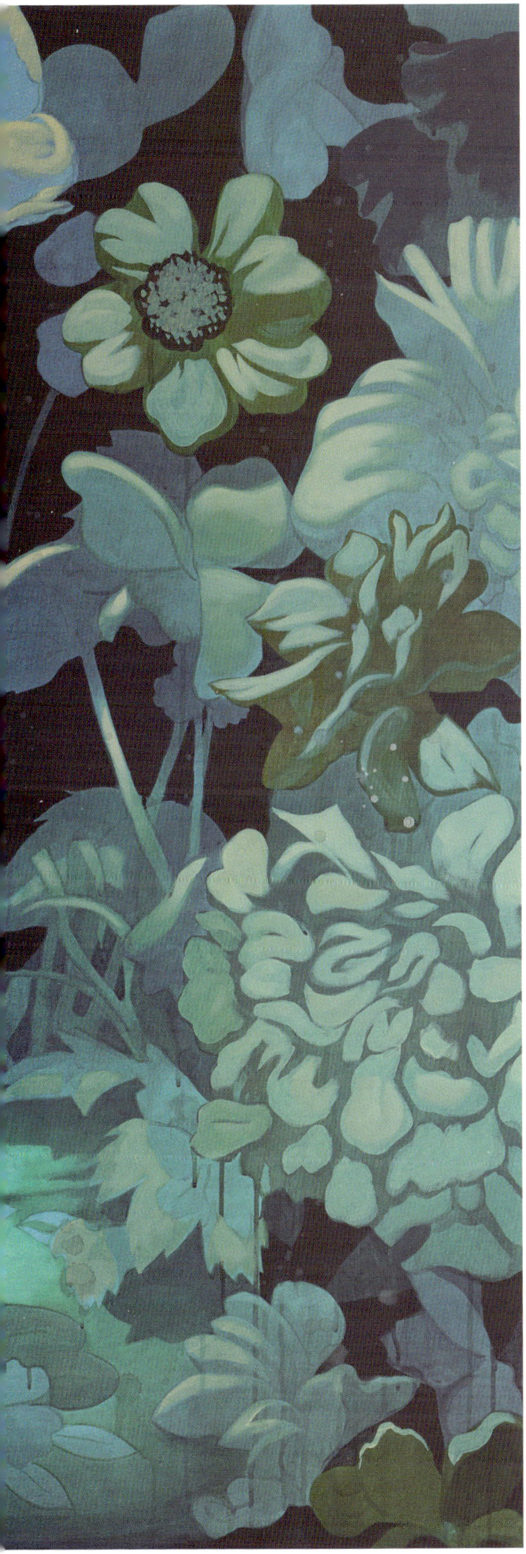

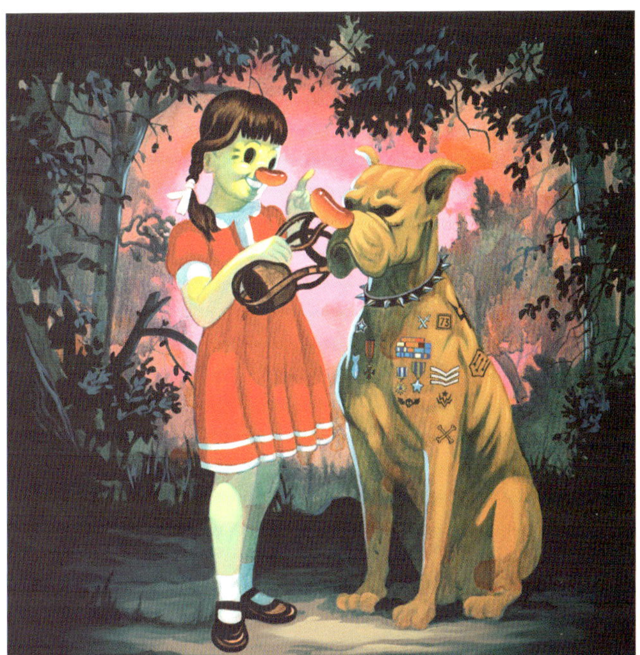

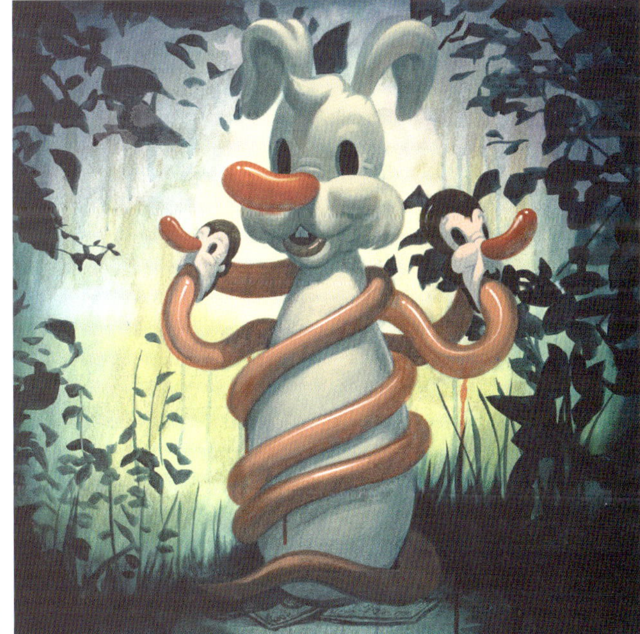

left: Sorry for Laughing (detail), acrylic on canvas
right, top: The Beast in the Jungle, acrylic on canvas
bottom: Your mind belongs to the State, acrylic on canvas

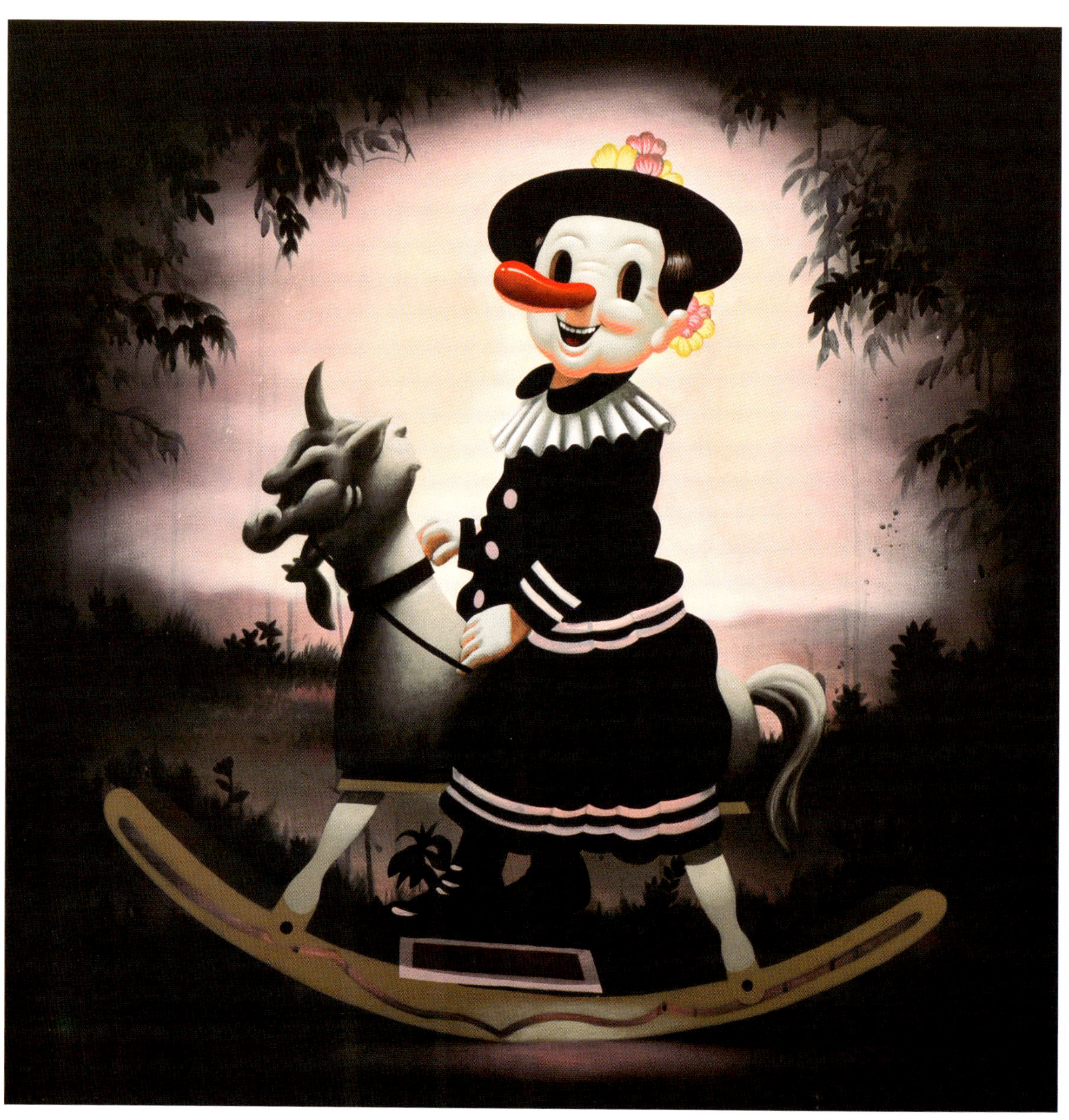

Stupid Anyway, acrylic on canvas

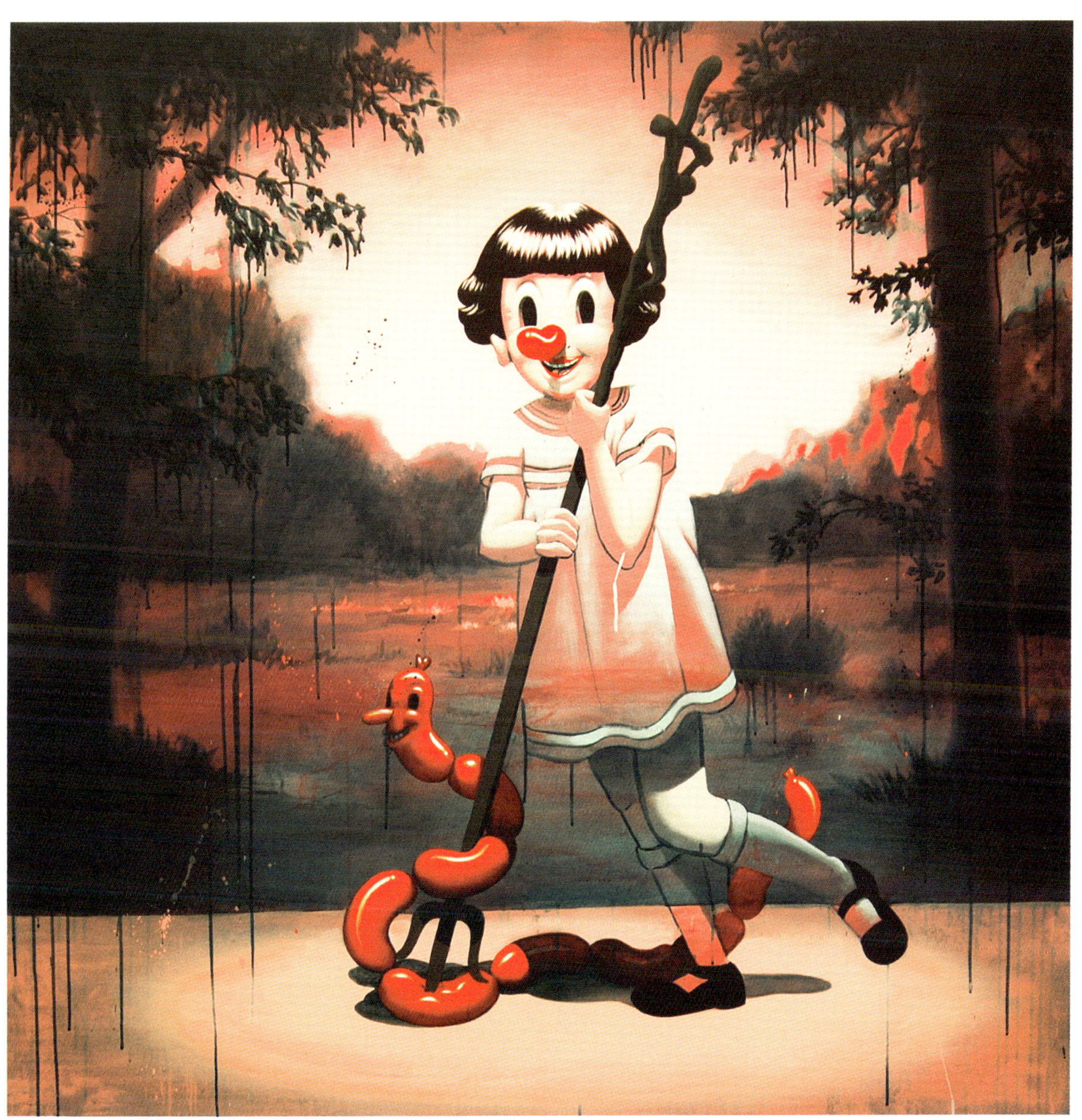

Sin in my heart, acrylic on canvas

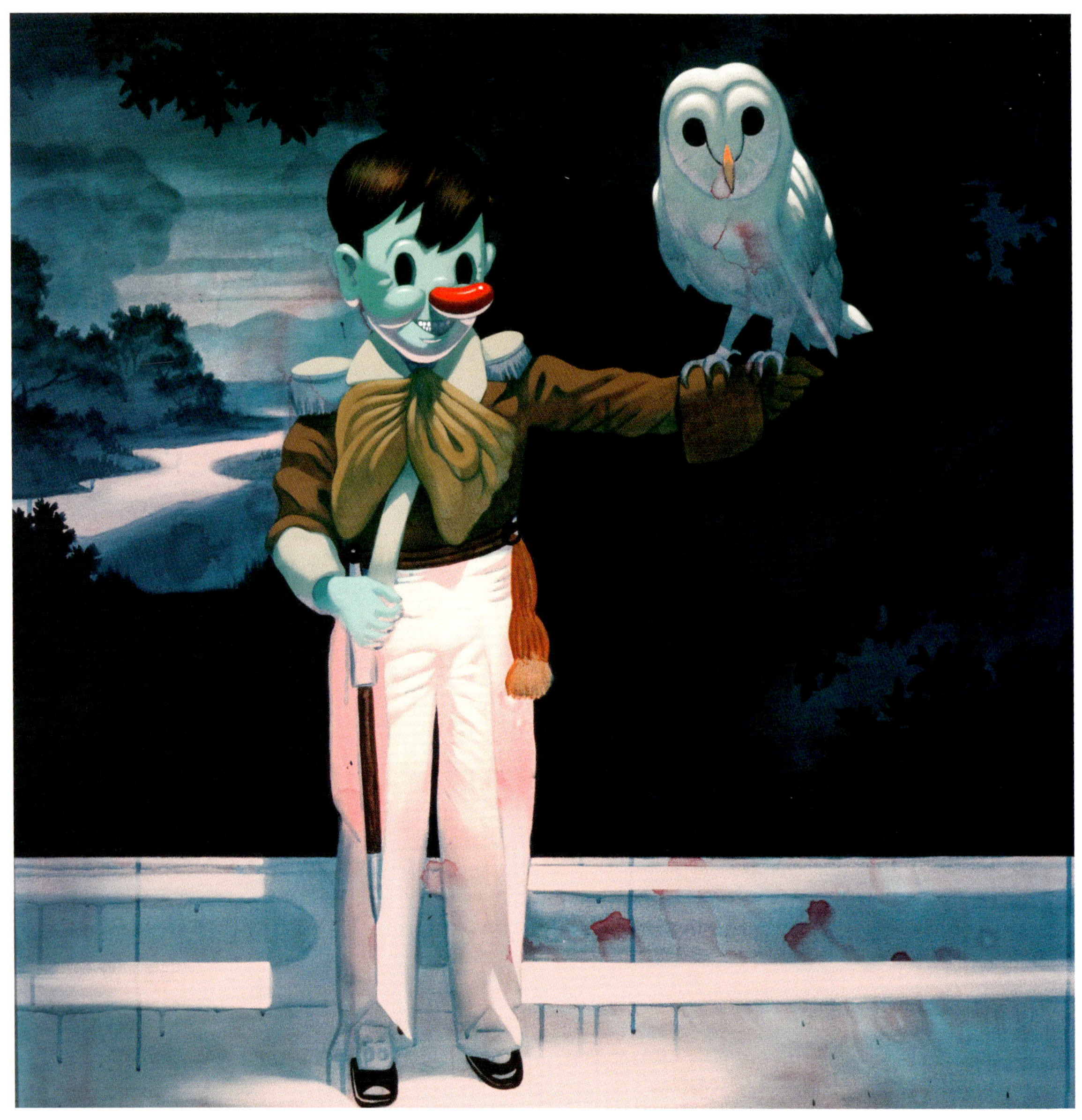

Superstition, acrylic on canvas

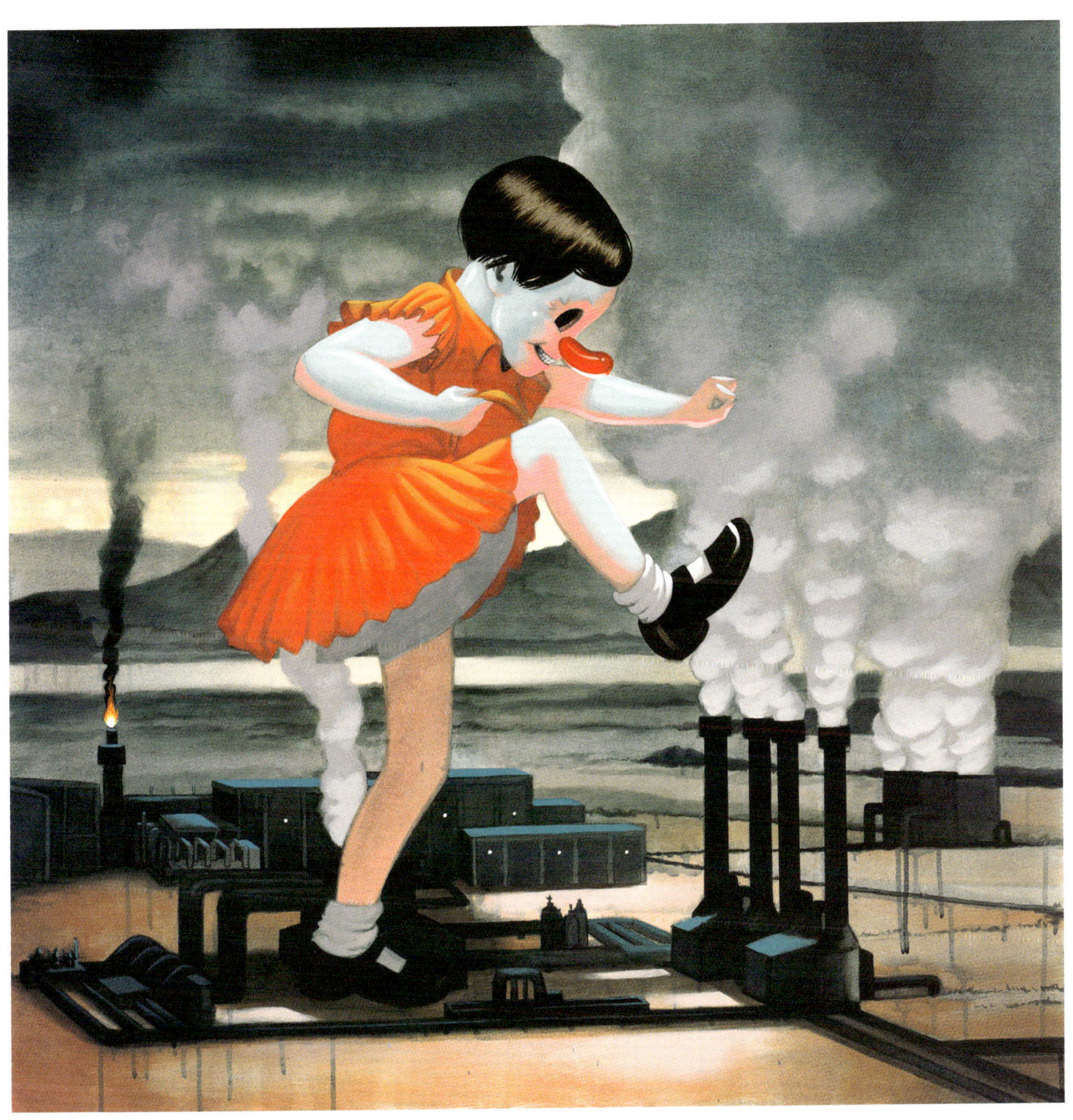

You are the Inspiration, acrylic on canvas

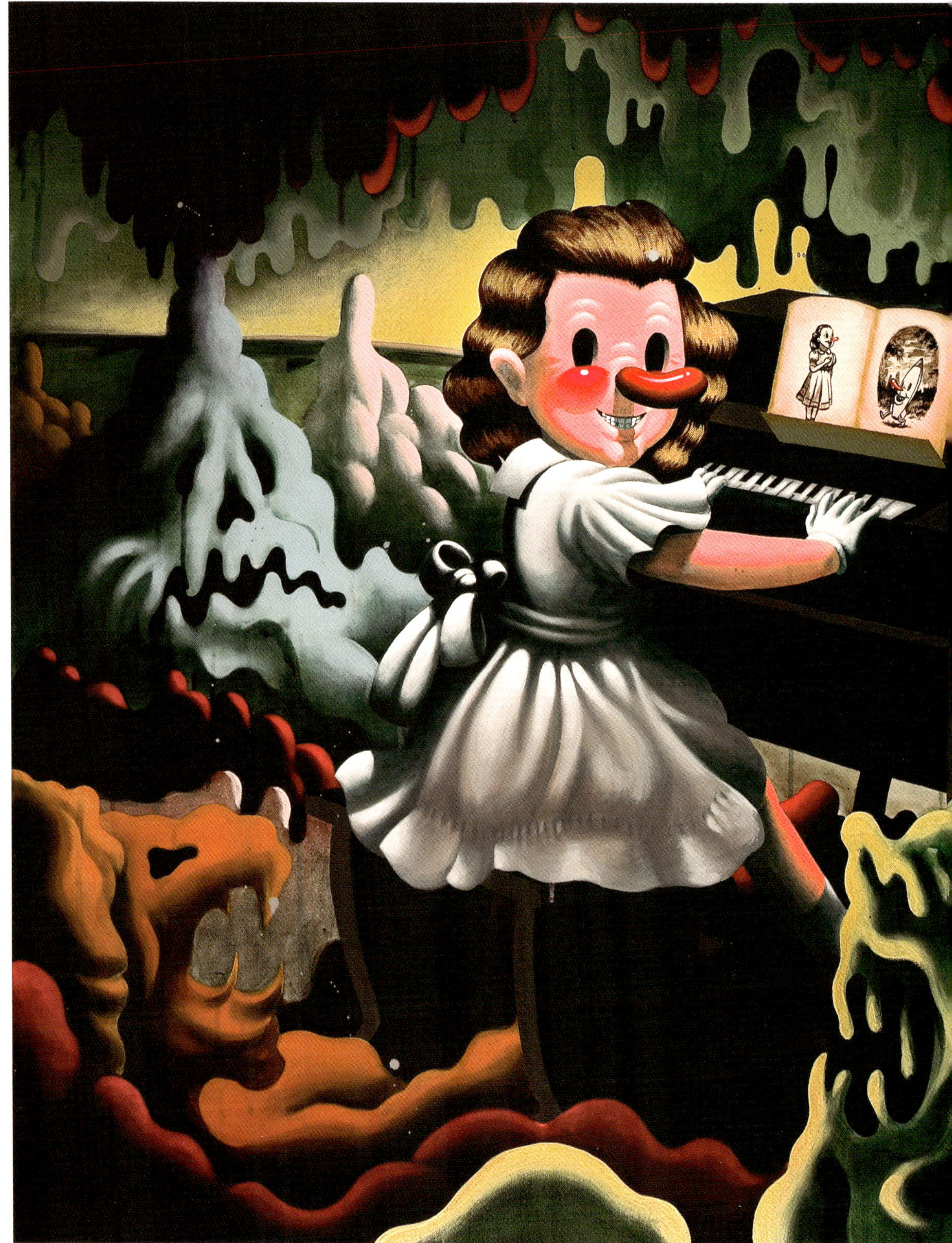

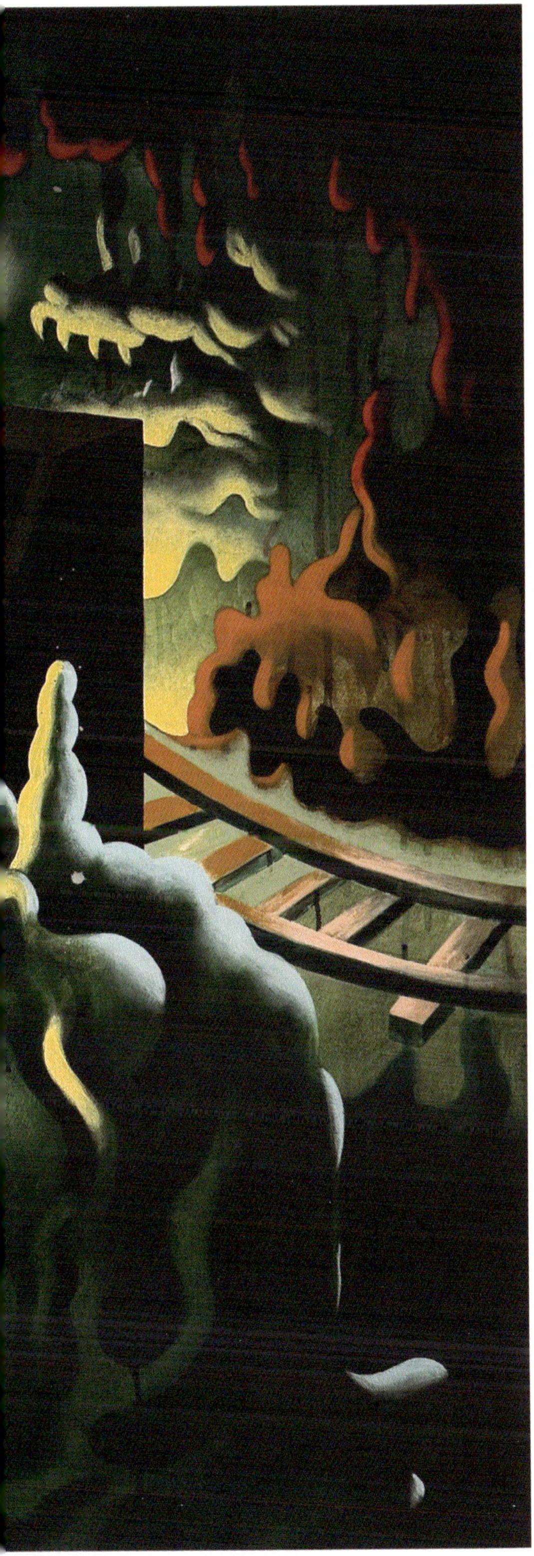

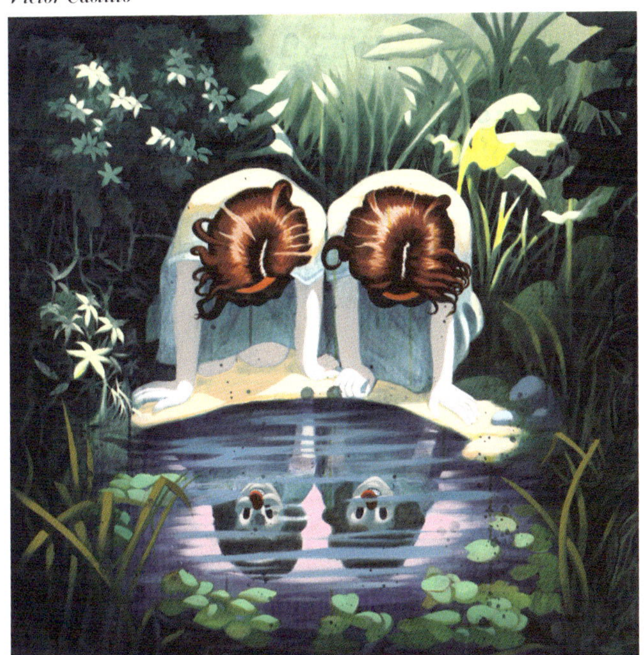

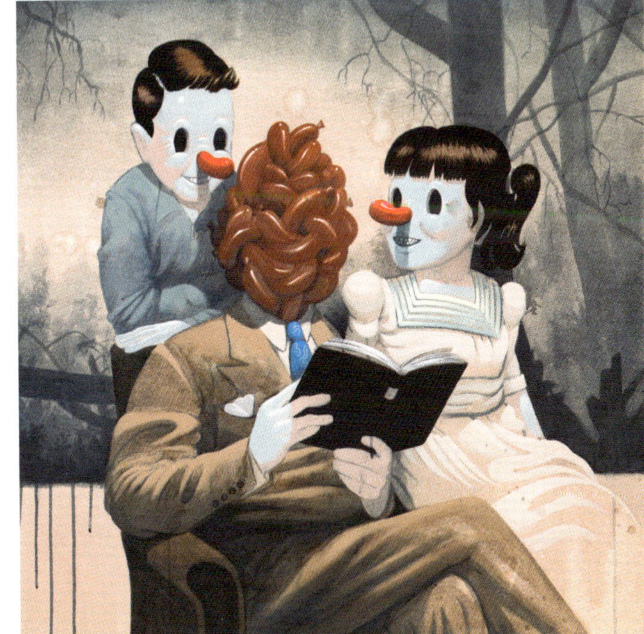

left: Horrible Fanfaria, acrylic on canvas
right, top: Quien es la mas bella, *bottom:* Written, forgotten

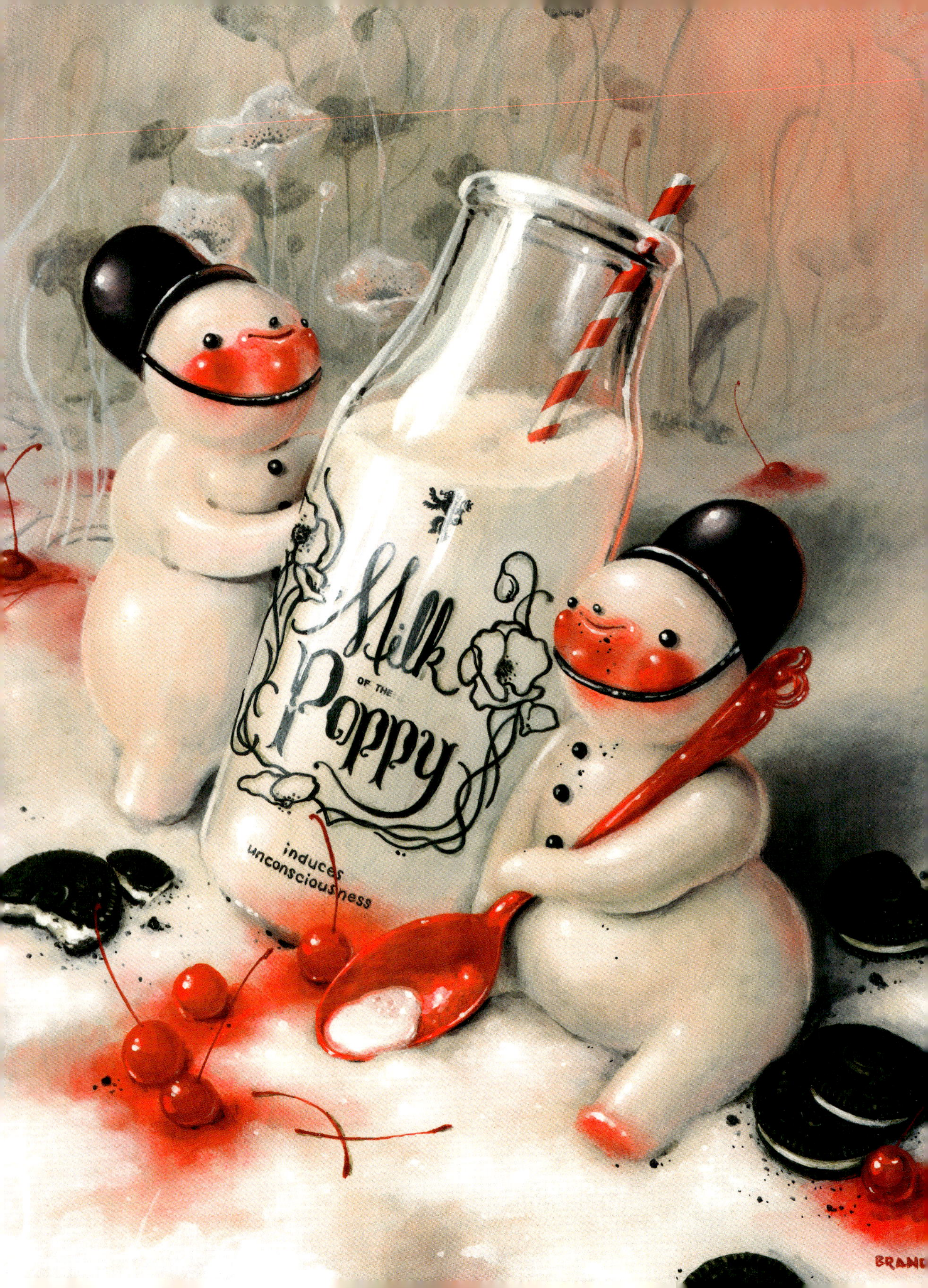
Milk
OF THE
Poppy
induces unconsciousness

www.brandimilne.com

Brandi Milne

Brandi Milne is an American painter. Born and raised in Anaheim California in the late 1970's, Milne's surrounding world of classic cartoons, toys, candies, Disneyland and joyous family Holidays fascinated and deeply influenced her young imagination.

Self-taught and emotionally driven, Brandi's work speaks of love, loss, pain and heartbreak underneath a beautiful candy-coated surface. Using elements as language from her child's mind, Brandi creates a unique surreal world that is undeniably hers.

Brandi's work is celebrated and supported in fine art galleries and museums internationally and across the US, and has been featured in both written and online publications such as *Hi Fructose* and *Bizarre Magazine*. She published her first book *So Good For Little Bunnies* in 2008 and her second, *Frohlich*, in 2014, both with Baby Tattoo Books. Brandi has collaborated with many companies including Hurley, Billabong, Disney, Sugarpill Cosmetics and Acme Film Works for CVS Pharmacy.

Brandi Milne es una pintora estadounidense. Nacida y criada en Anaheim (California) a finales de 1970, su mundo lleno de dibujos animados, juguetes, caramelos, Disneyland y vacaciones de familia feliz le fascinaron e influyeron profundamente en su joven imaginación.

Autodidacta y motivada, la obra de Brandi habla del amor, la pérdida, el dolor y la angustia que subyace por debajo de una apariencia hermosa revestida de dulzura. Utilizando elementos como el lenguaje de la mente de un niño, Brandi crea un mundo surrealista único.

La obra de Brandi se expone en galerías de arte y museos a nivel internacional y en los Estados Unidos, y ha sido presentada tanto en publicaciones escritas como en línea, tales como *Hi Fructose* y *Bizarre Magazine*. Publicó su primer libro *So Good For Little Bunnies* en 2008 y su segundo, *Frohlich*, en 2014, ambos con la editorial Baby Tattoo Books. Brandi ha colaborado con muchas empresas, incluyendo Hurley, Billabong, Disney, Sugarpill Cosmetics y Acme Film Works para CVS Pharmacy.

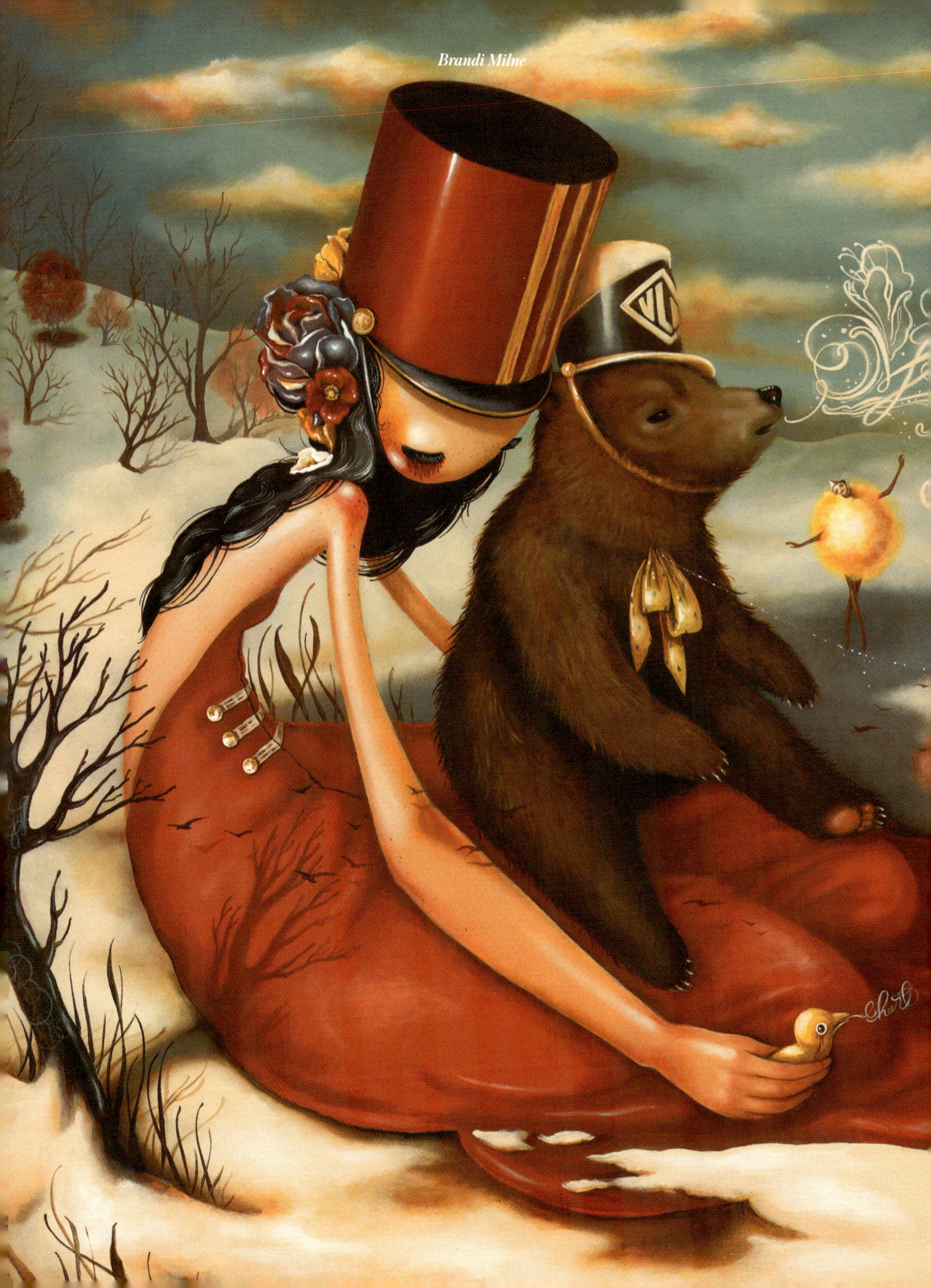

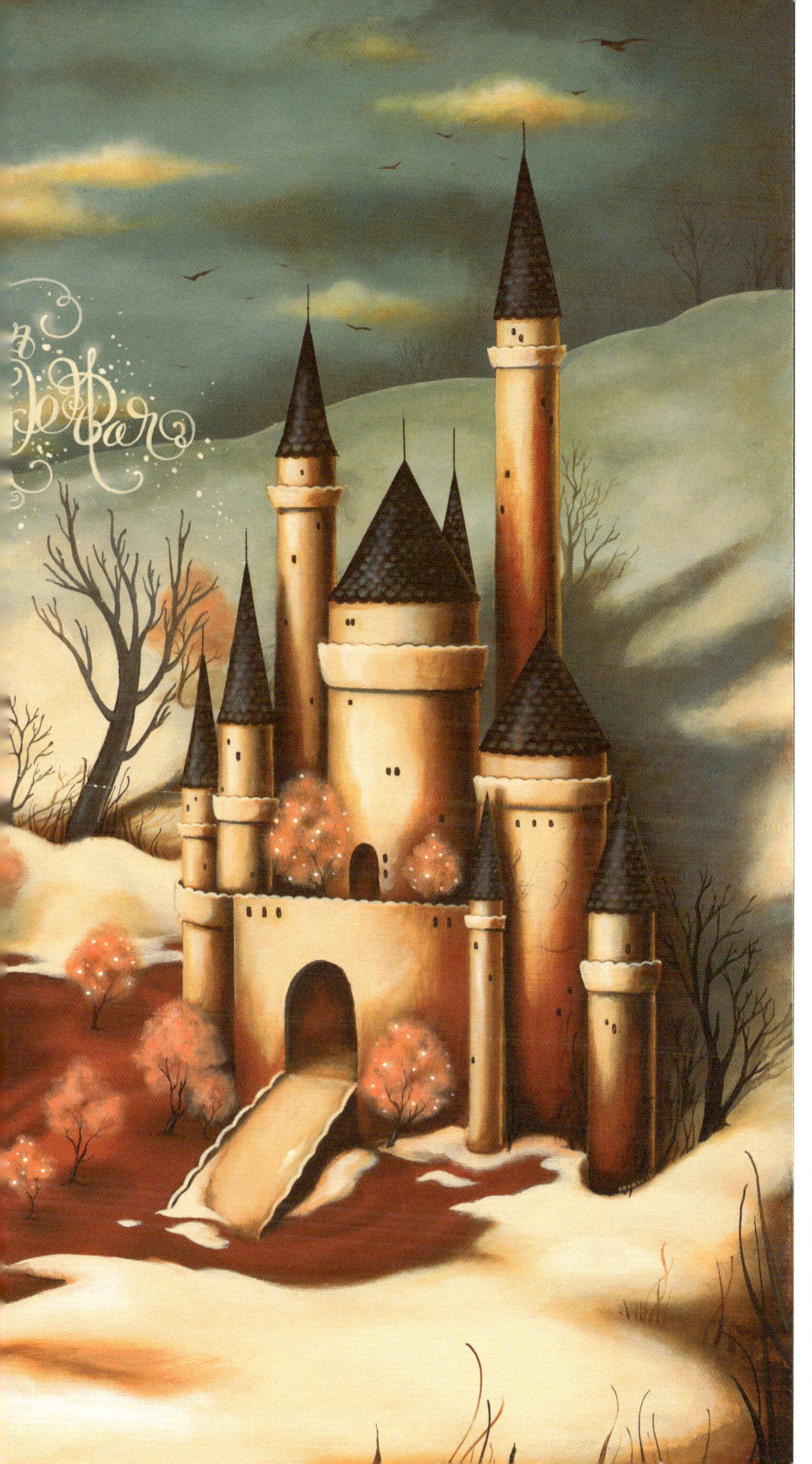

How Can I Shine Without You

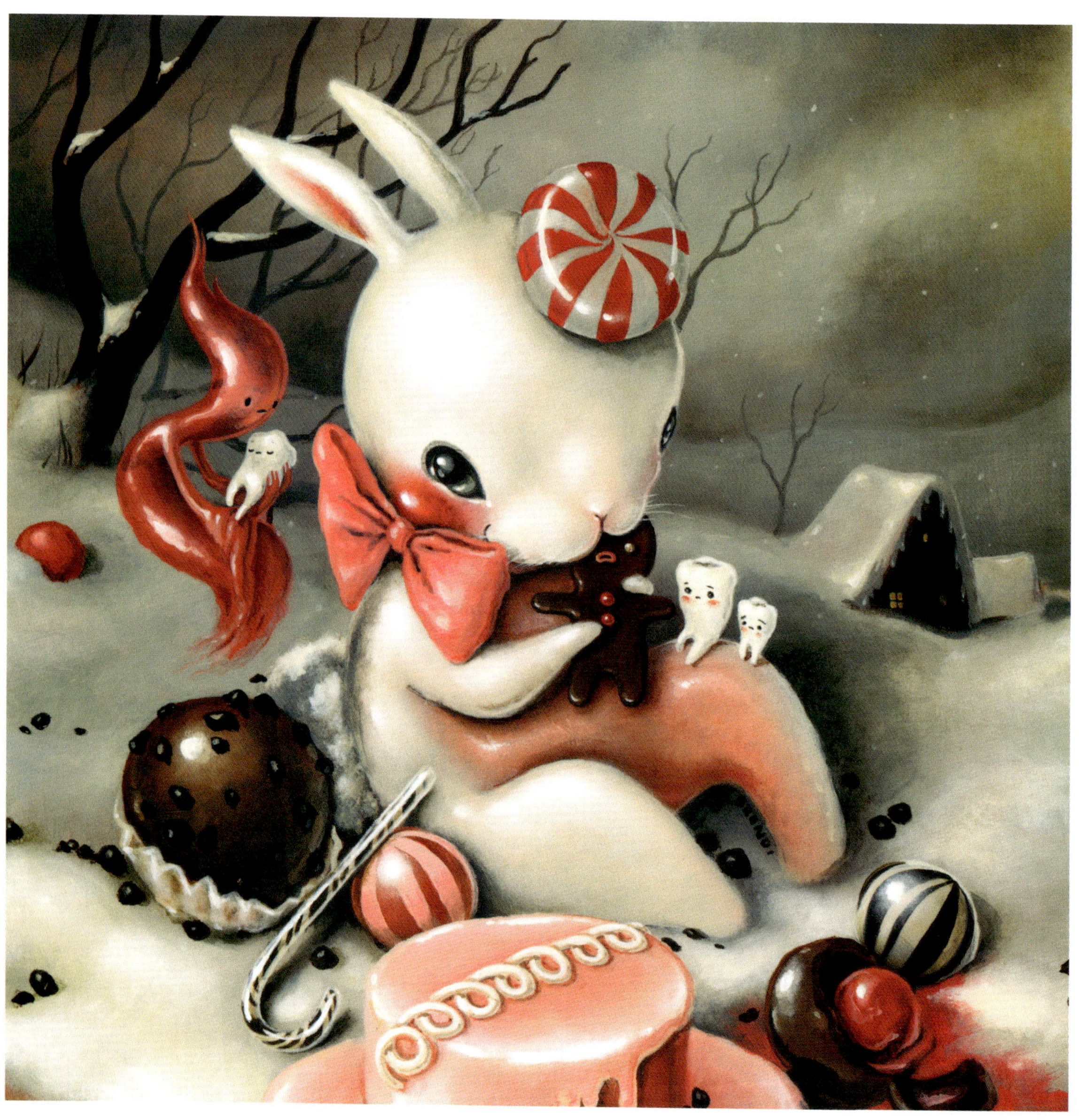

Soothe Yourself

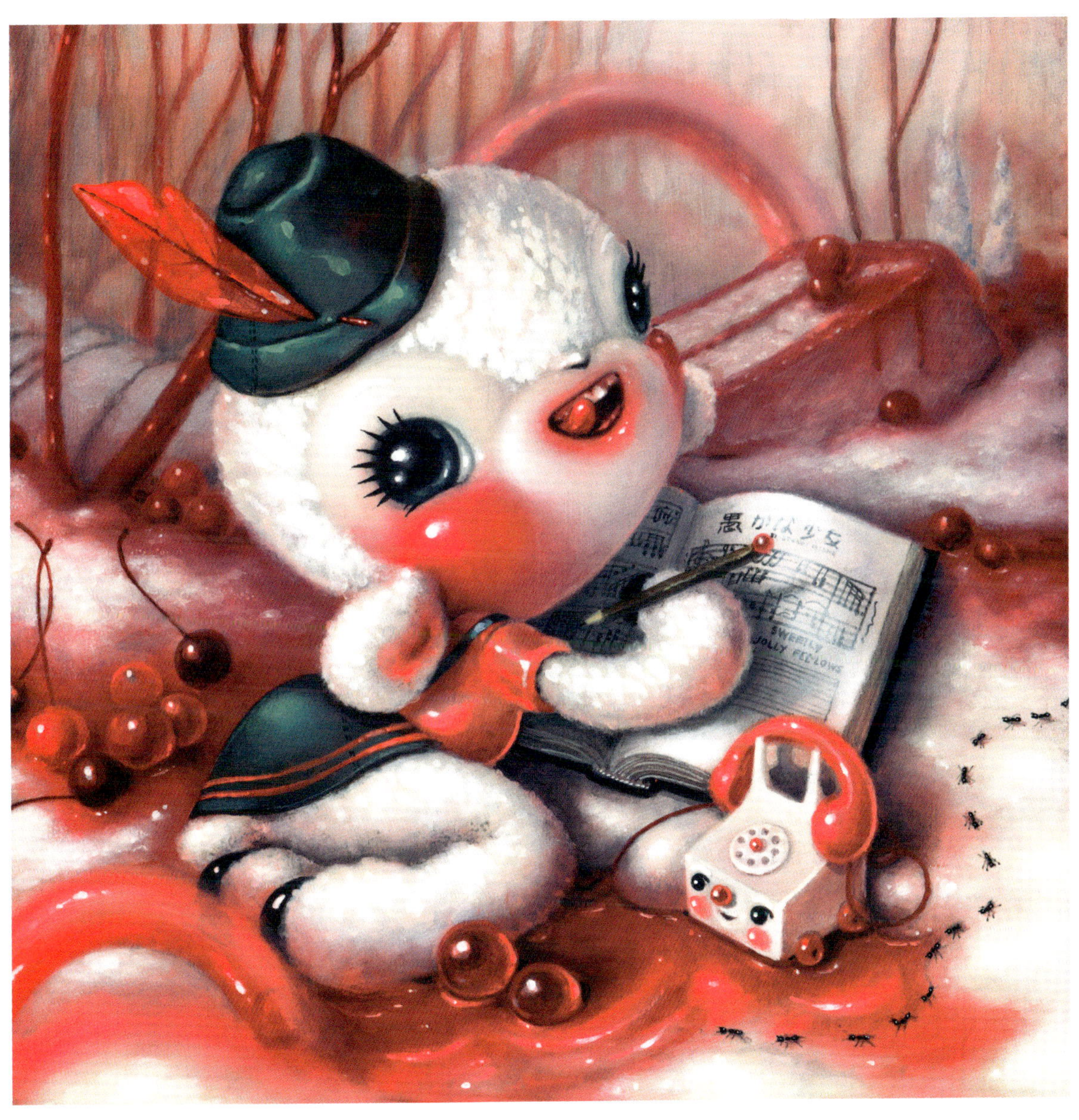

Once Upon A Time, Life Was Sweeter Than We Knew
next page: The Little Death // ***next one:*** I Never Dreamed Of Such A Place

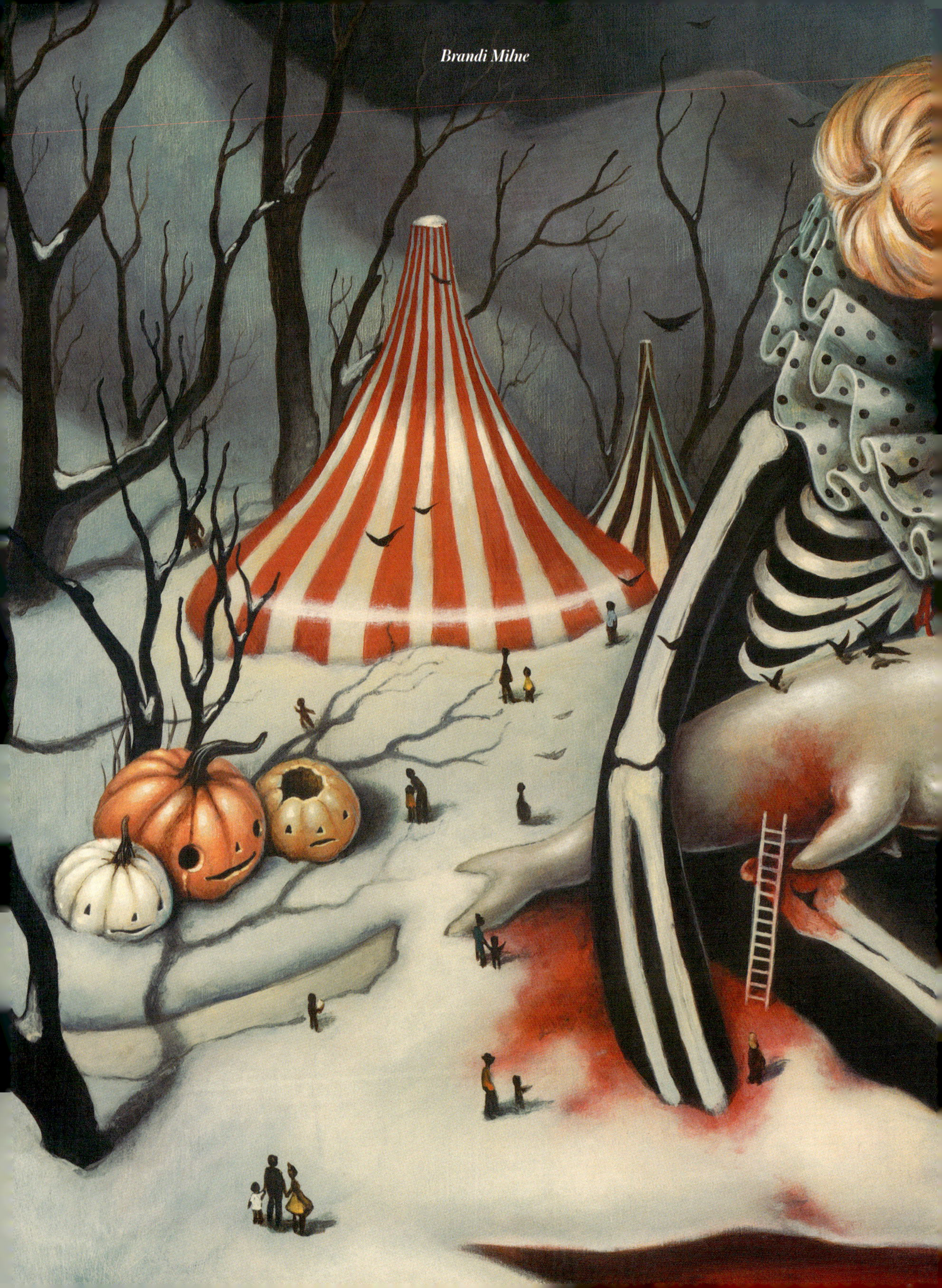

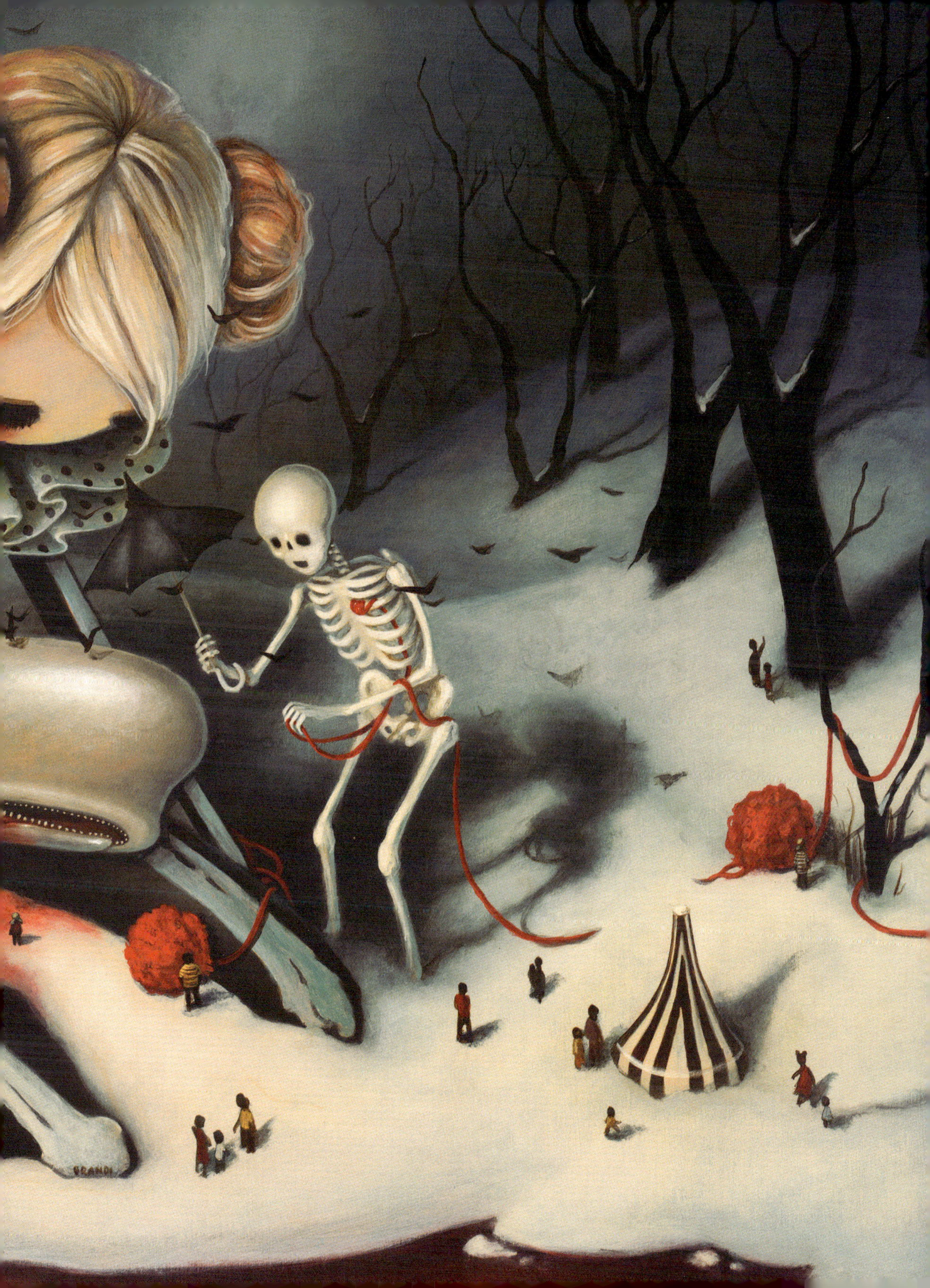
BRANDI

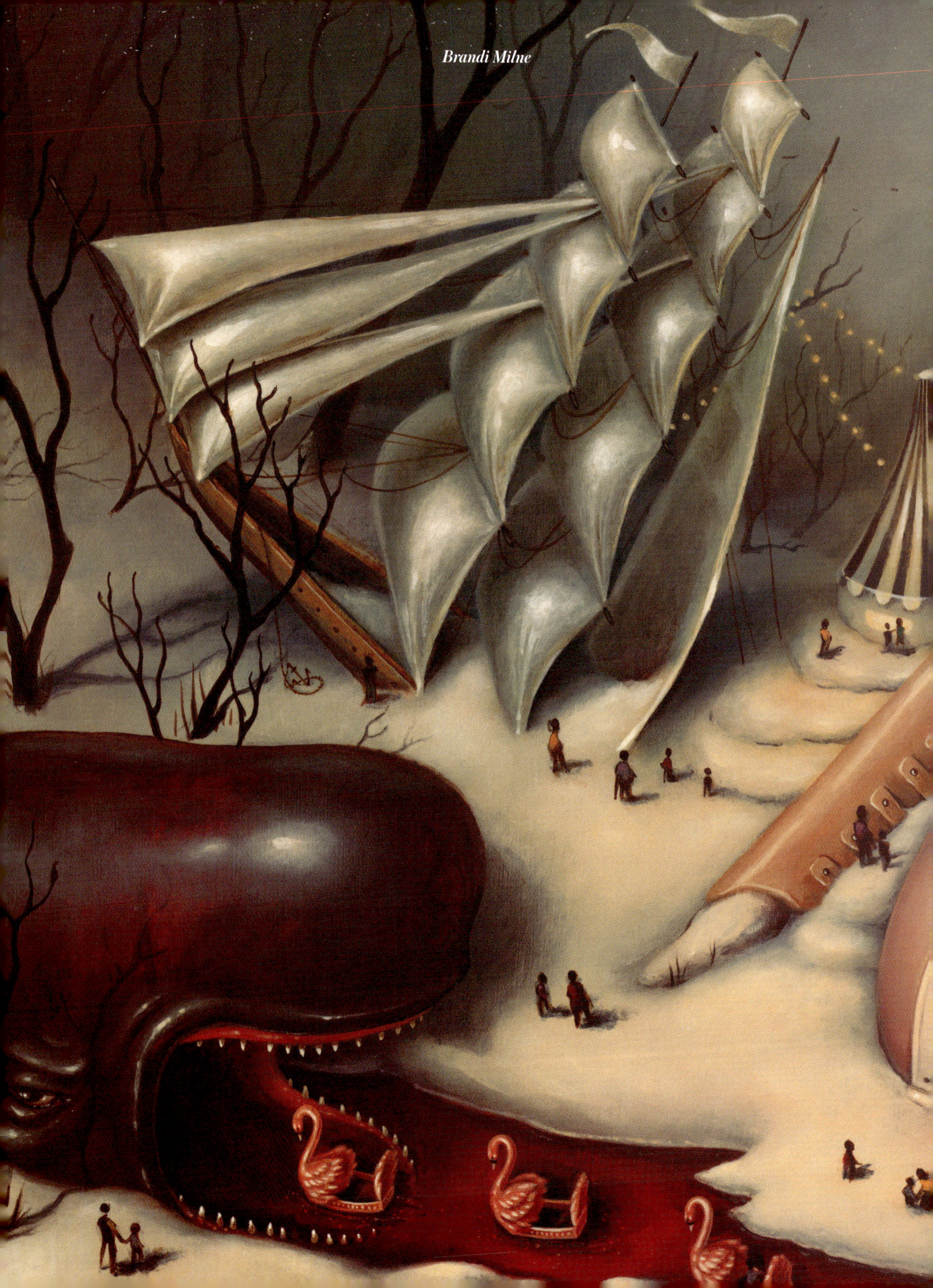

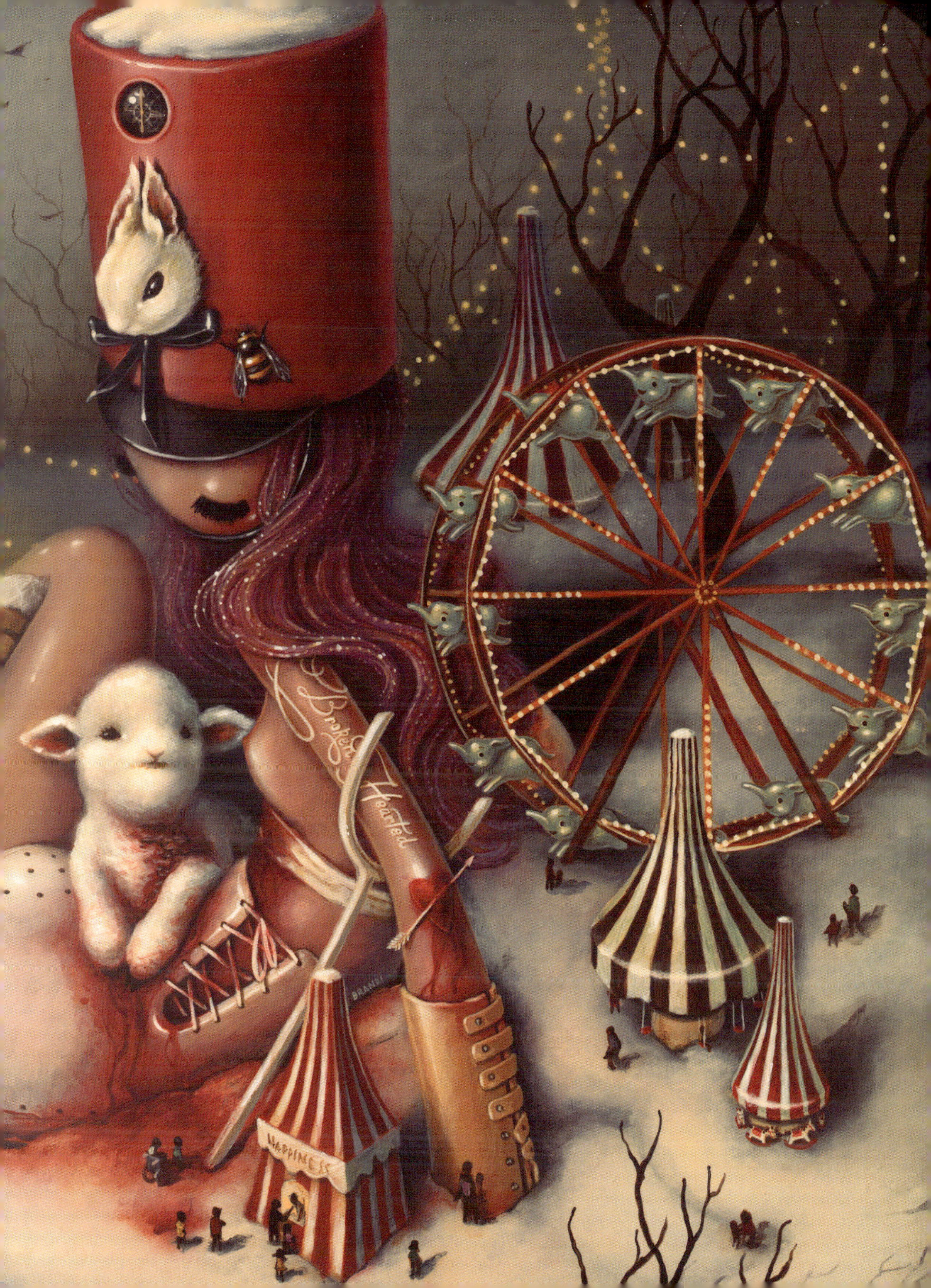
Broken Hearted
BRANDI
HAPPINESS

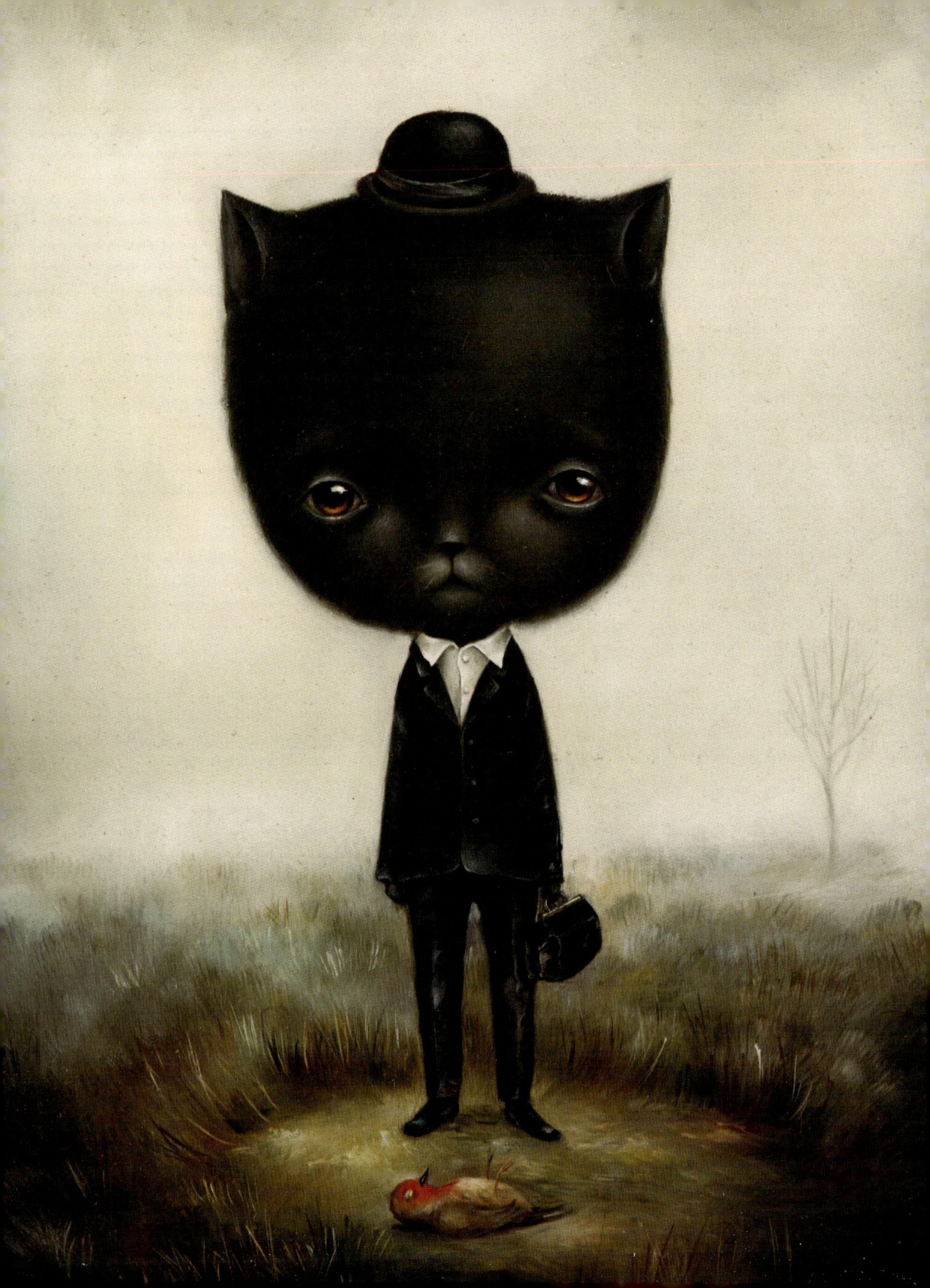

dilkabear.tumblr.com

Dilka Bear

Dilka was born in Almaty, in present day Kazakhstan, when it was still the Soviet Union. Drawing has always been her passion; she used to draw very much when she was little, and this really didn't make her parents very happy because she used to draw on books and newspaper, even on the walls of their house, or on her mother's dresses!

When she finally grew up a little, she decided to study architecture, because she let herself be talked into studying something "serious". However, after two years she decided that it had been a bad decision and so she began to study art instead.

Dilka graduated not very long after that, and she found herself working as a graphic designer, and finding it very boring indeed, she moved to italy when she was 28, but there she couldn't find any kind of job at all. She was lucky though: a friend gave her a few old tubes of acrylic paint and some small pieces of wood that she had found in a street market, cut to a proper size. Dilka started to paint, just some paintings of animals at first, mainly bears, but they were kind of ugly. She hadn't quite come up with her own style yet, although her first works were kind of sweet. Then she tried to paint people: her characters always looked like children because there's something of her own in each of them, and she never wanted to grow up. She is still a child, deep down. Most of her works tells stories, she feels that she is a painter and a storyteller all at once.

Sometimes she can be inspired by people or by things that happen around her, with books that she read, or by stories that just materialize in her mind.

Dilka nació en Almaty, en la actualidad Kazajstán, cuando aún era la Unión Soviética. El dibujo siempre ha sido su pasión; solía dibujar mucho cuando era pequeña y esto era algo que a sus padres no les hacía demasiada gracia ya que solía dibujar en libros y periódicos, ¡incluso en las paredes de su casa y los vestidos de su madre!

Cuando finalmente creció un poco, decidió estudiar arquitectura, ya que se convenció a si misma para estudiar algo "serio". Sin embargo, dos años después decidió que había sido una mala decisión y empezó a estudiar arte.

Dilka se graduó poco después y se encontró trabajando como diseñadora gráfica, lo cual, de hecho, encontraba muy aburrido. Se mudó a Italia cuando tenía 28 años pero allí no pudo encontrar ningún tipo de trabajo. Aún así, tuvo suerte: un amigo le dio unos tubos viejos de pintura acrílica y algunos trozos pequeños de madera que había encontrado en un mercado callejero. Dilka comenzó a pintar animales, generalmente osos, pero eran algo feos. Aún no había alcanzado su propio estilo. Entonces intentó pintar gente: Sus personajes siempre parecían niños porque hay algo suyo en cada uno de ellos y ella nunca quiso crecer. En el fondo aún es una niña. La mayoría de sus obras cuentan historias, ella siente que es pintora y a la vez narradora.

A veces puede verse inspirada por personas o por cosas que suceden a su alrededor, por libros que lee o por historias que sólo se materializan en su mente.

▸ Mr. Reaper

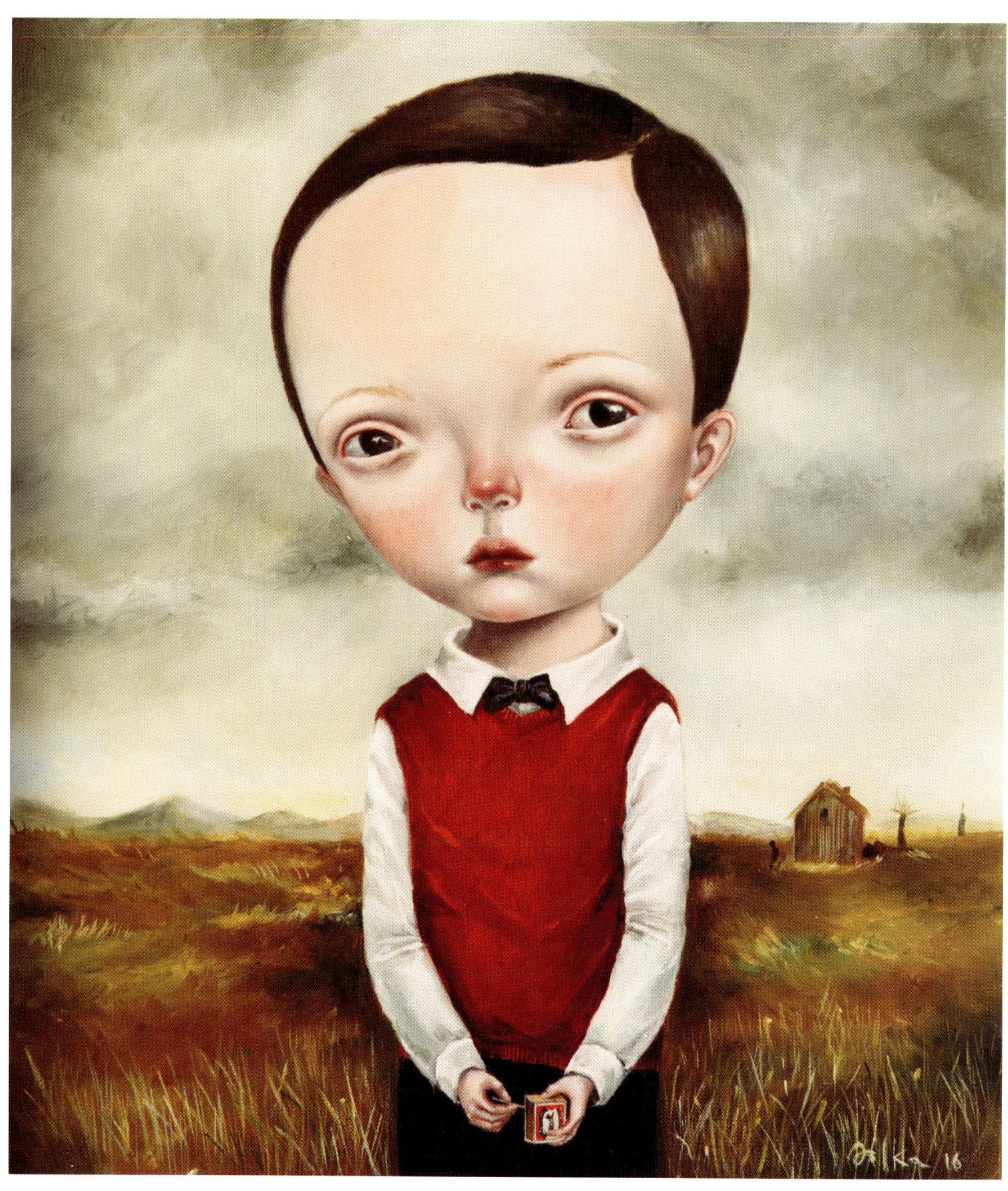

The good son

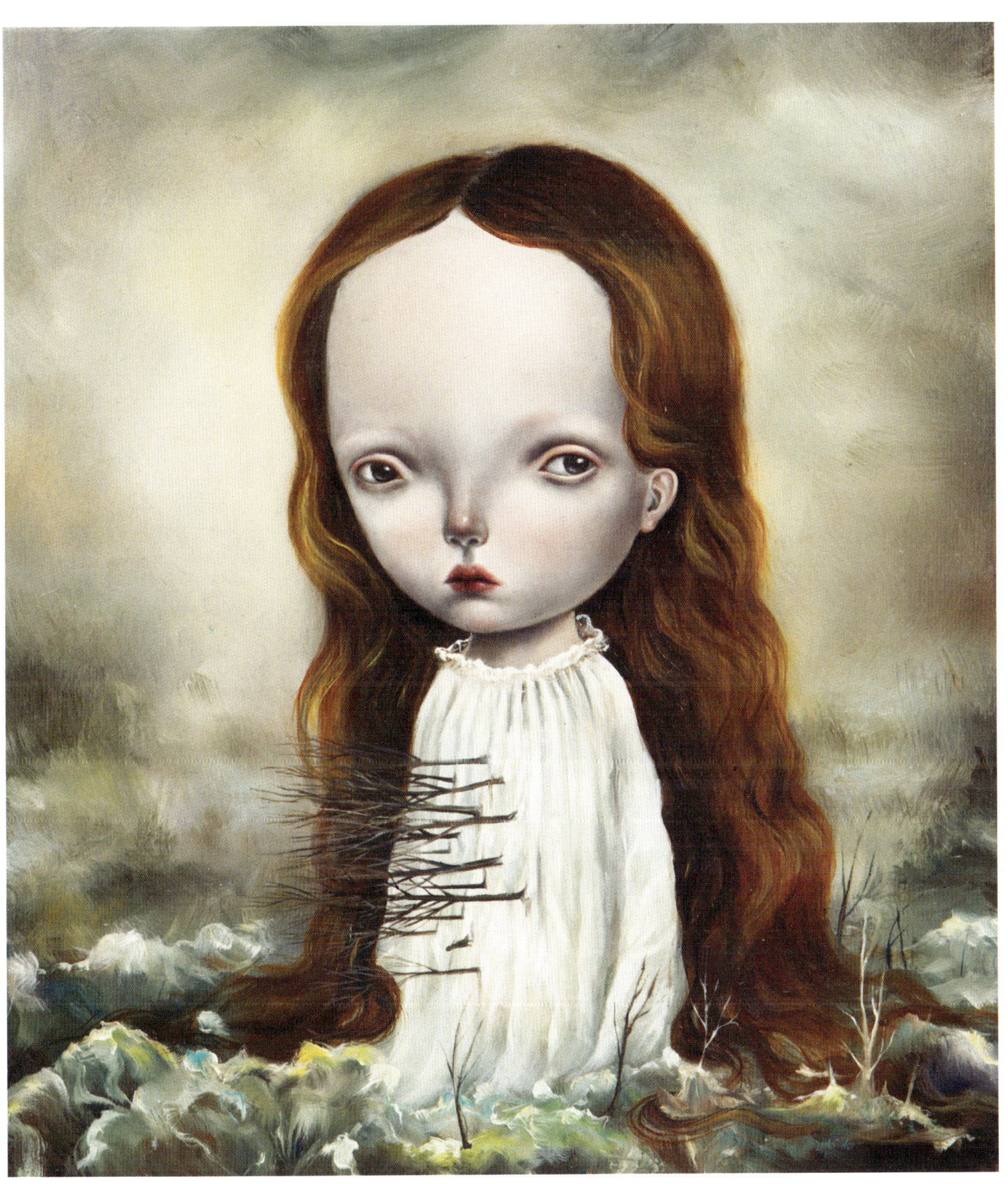

My dead forest

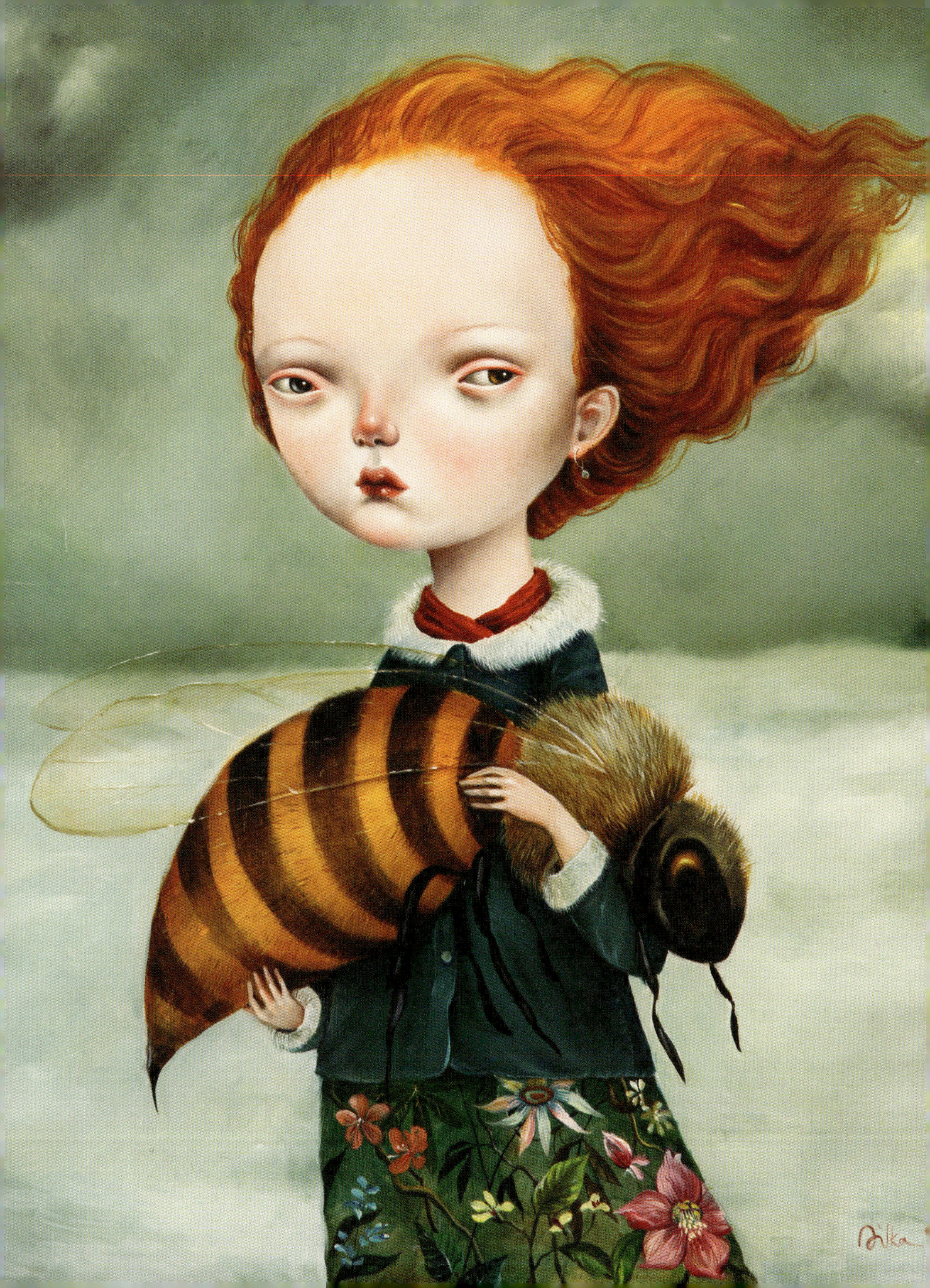

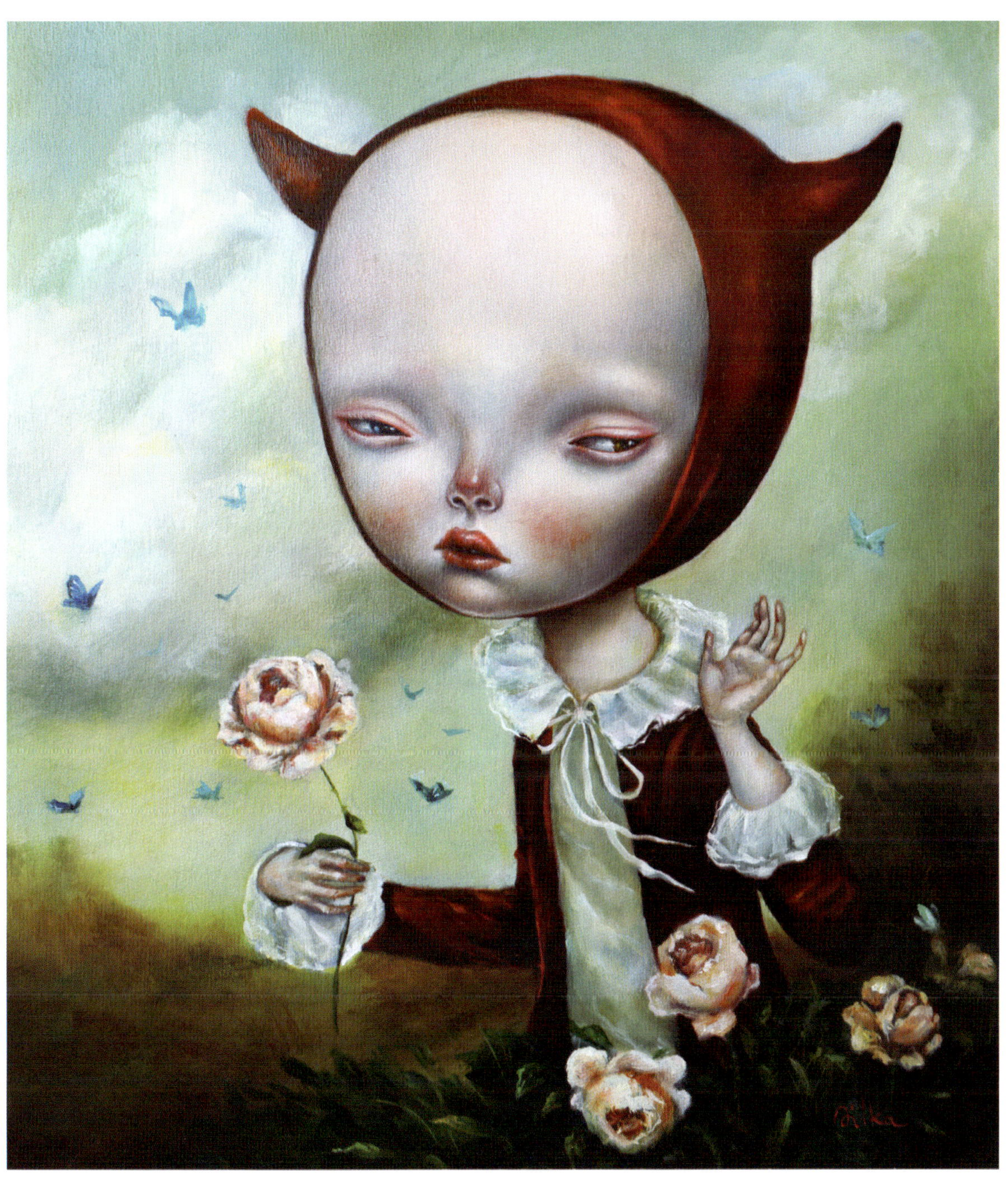

left: Hunter // ***right:*** Devil and butterflies

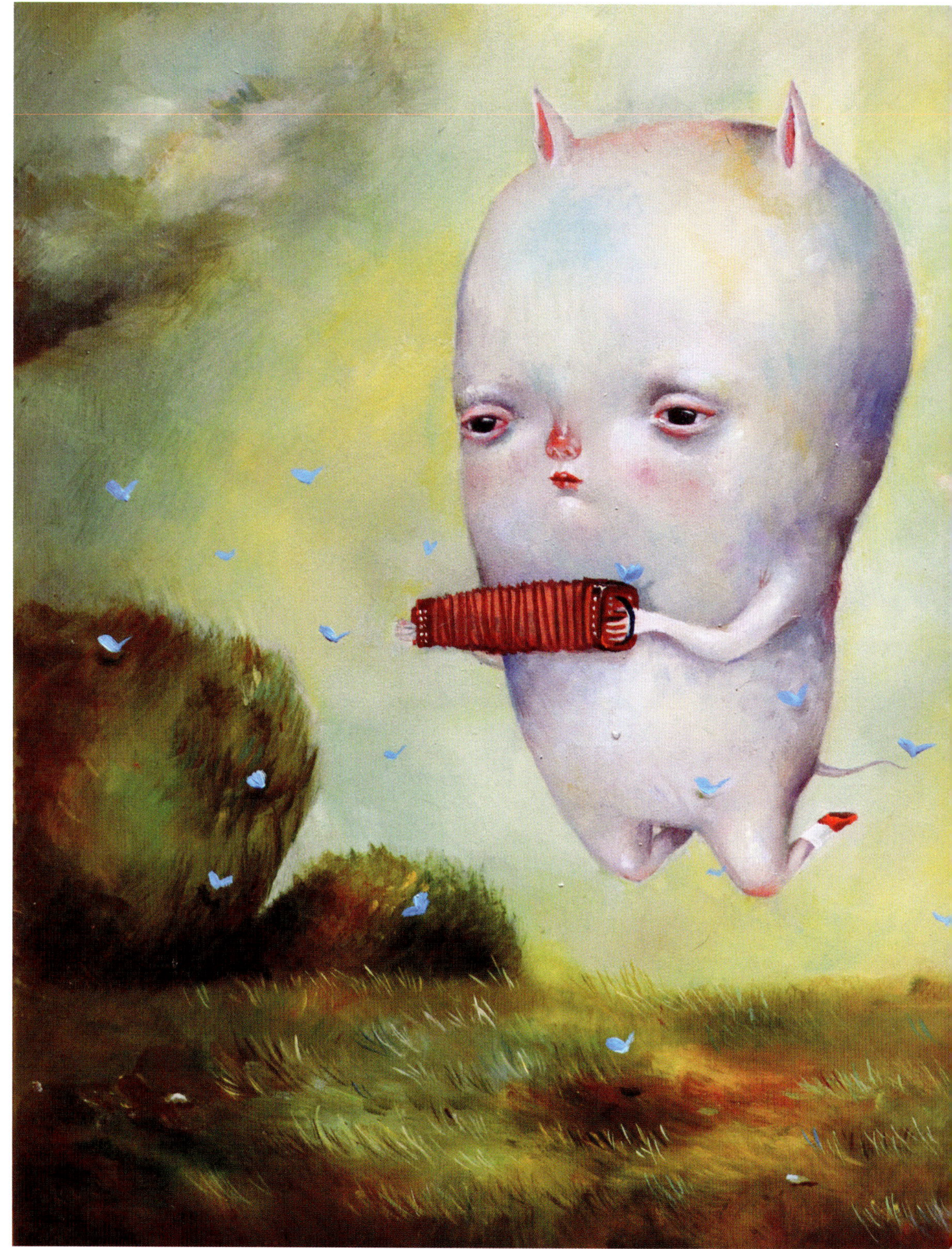

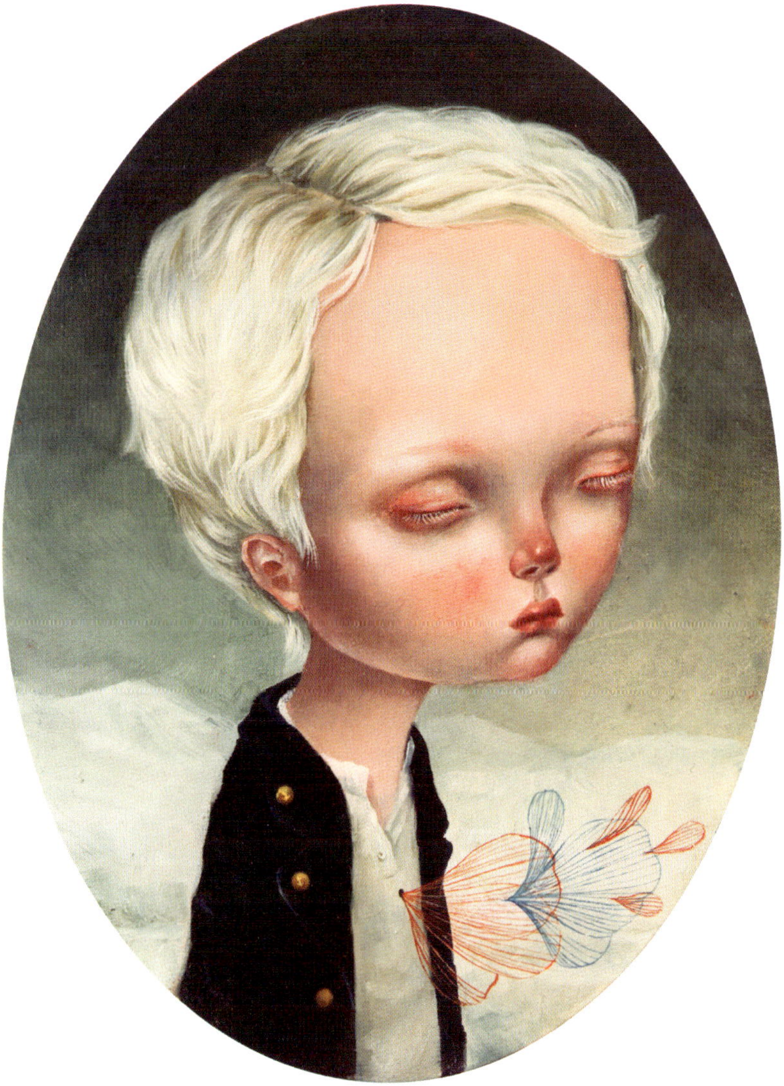

left: Lalaland // *right:* Lovers part one

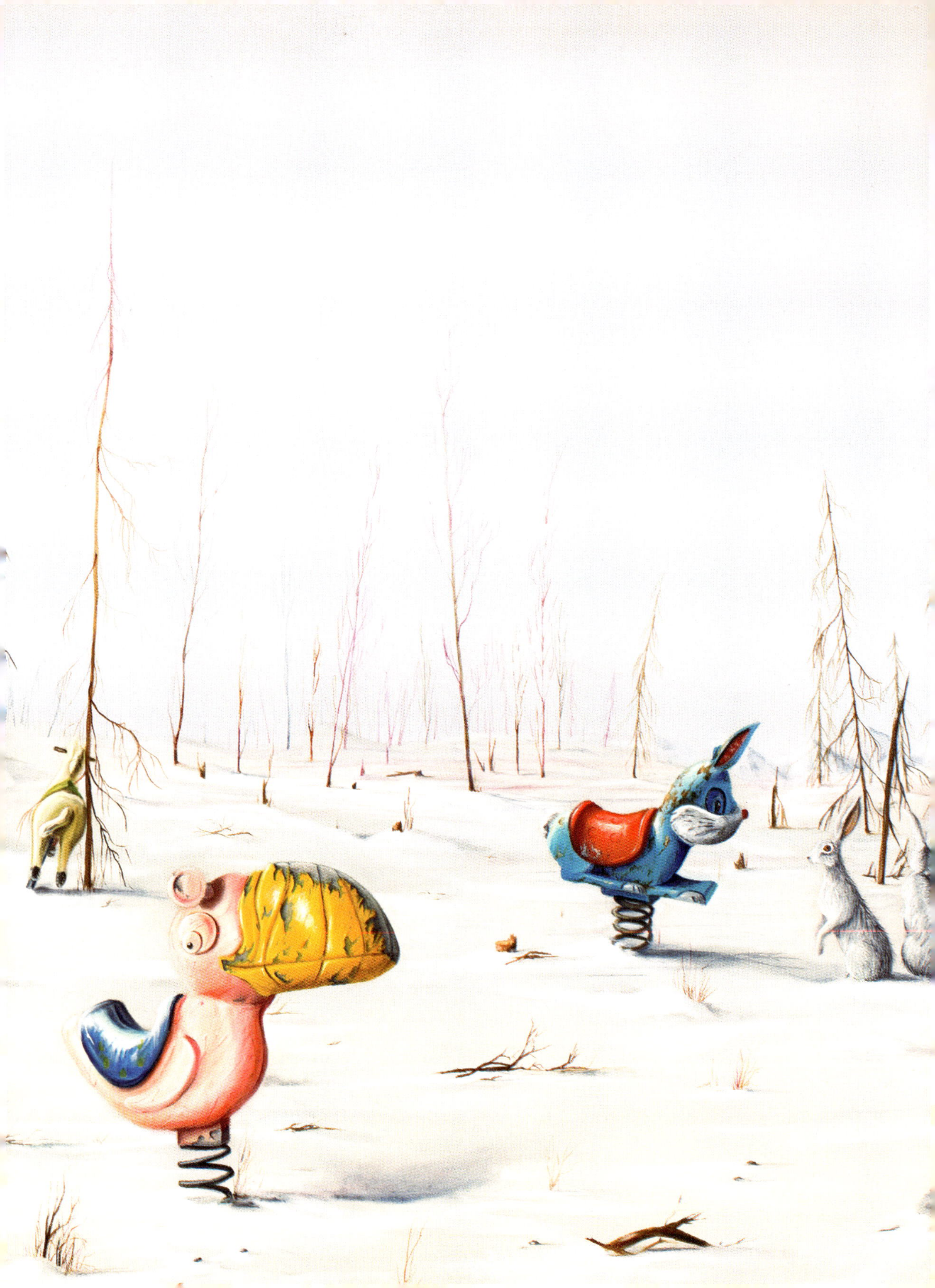

ewapronczukkuziak.pl

Ewa Pronczuk-Kuziak

Ewa Prończuk-Kuziak is a Polish contemporary artist, who lives and works in Warsaw, Poland.

She studied Polish Philology at the Warsaw University, Fine Arts at the Royal Academy of Fine Arts (Antwerp, Belgium) and Painting at the Academy of Fine Arts (Warsaw, Poland) where she obtained an MFA in Painting.

Ewa's oil paintings are a combination of still life, nature and fantasy. She creates rainbow-colored visions of animals that are made of materials, woven out of thread and decorative fabrics. Build on contrast, they are full of life, energy, and fantasy, always ideal in their complicated nature and continuous transformation. In her works, Ewa uses intensely saturated colors which illustrate the vibrancy of the world her characters inhabit.

Ewa Prończuk-Kuziak es una artista polaca contemporánea que vive y trabaja en Varsovia (Polonia).

Estudió Filología Polaca en la Universidad de Varsovia, Bellas Artes en la Real Academia de Bellas Artes (Amberes, Bélgica) y Pintura en la Academia de Bellas Artes (Varsovia, Polonia), donde obtuvo un Máster de Bellas Artes en Pintura.

Las pinturas al óleo de Ewa son una combinación de vida inerte, naturaleza y fantasía. Crea visiones de color arco iris de animales que están hechos de materiales, tejidos de hilo y telas decorativas. Creadas sobre contrastes, sus pinturas están llenas de vida, energía y fantasía, siempre ideales en su complicada naturaleza y transformación continua. Ewa utiliza colores intensamente saturados que ilustran la vitalidad del mundo que habitan sus personajes.

▸ No title (detail), oil on linen

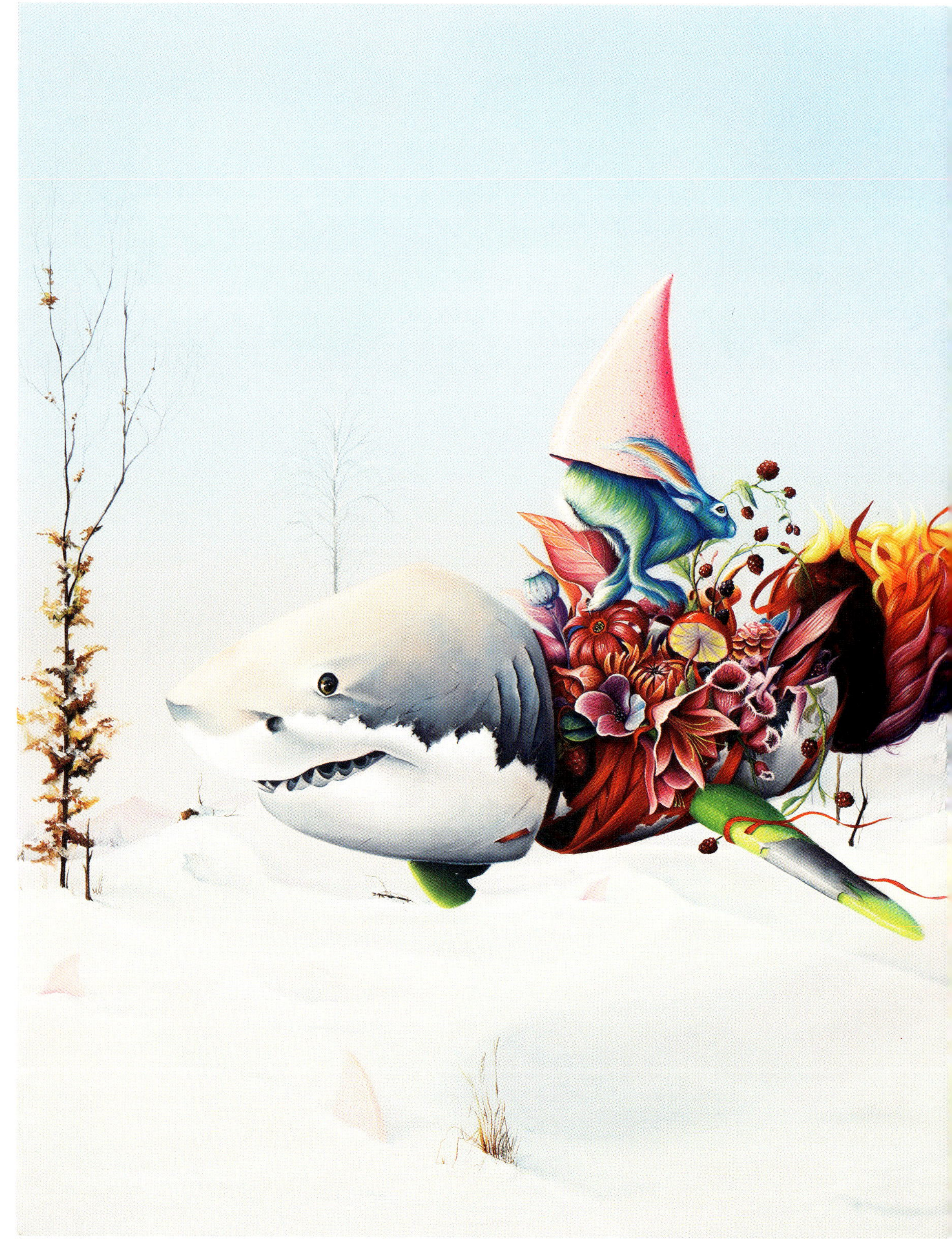

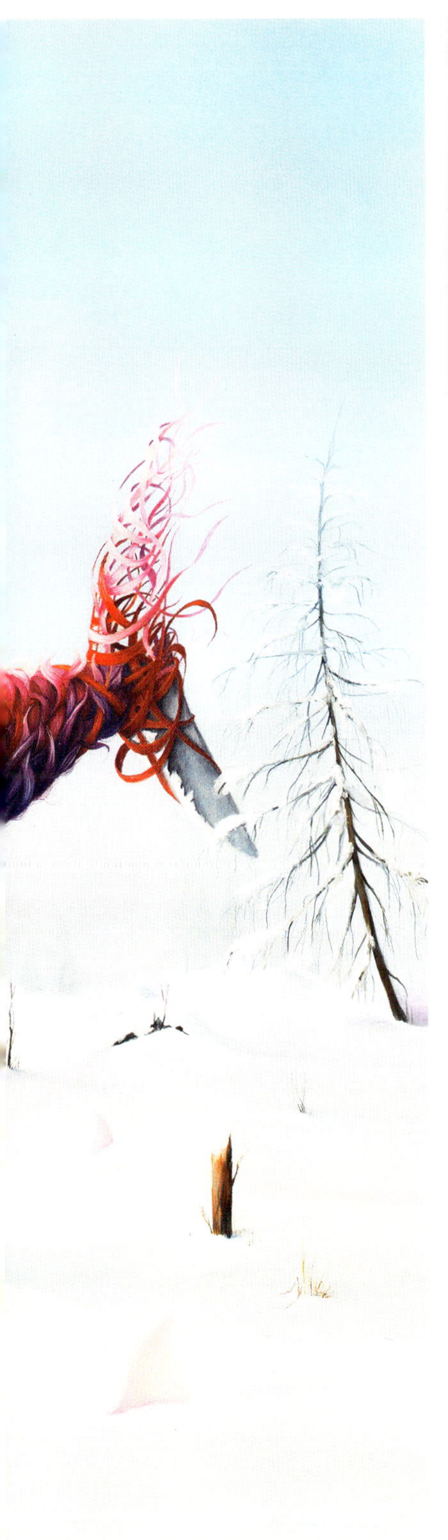

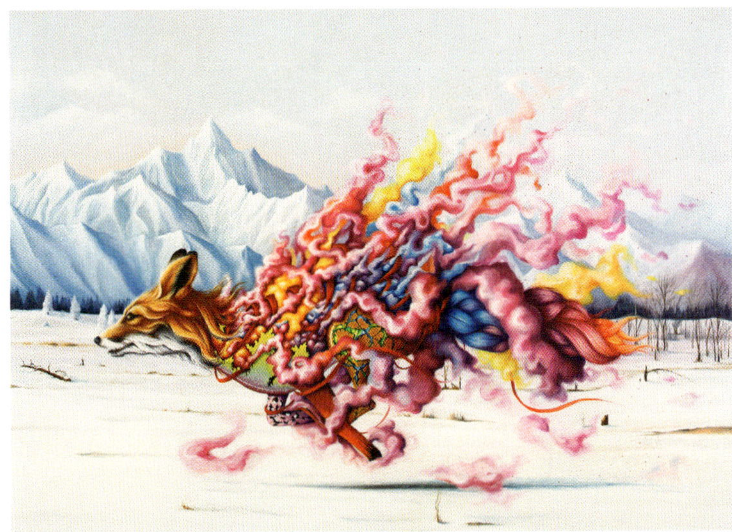

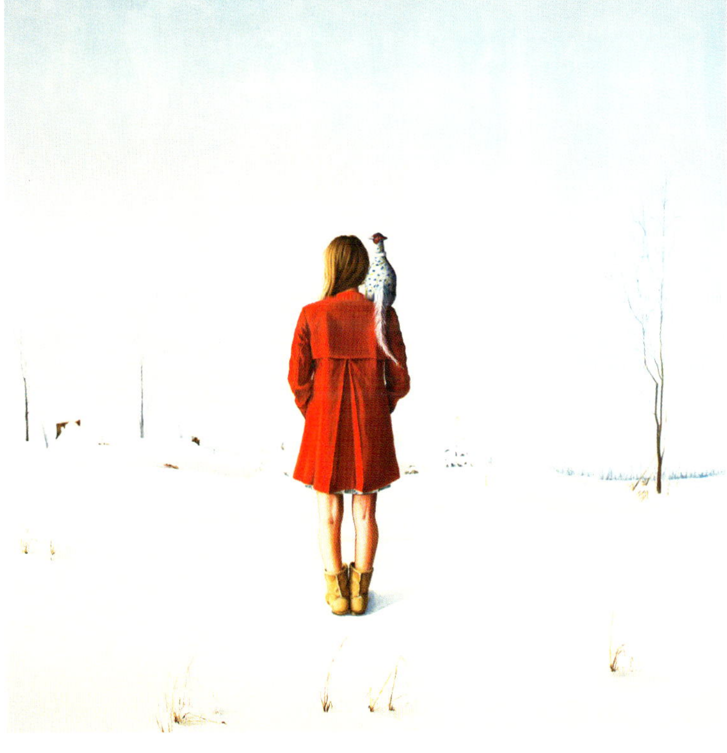

left: Where is my mind, oil on linen
right, top: Phoenix, oil on linen, ***bottom:*** The Immensity series, oil on canvas

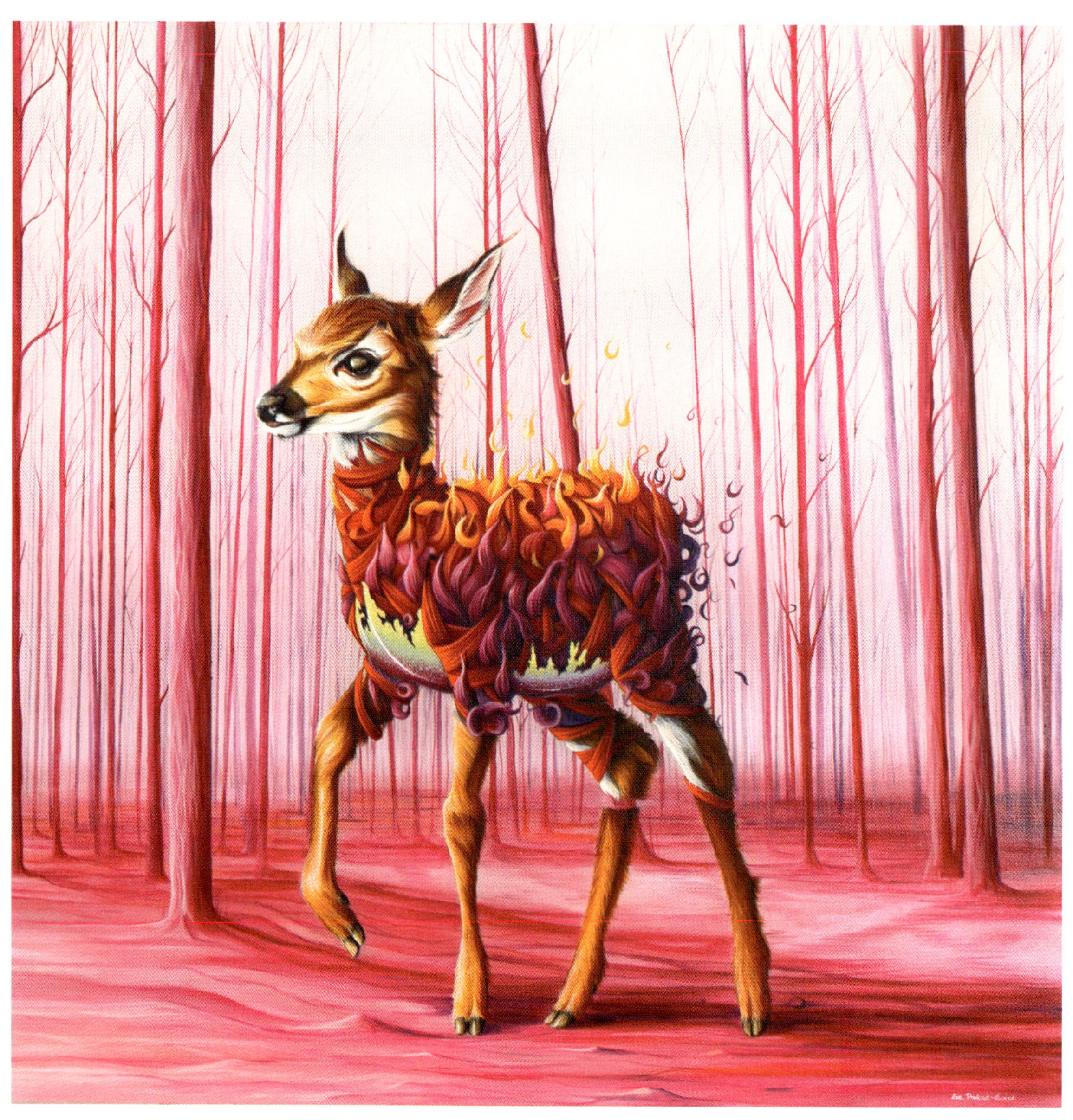

The Still life series: Who killed Bamby, oil on linen

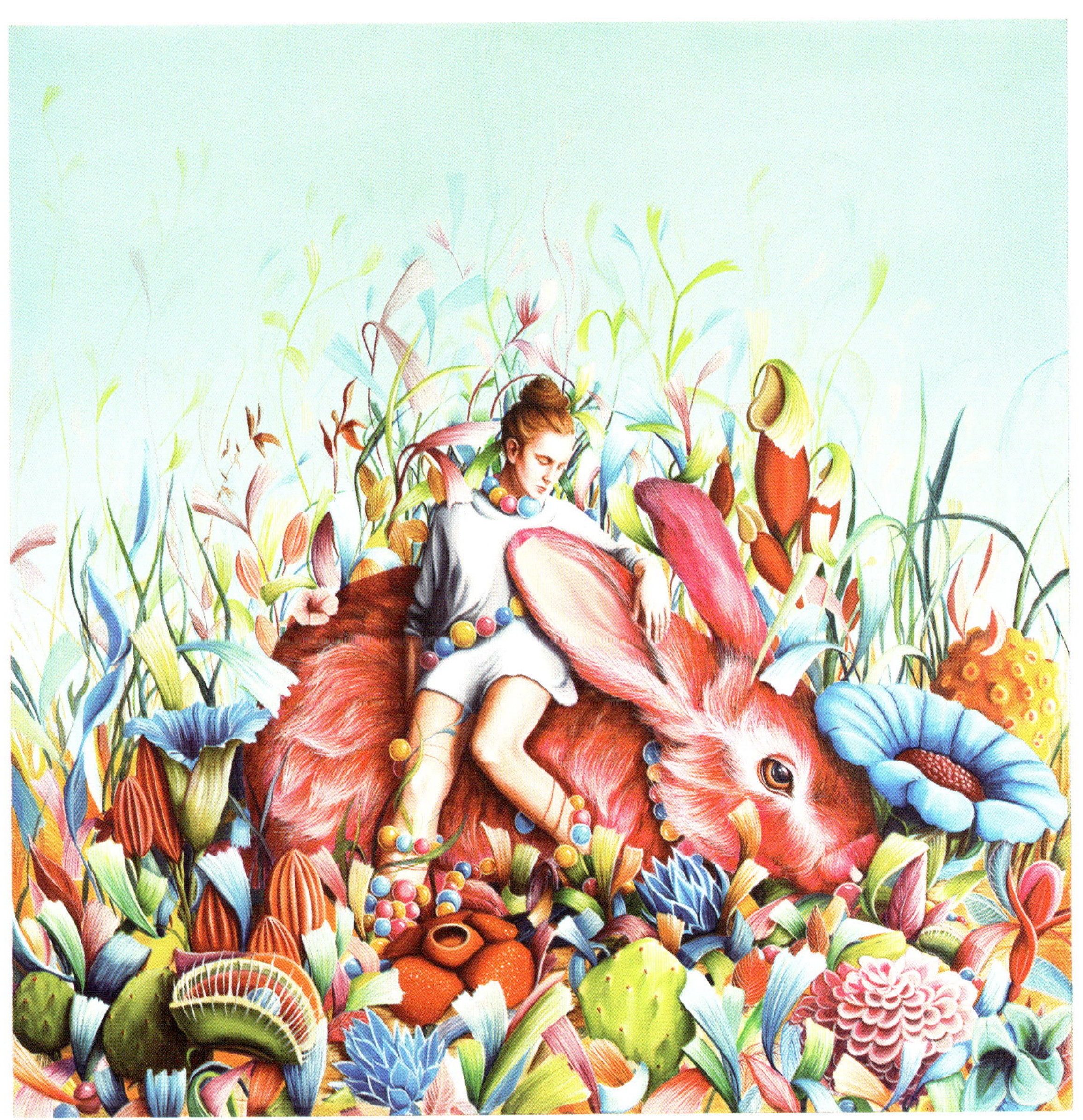

Dreamer, oil on canvas

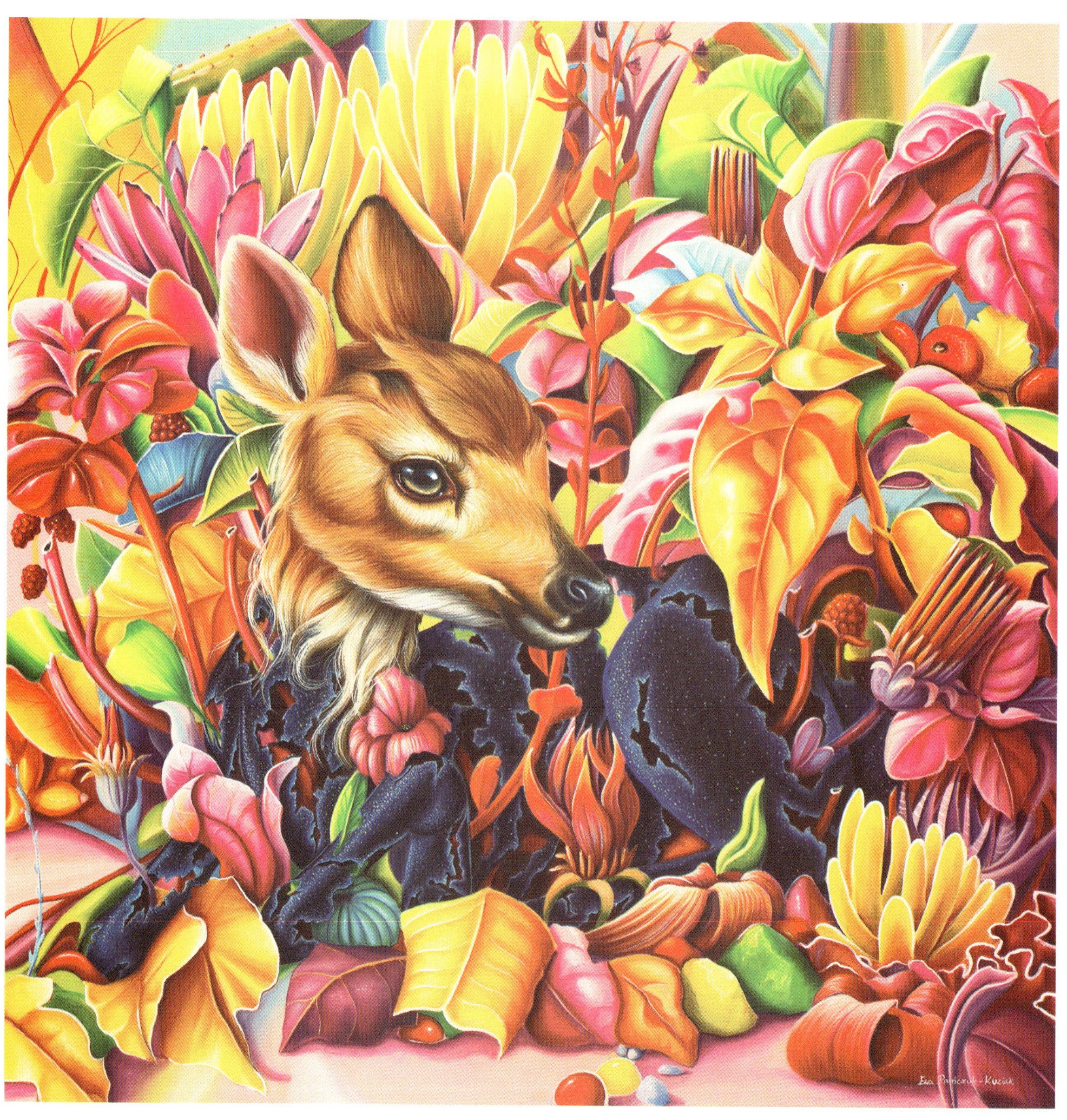

Bitter secrets, oil on linen

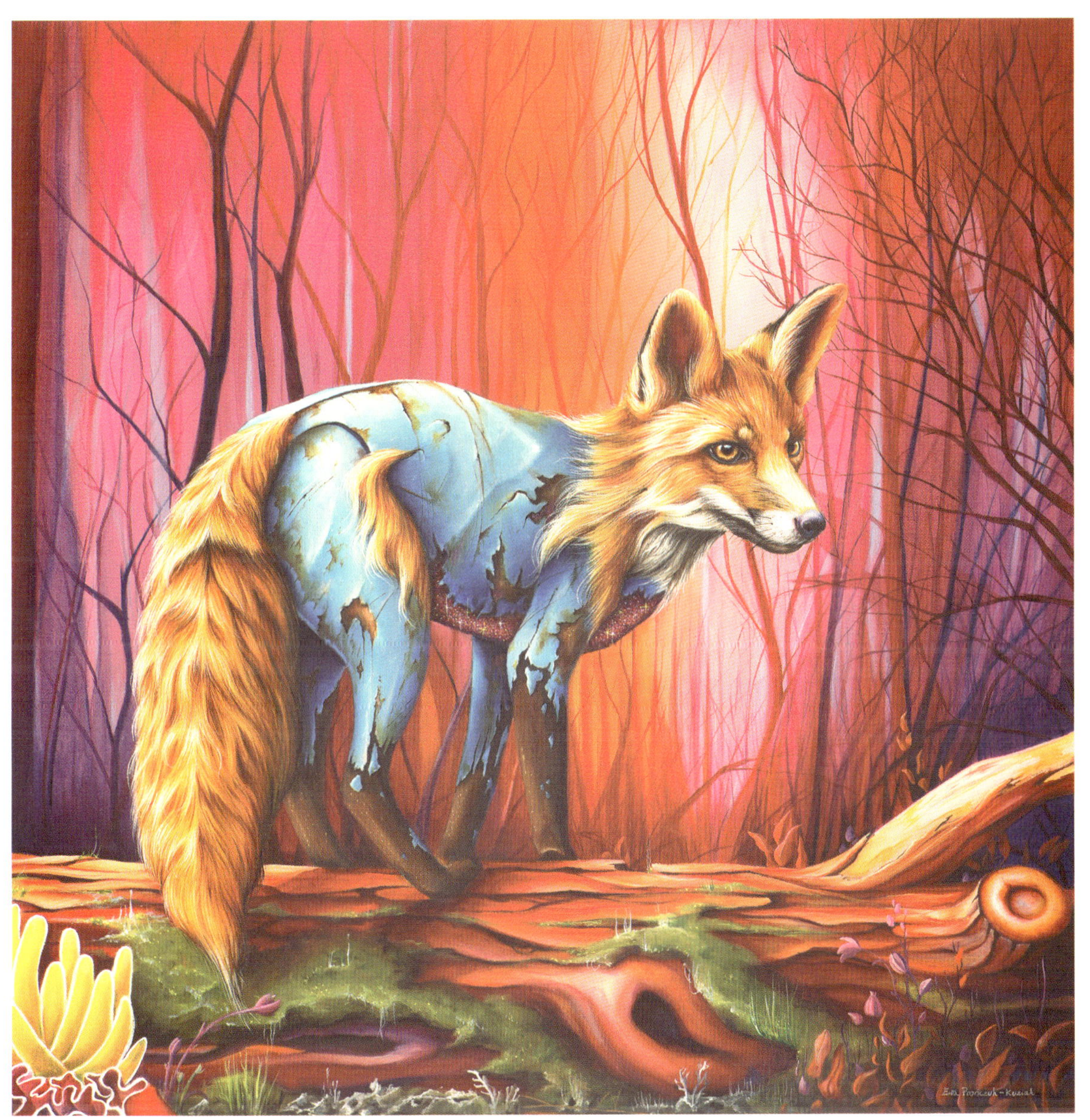

Sweet secrets, oil on linen

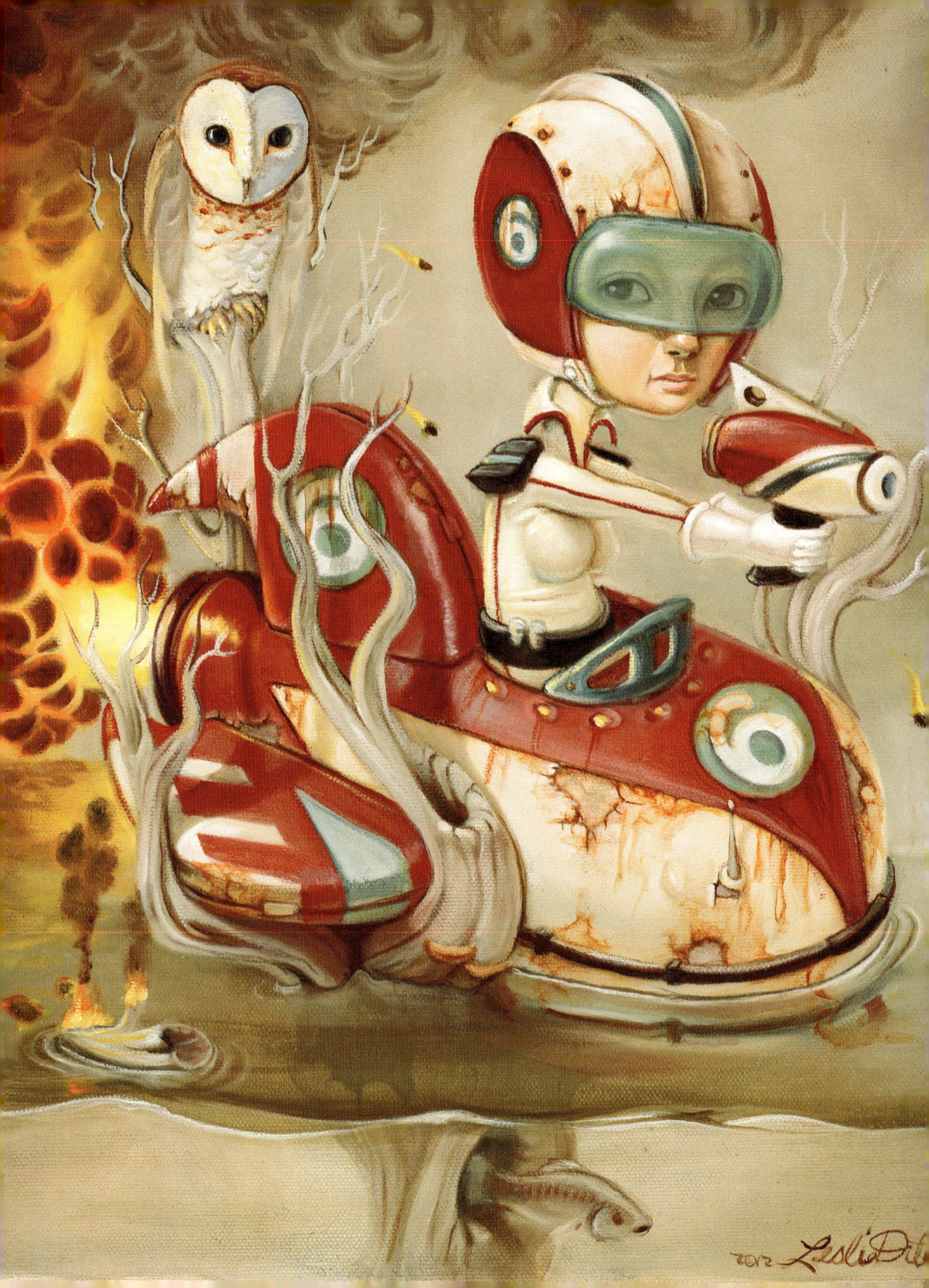

www.leslie-ditto.com

Leslie Ditto

The self taught contemporary arrtist, Leslie Ditto.

Using oil paints as her chosen media, Leslie Ditto creates thought provoking surreal paintings to communicate a deeper message regarding social, political, and personal struggles with the use of symbolism. Many of her paintings take several pain staking months for her to complete. Working passionately for 13 to 17 hours a day, 7 days a week until complete, she finds herself obsessed with details. Utilizing the techniques of the "Old Masters" to achieve her highly detailed images she is known for.

Leslie not only creates unique images with a touch of beauty filled with light & color but she also embraces the darker side of the human spirit.

Born in Memphis, Tennessee, Leslie was raised as a young "southern" girl around the unconventional environment of a "Old School" Harley Davidson Motorcycle shop that was owned by her family. It was in their shop that her fascination with surrealism can be rooted, where motorcycles where often painted by her father & uncle with surrealistic fantasy themed images inspired by legendary artist Frank Frenzetta and Boris Valleo. Since beginning her fine art career in 2008, Leslie has quickly excelled. She has exhibited her paintings in some of the most cutting edge contemporary galleries around such as Copro Gallery in Santa Monica, California and Last Rites Gallery NYC. Her work has been featured in numerous publications, art magazines, and art books distributed across the globe...

La artista contemporánea autodidacta, Leslie Ditto.

Utilizando pinturas al óleo como medio elegido. Leslie Ditto crea pensamientos que provocan pinturas surrealistas para comunicar un mensaje más profundo con respecto a las luchas sociales, políticas y personales con el uso del simbolismo. Muchas de sus pinturas le provocaron sufrimiento durante meses hasta finalizarlas. Trabajando de 13 a 17 horas al día, 7 días a la semana hasta terminarlo. Leslie se obsesiona con los detalles. Se la conoce por utilizar las técnicas de los "Viejos Maestros" para lograr sus ilustraciones extremadamente detalladas.

Leslie no sólo crea imágenes únicas con un toque de belleza lleno de luz y color, sino que también abraza el lado más oscuro del espíritu humano.

Nacida en Memphis (Tennessee), Leslie fue criada como una joven "sureña" alrededor del ambiente poco convencional de la "Vieja Escuela" que era una tienda de motocicletas Harley Davidson, propiedad de su familia. Fue, en su tienda, donde pudo arraigarse su fascinación por el surrealismo, donde su padre y su tío a menudo pintaban las motocicletas con imágenes de fantasía surrealista inspiradas por el legendario artista Frank Frenzetta y Boris Valleo. Desde el comienzo de su carrera artística en 2008, Leslie ha sobresalido rápidamente. Ha expuesto sus pinturas en algunas de las galerías contemporáneas más vanguardistas, como la Copro Gallery en Santa Mónica, California y Last Rites Gallery de Nueva York. Su obra ha aparecido en numerosas publicaciones, revistas y libros de arte distribuidos en todo el mundo...

▸ Crash and burn (detail) // ***next page:*** Pop

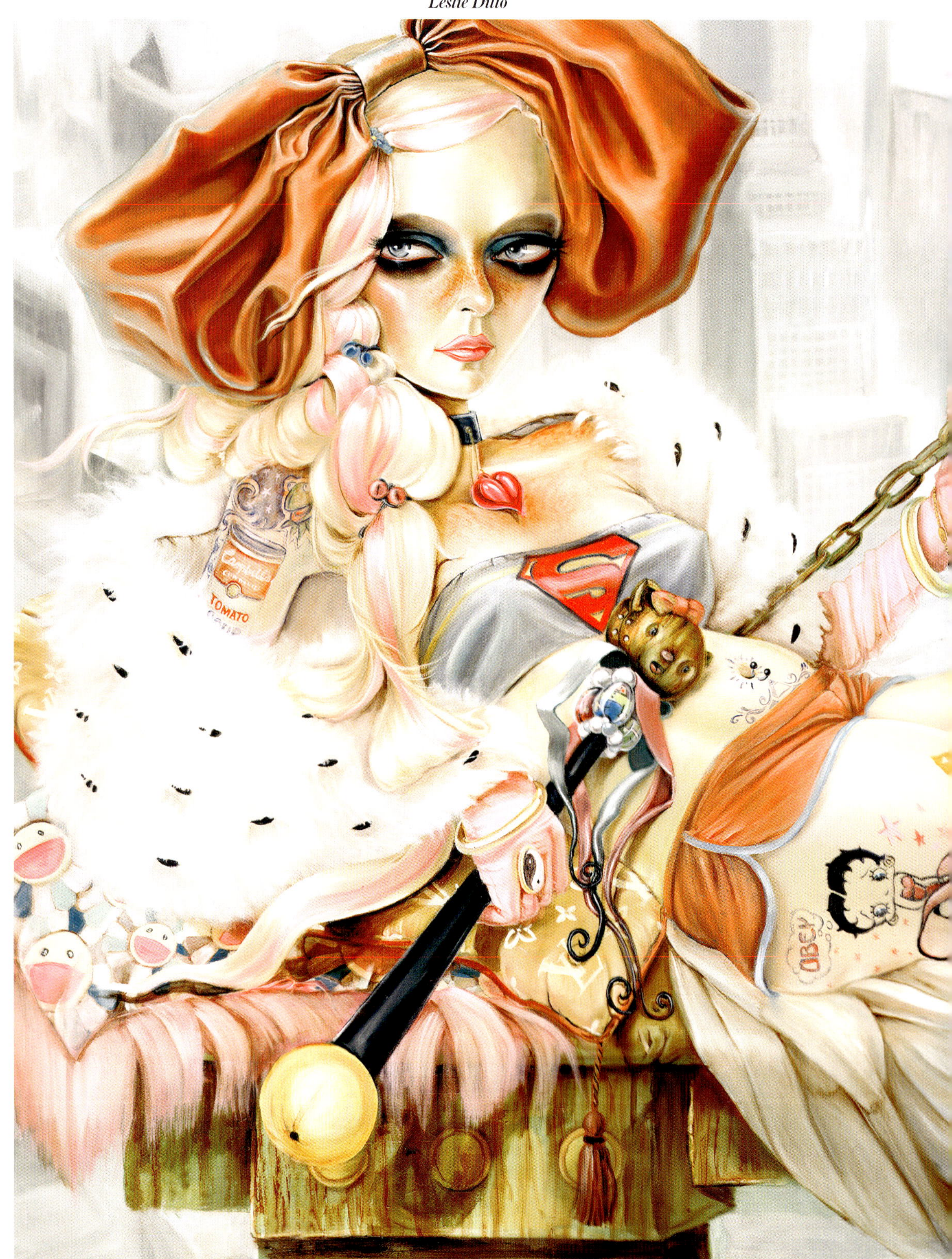
TOMATO
OBEY

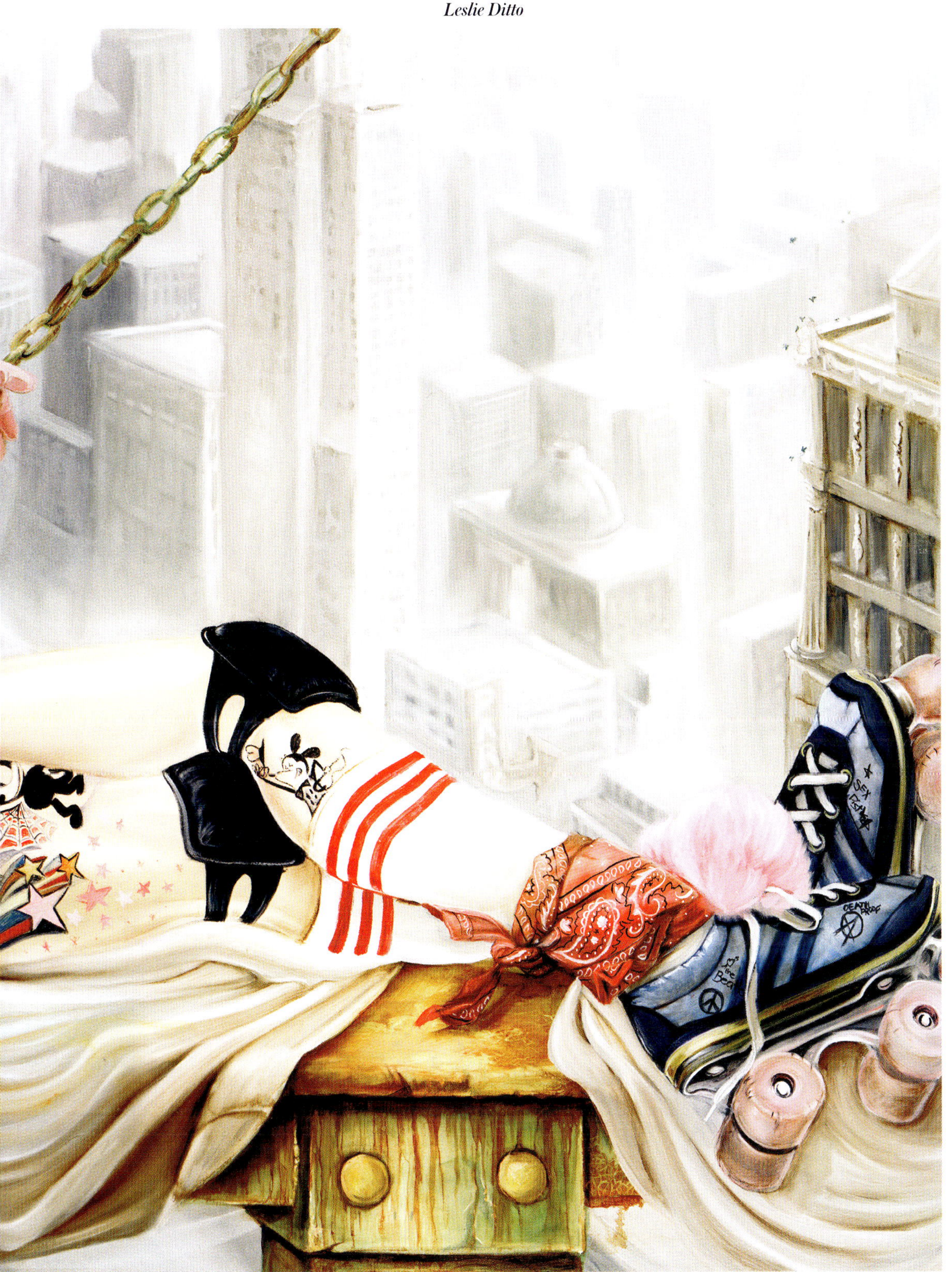

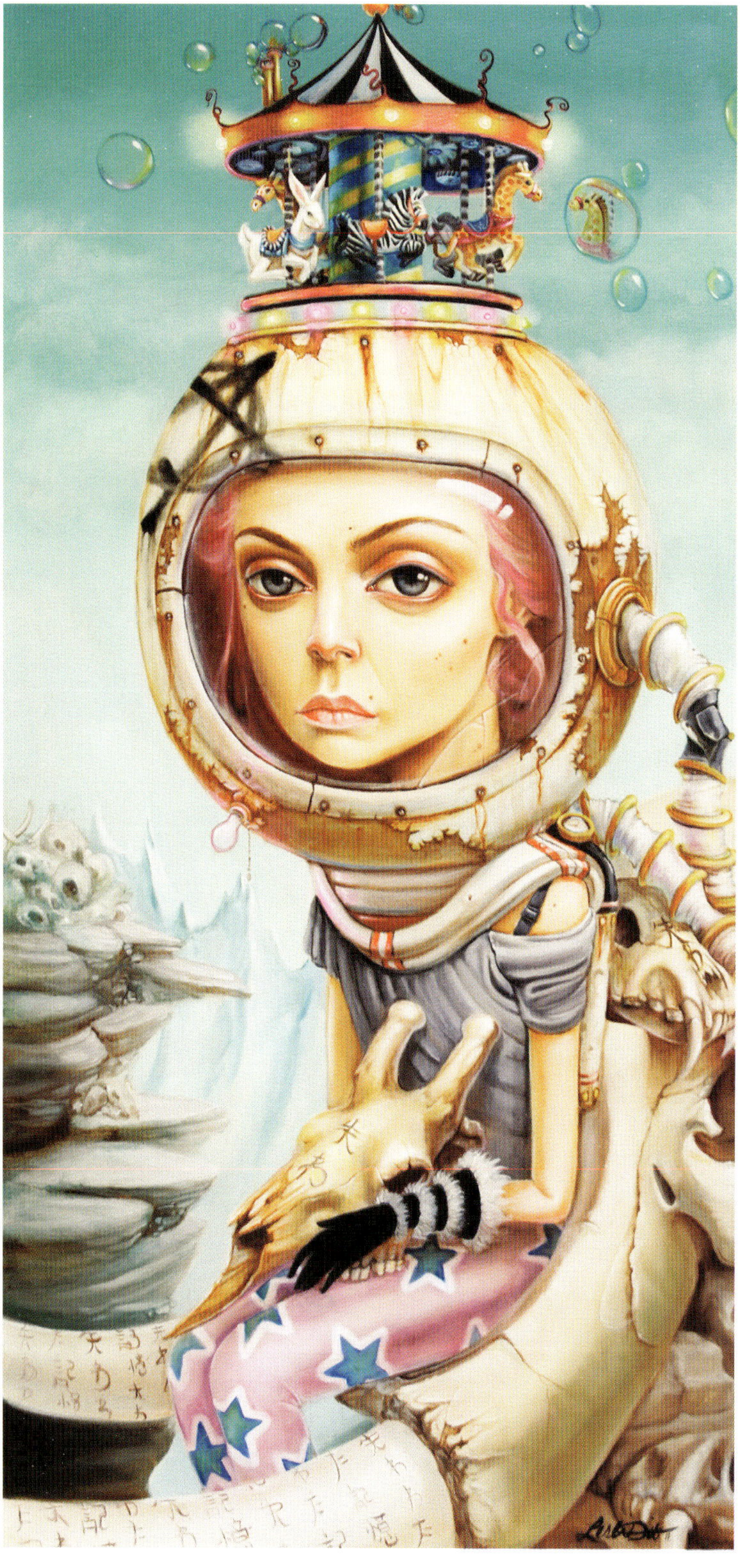

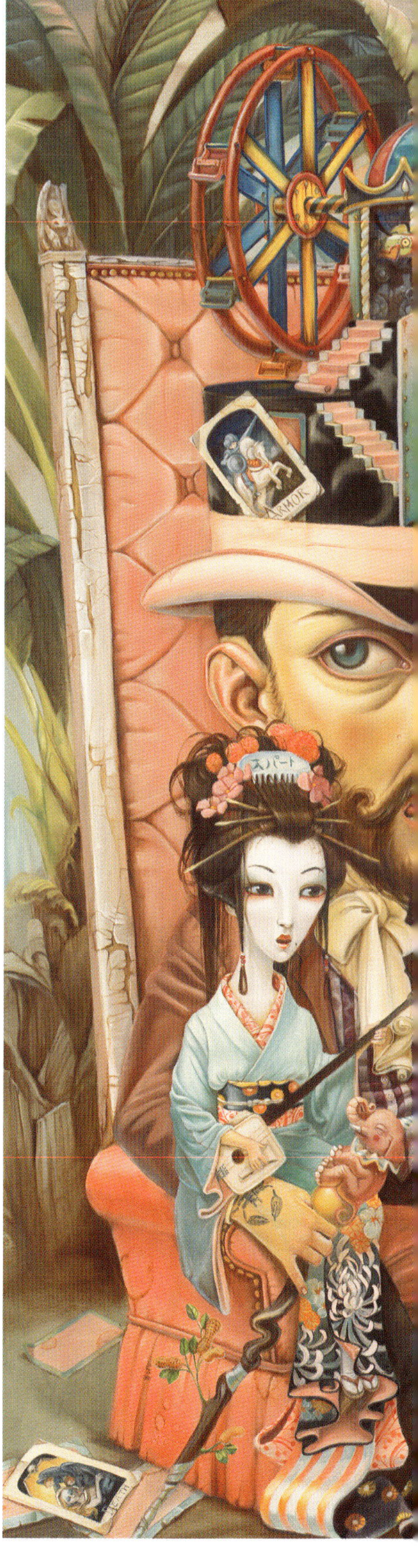

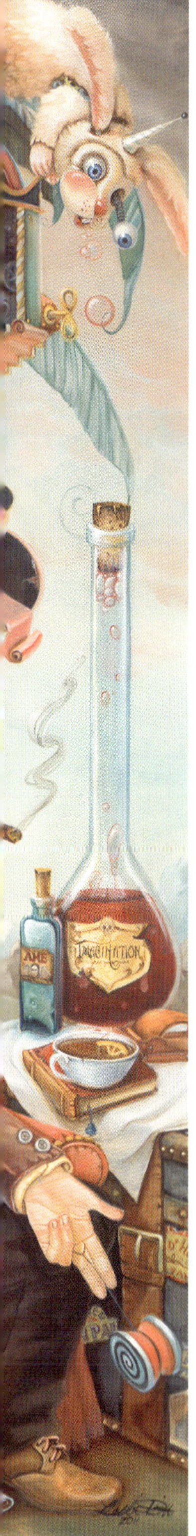

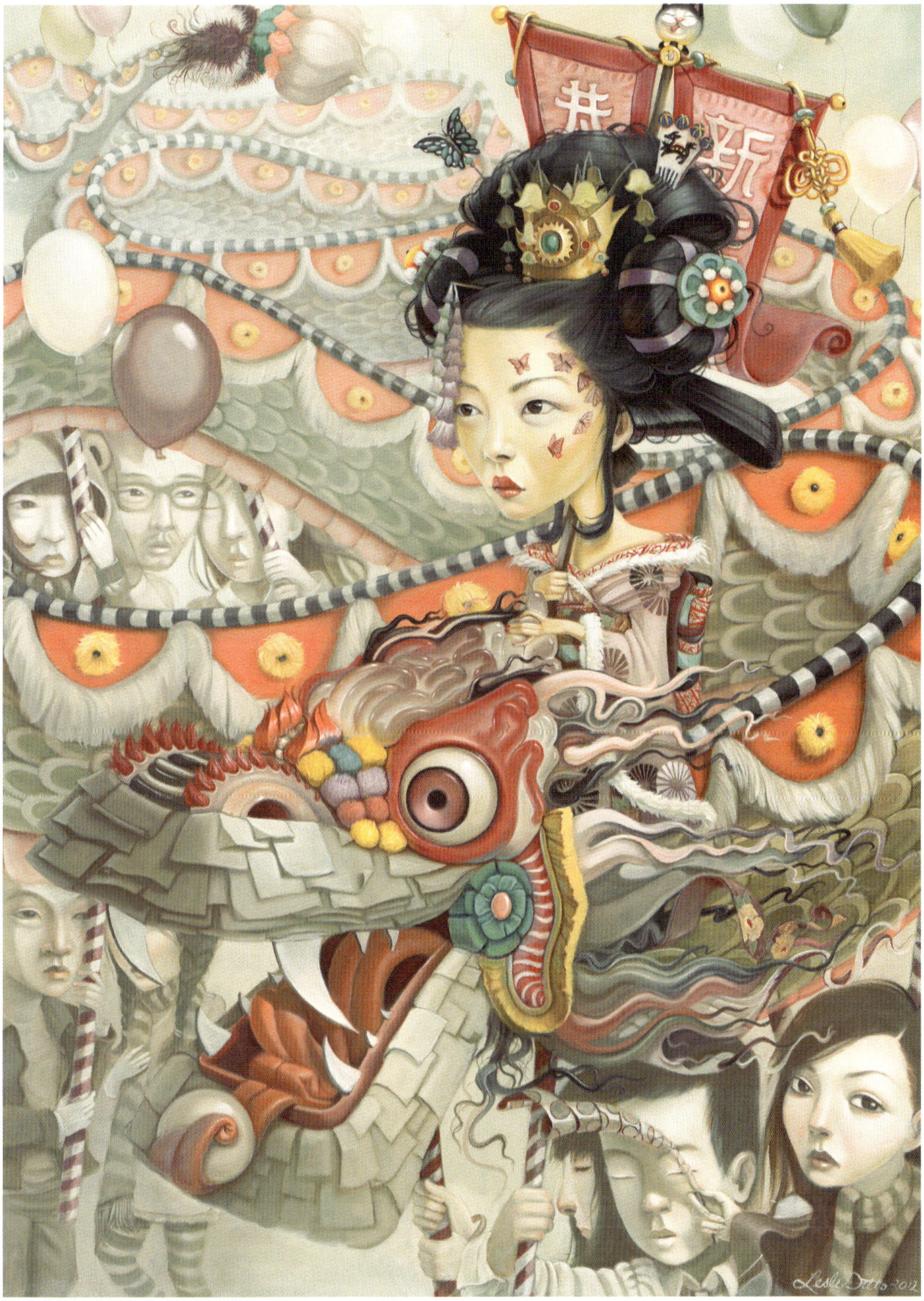

left: Bell Toll, Magician, *right:* Riding

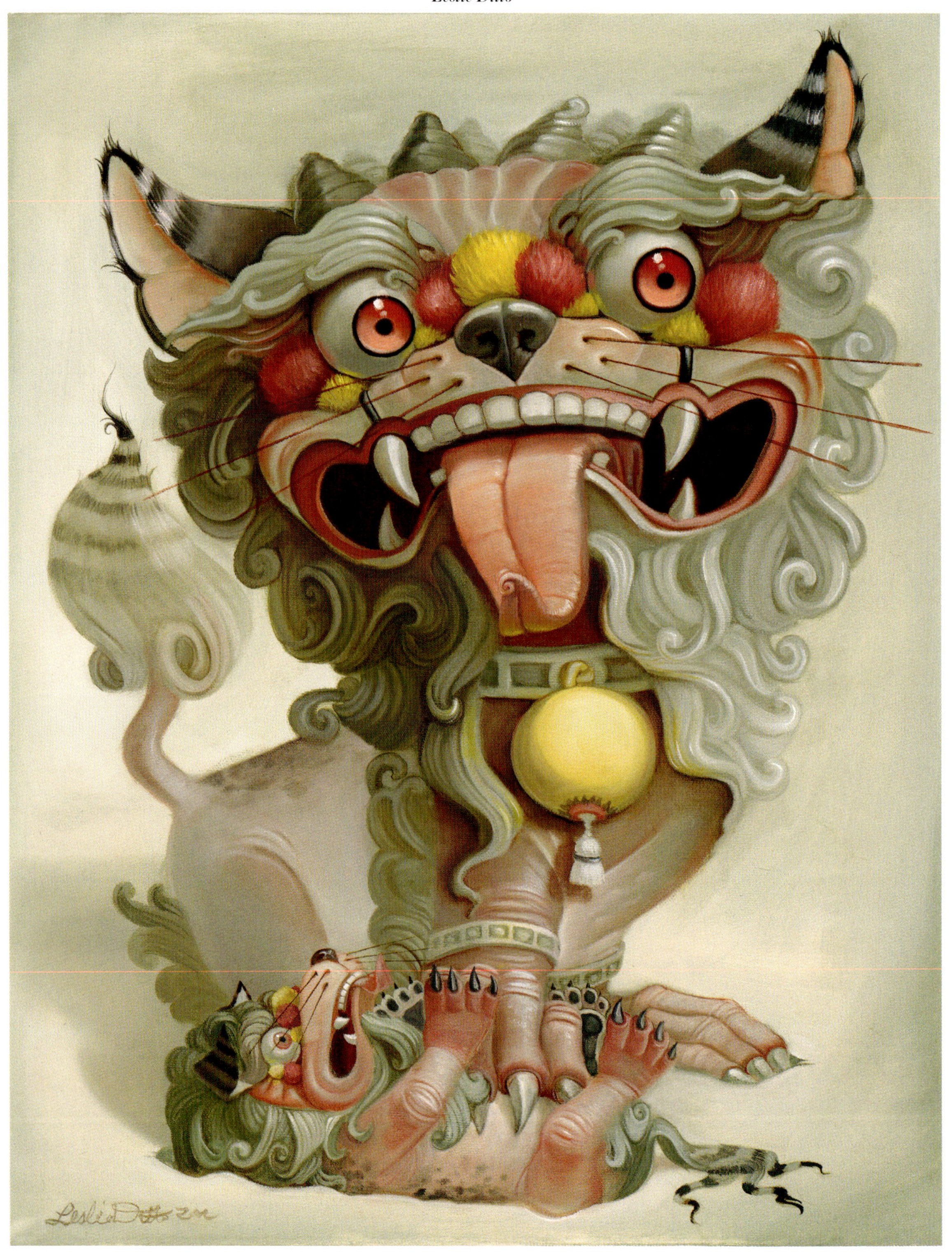

left: Shishi, ***right:*** China sang

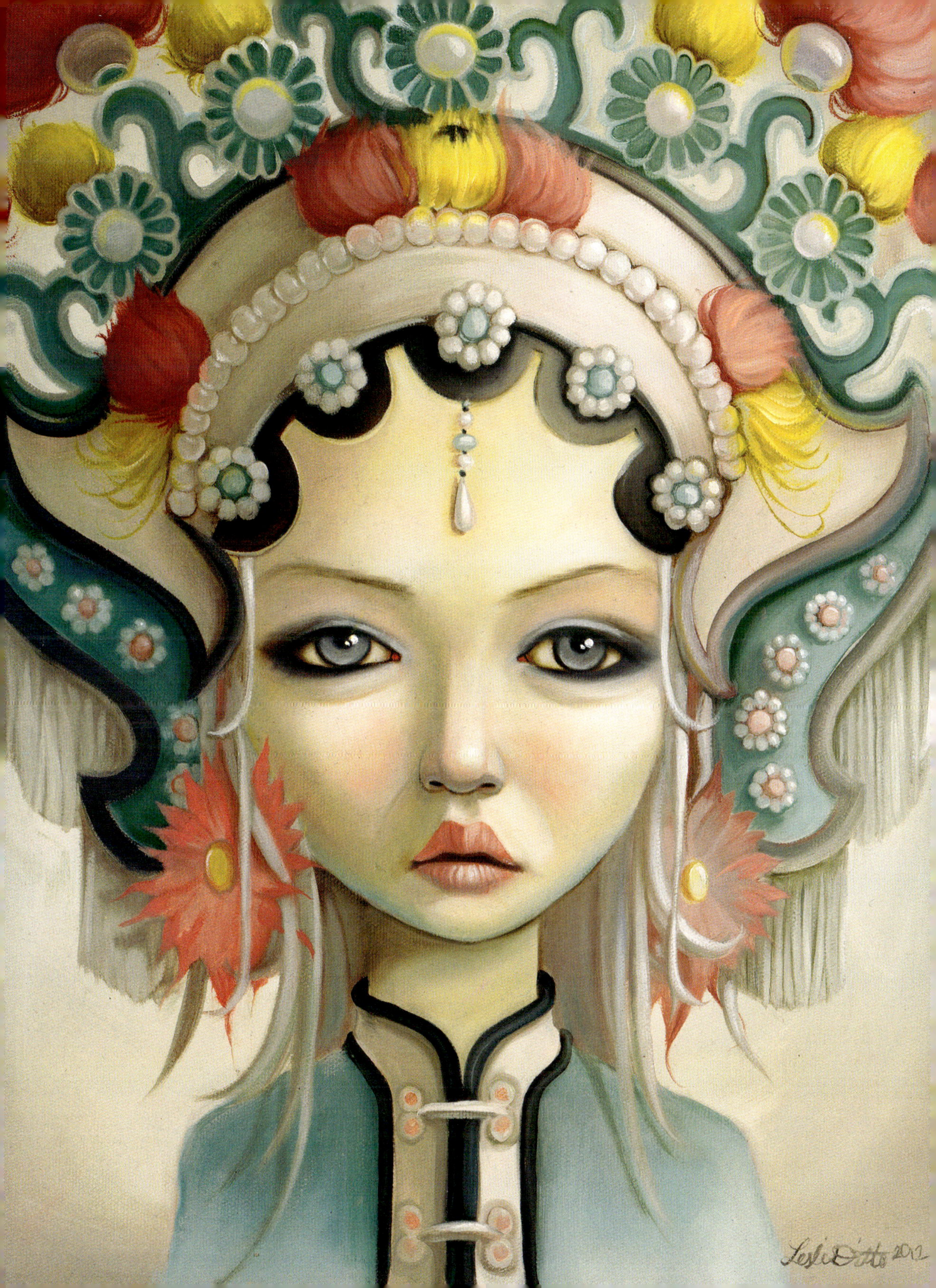

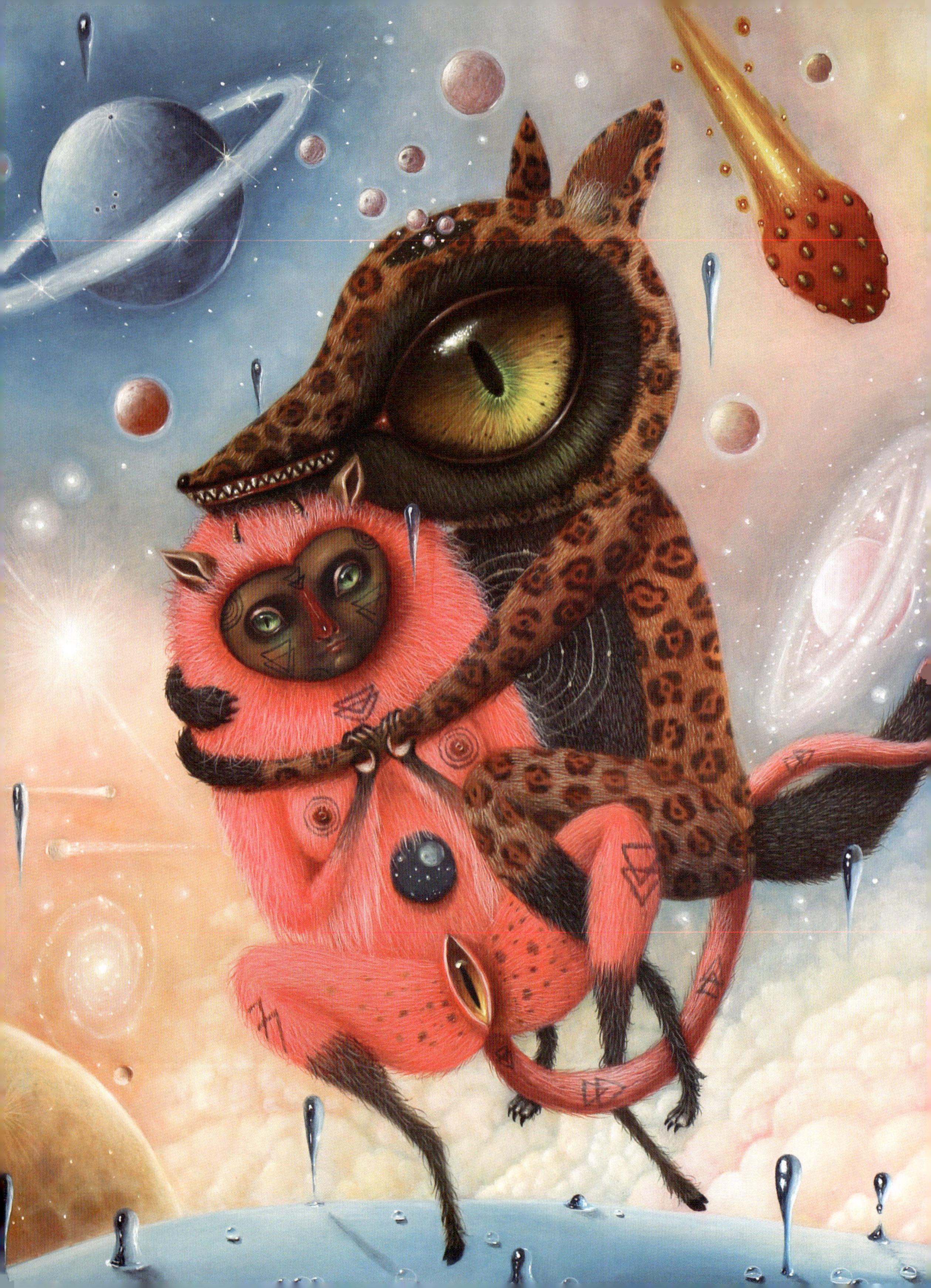

artbypeca.com

Peca

Born in Argentina & based in Barcelona, Peca is a painter, illustrator & stop-motion filmmaker. She studied Fine Arts University of La Plata city in Argentina. Working in pop surrealism. She uses a variety of materials/surfaces to create her surreal cosmos, full of mystical subjects & unusual situations. The characters in Peca's art are furry wide-eyed creatures on a quest to explore the universe. Though located in a galaxy far away, her subjects reveal some of the artist's personal experiences, thoughts & emotions.

Her childhood was marked by the military dictatorship in Argentina when the artist turned to music for refuge from the circumstances surrounding her. Her love for music drove her to enroll in music studies, but after 2 years Peca shifted her education & began to study engraving instead. From this her love of art grew & she tried many different types.

Peca's artistic process is rooted in introspection. Her paintings reflect visions from her dreams & meditations onto canvas. She uses an array of mediums including oils, acrylics & pencils. Peca's unusual characters cry birds from their many eyes, shoot galaxies from their mouth & bleed strawberry juice. Her surreal artwork has traveled all over the world & exhibited in various venues in USA like La Luz de Jesus and Copro Gallery, also her art was showed in Japan, Germany, Spain, London, France and Australia.

Nacida en Argentina y asentada en Barcelona, Peca es pintora, ilustradora y cineasta de la técnica stop-motion. Estudió Bellas Artes en la Universidad de La Plata, en Argentina. Trabaja el surrealismo pop. Utiliza una gran variedad de materiales/superficies para crear su cosmos surrealista, lleno de temas místicos y situaciones inusuales. Los personajes en el arte de Peca son criaturas peludas de ojos anchos dispuestos a explorar el universo. Aunque están situados en una galaxia lejana, sus temas revelan experiencias personales, pensamientos y emociones de la artista.

Su infancia estuvo marcada por la dictadura militar en Argentina, cuando la artista recurrió a la música para refugiarse de las circunstancias que la rodeaban. Su amor por la música la llevó a inscribirse a clases de música, después de 2 años, Peca cambió su educación y comenzó a estudiar el arte del grabado. Desde entonces su amor por el arte creció.

El proceso artístico de Peca está cimentado en la introspección. Sus pinturas reflejan visiones de sus sueños y meditaciones. Utiliza una variedad de medios incluyendo óleos, acrílicos y lápices. Los personajes inusuales de Peca lloran pájaros de sus ojos, disparan galaxias desde su boca y sangran jugo de fresa. Su obra de arte surrealista ha sido expuesta en varios lugares de Estados Unidos como La Luz de Jesús y la Copro Gallery; su arte también se exhibió en Japón, Alemania, España, Londres, Francia y Australia.

▸ Saturnalia, oil on canvas

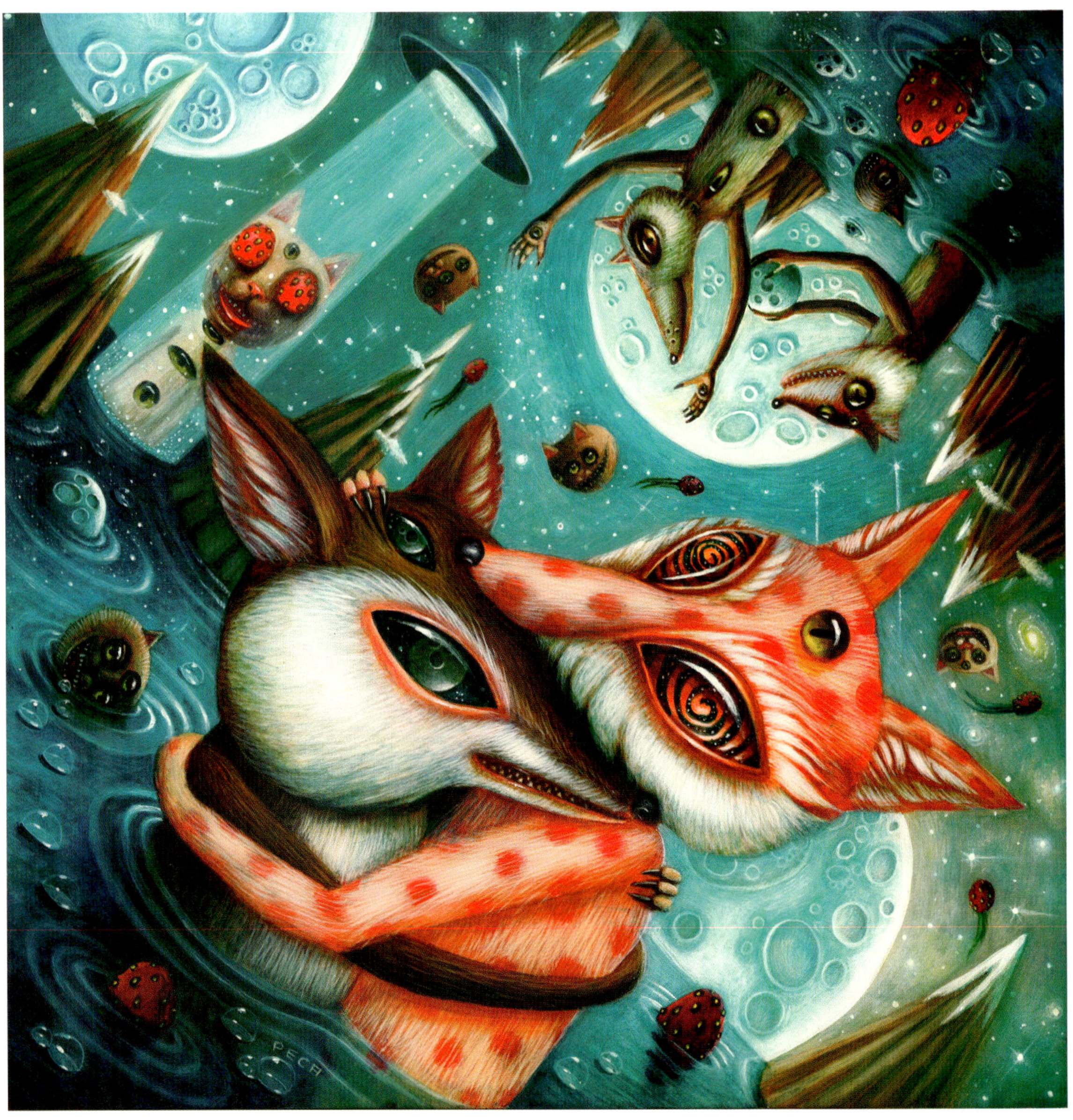

Hopi Dream "Royalty", acrylic on woodenboard

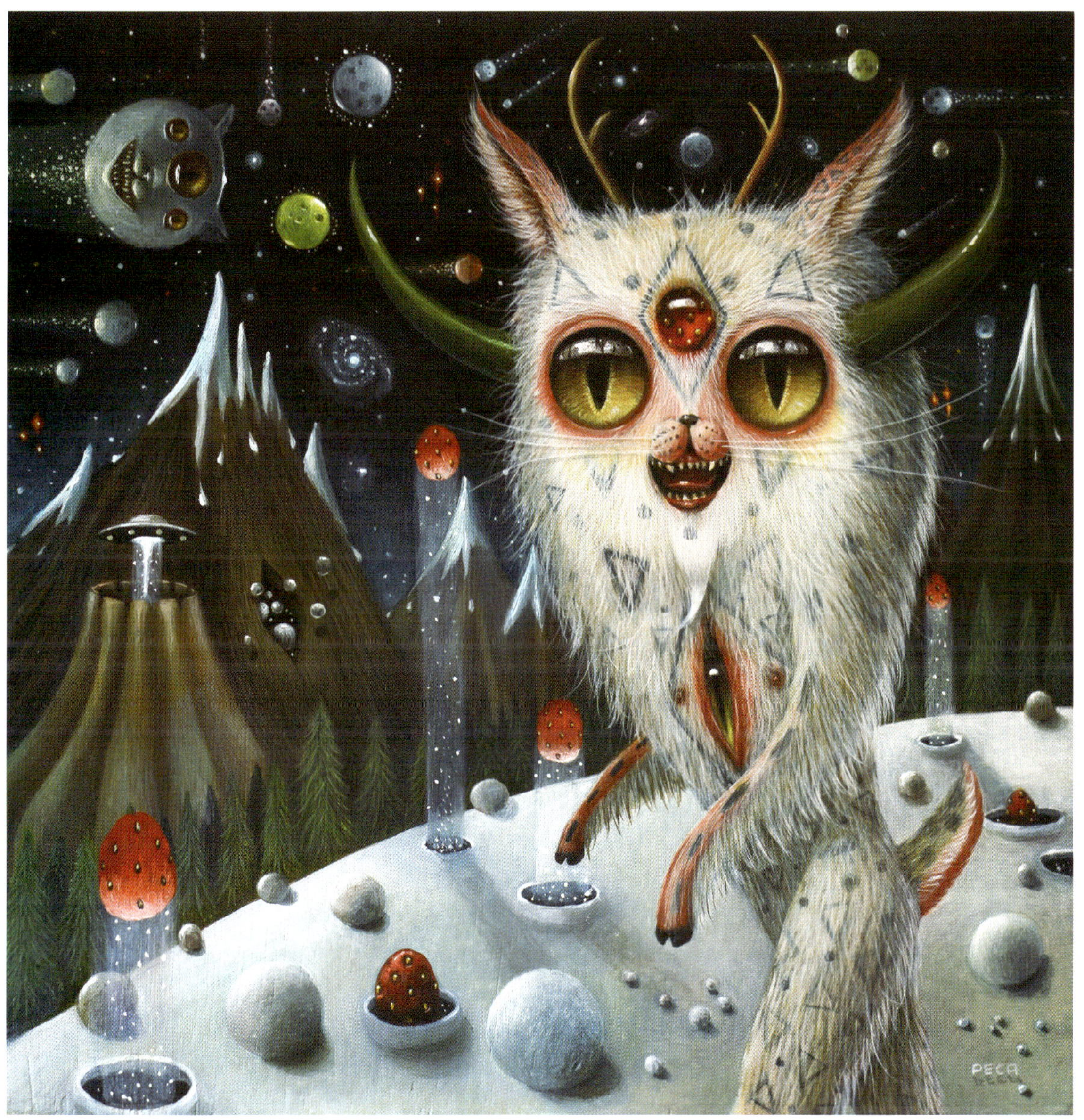

Beat, oil on woodenboard

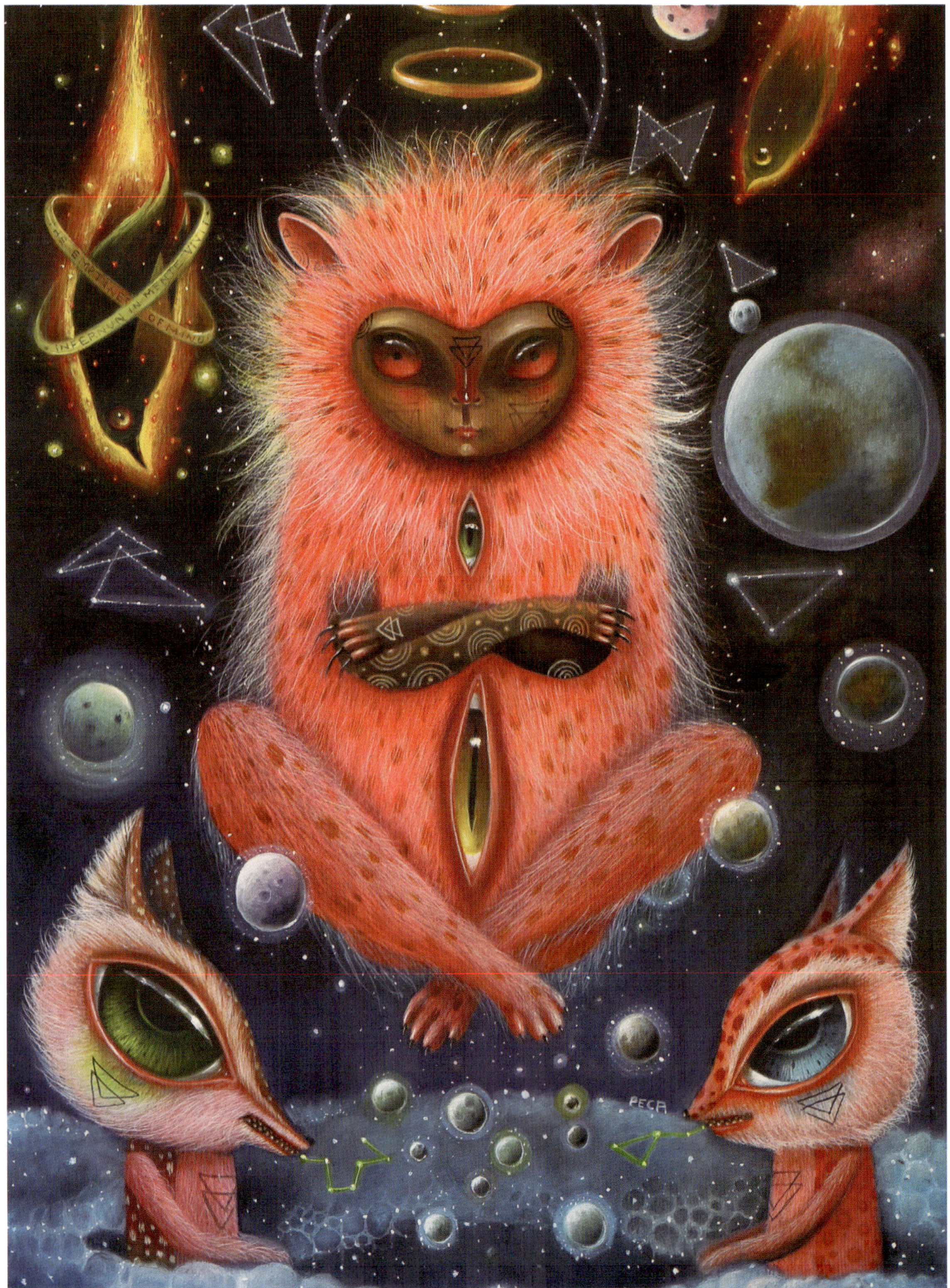

The Hierophant, oil on woodenboard

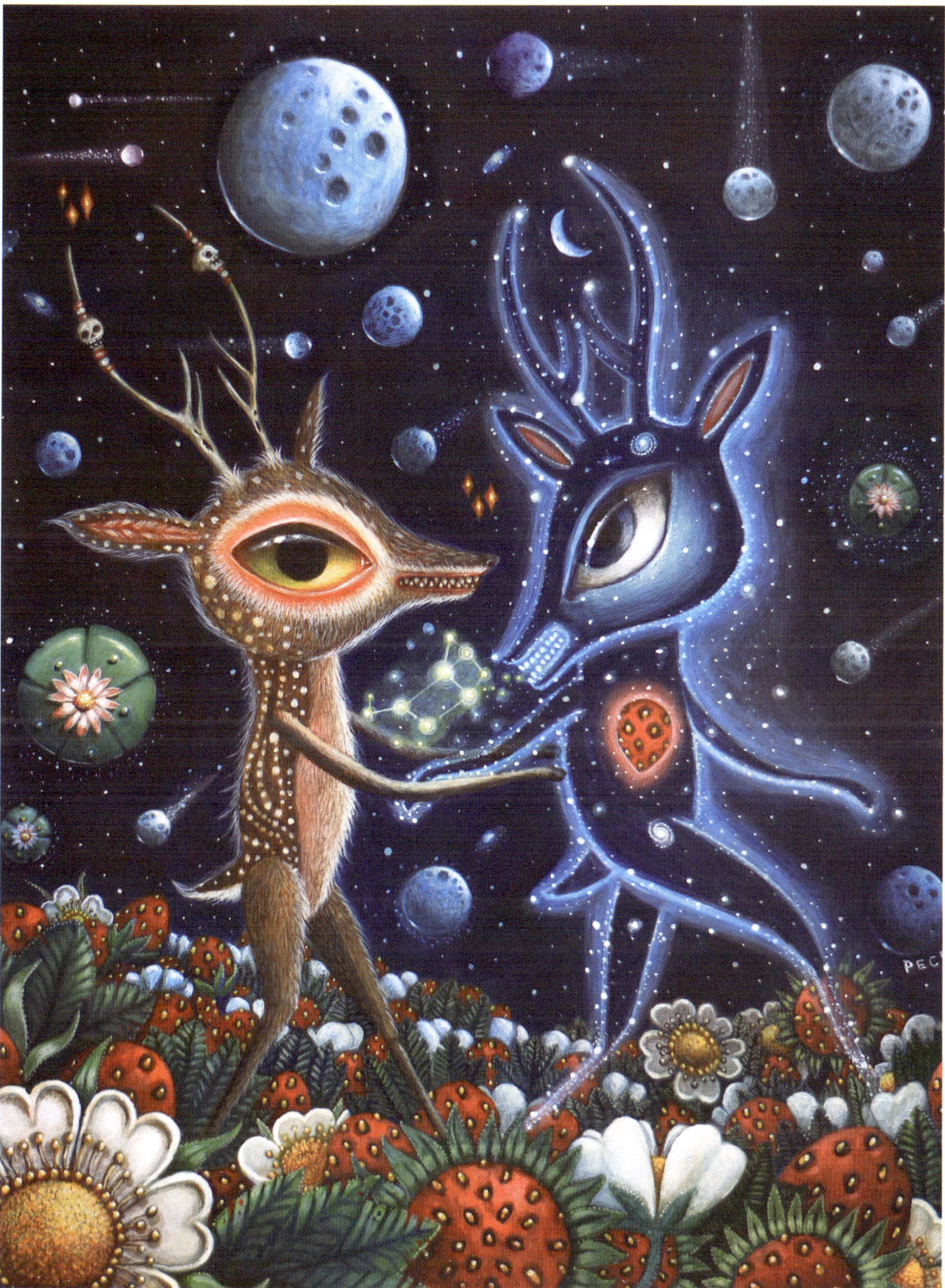

The Messagge, acrylic on canvas

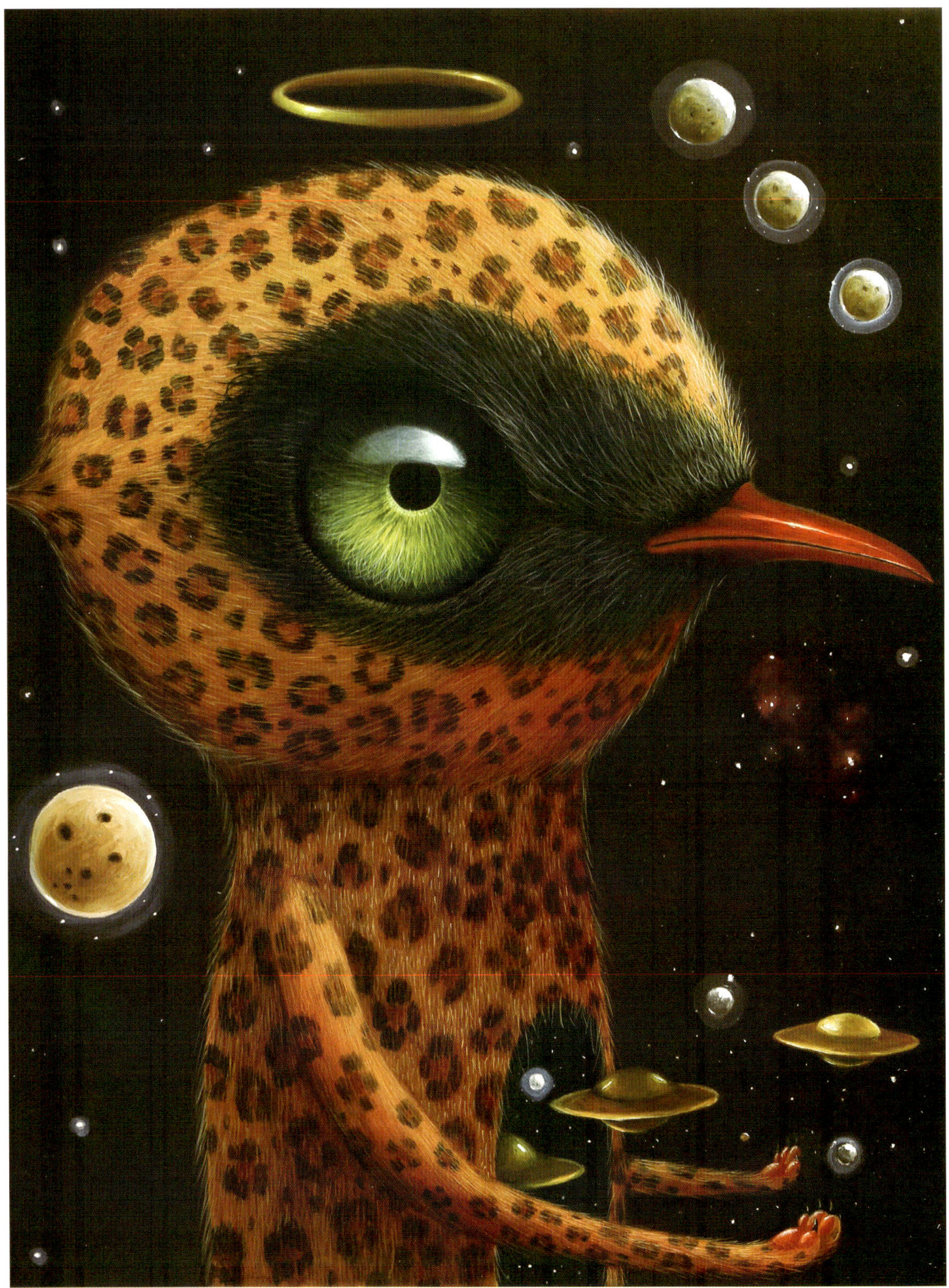

The big Organism, oil on canvas

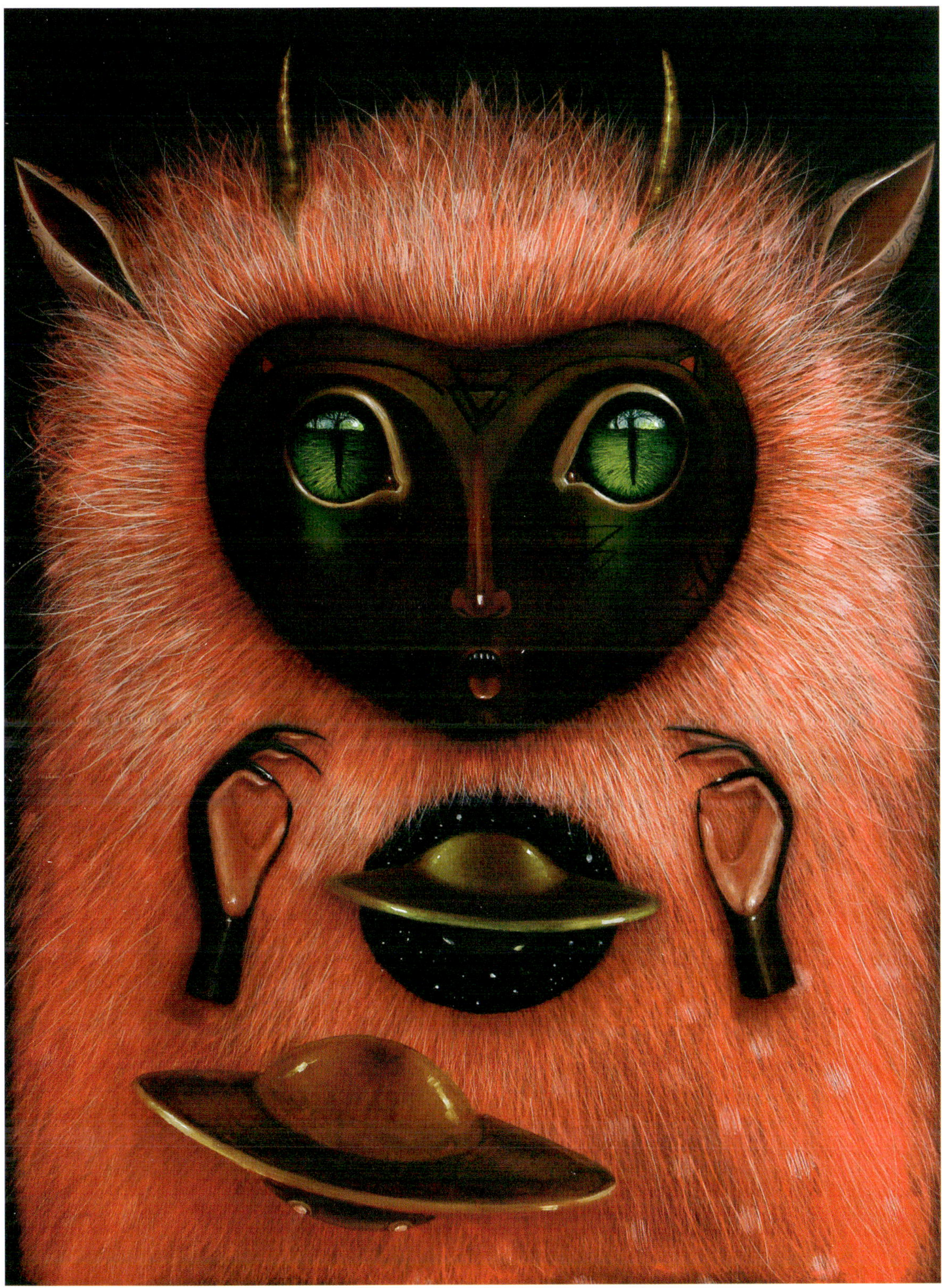

Universal Mother, oil on canvas

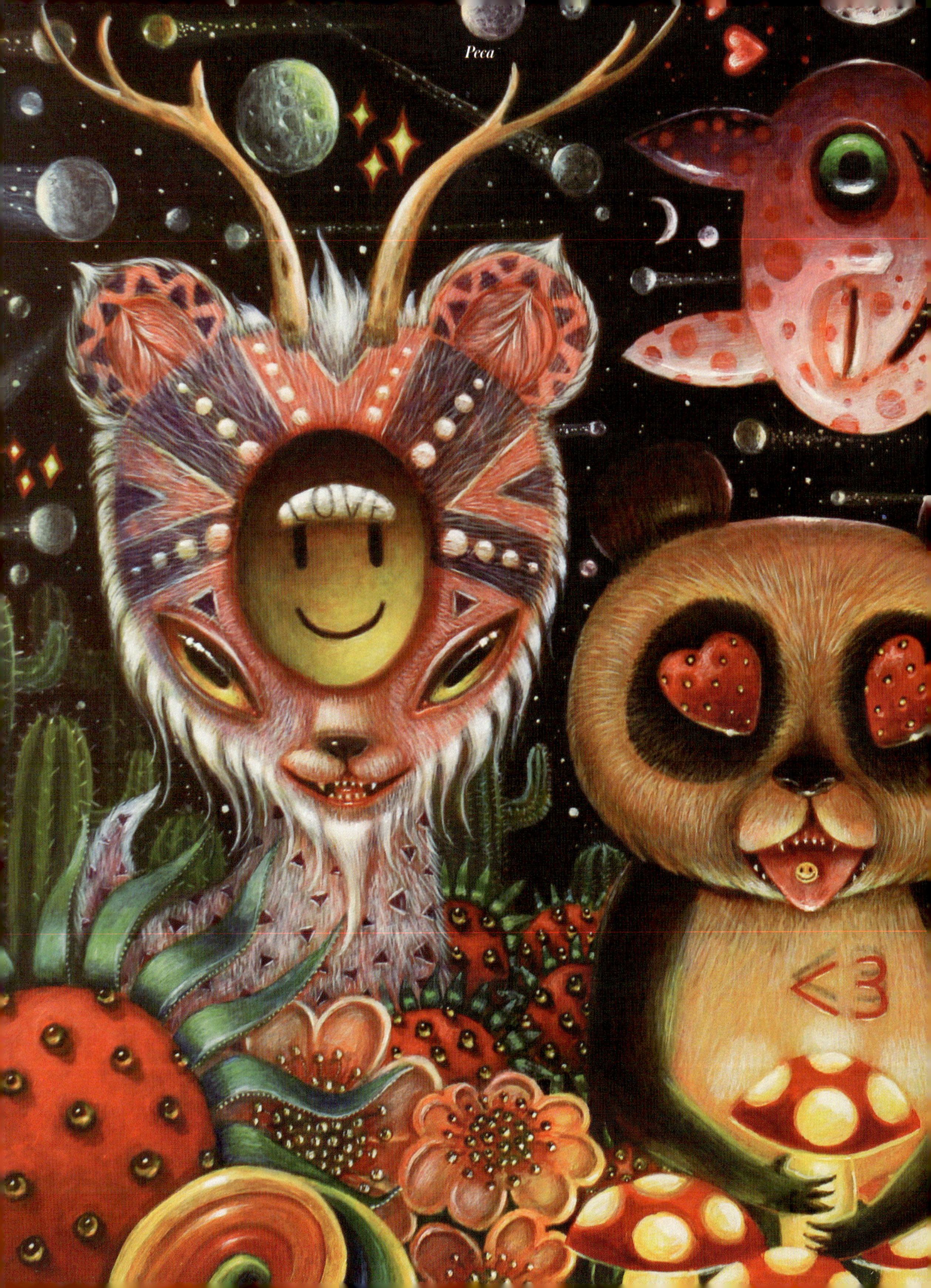

Peca

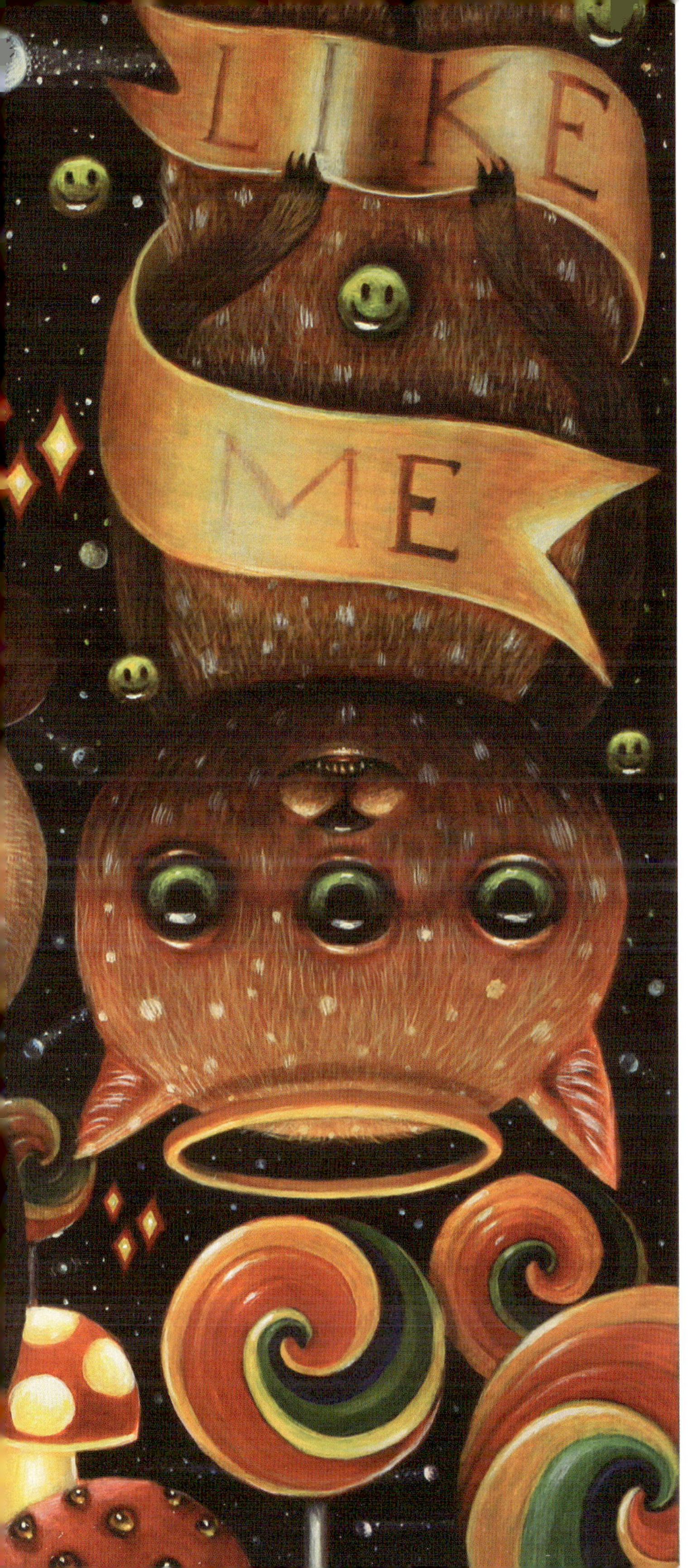

We are the love

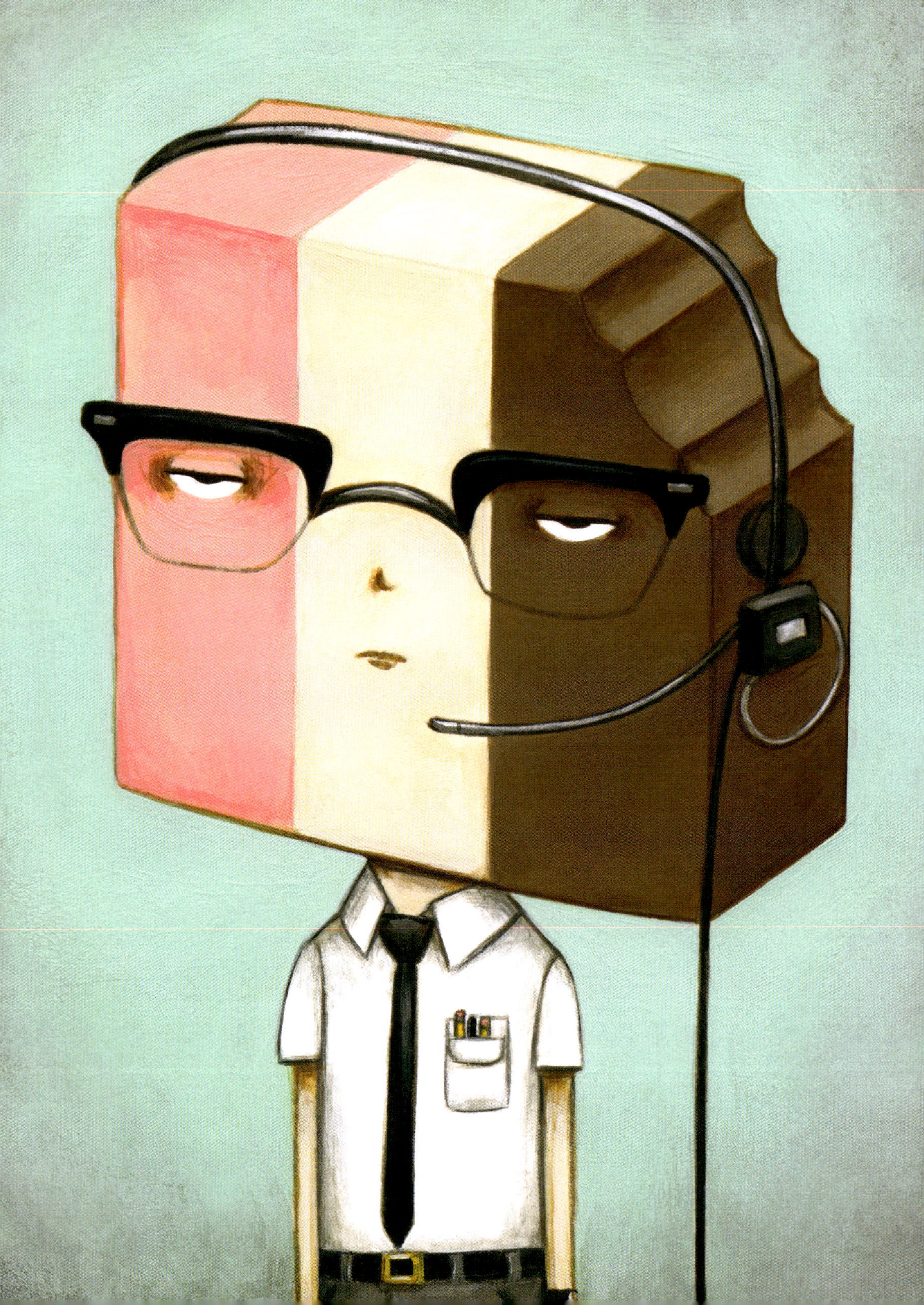

www.annatillettdesigns.com

Anna Tillett

Anna Tillett was born in Florida, where she spent the majority of her life until attending college at Memphis College of Art in Memphis, TN. It was there that she earned a B.F.A. in illustration, and solidified her love for all things BBQ, and Elvis. Since college she's spent her days creating illustrations for popsicle shops, tees, films, and children's books.

You can currently find her painting her next sour-faced sweet and eating all the pizza in the Beehive State of Utah.

Anna Tillett nació en Florida, donde pasó la mayor parte de su vida hasta que fue a la universidad en la Escuela de Arte de Memphis (Tennessee). Fue allí donde obtuvo una Licenciatura en ilustración y solidificó su amor por la barbacoa y Elvis. Desde la universidad, ha pasado sus días creando ilustraciones para tiendas de helados, camisetas, películas y libros infantiles.

Actualmente esta pintando su próximo "sour-faced sweet" y comiéndo pizza en el Estado de Utah.

▸ Astronaut Ice Cream Mission Control

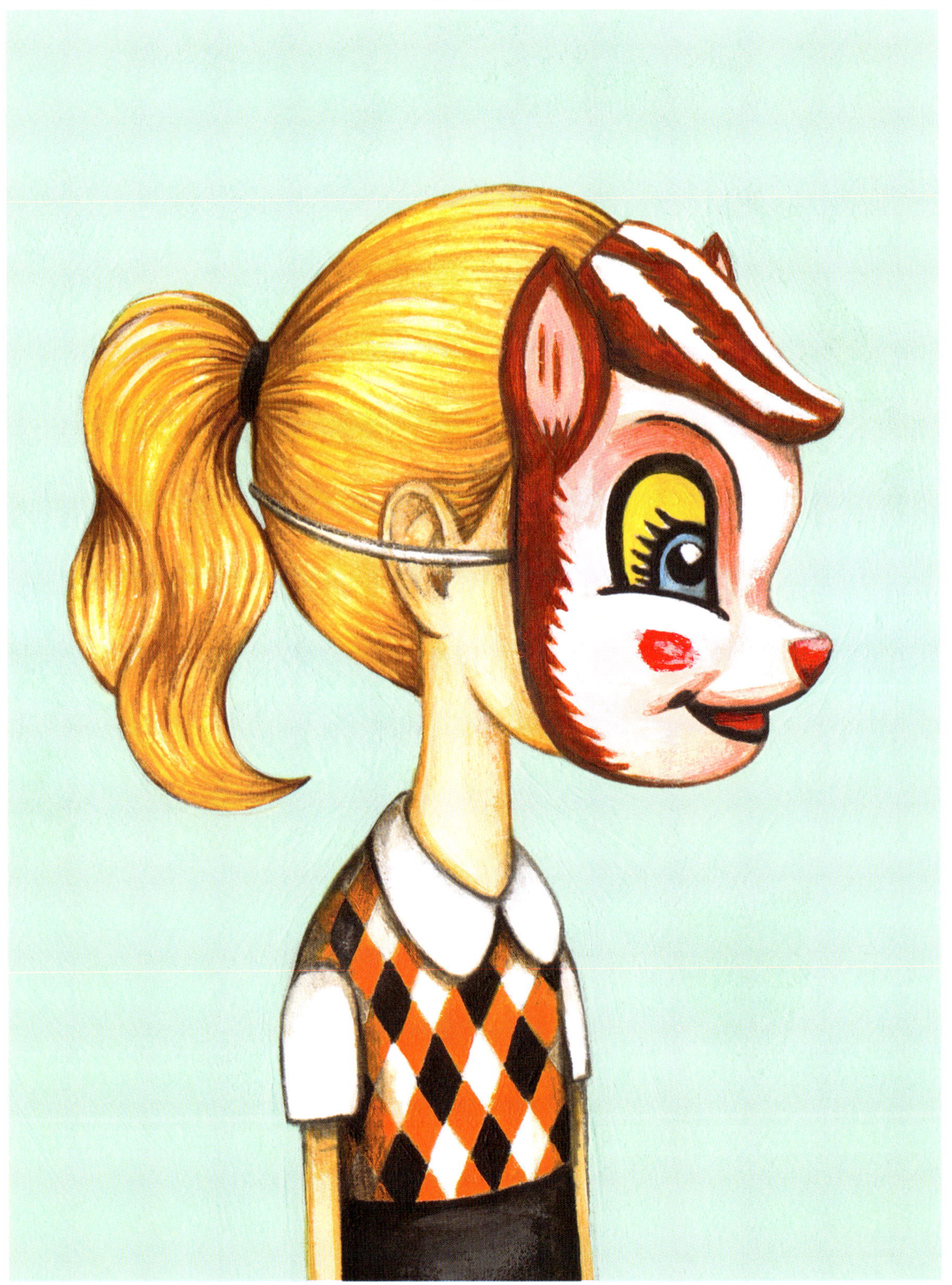

left: Candy Bandit Girl // *right:* Candy Bandit Boy

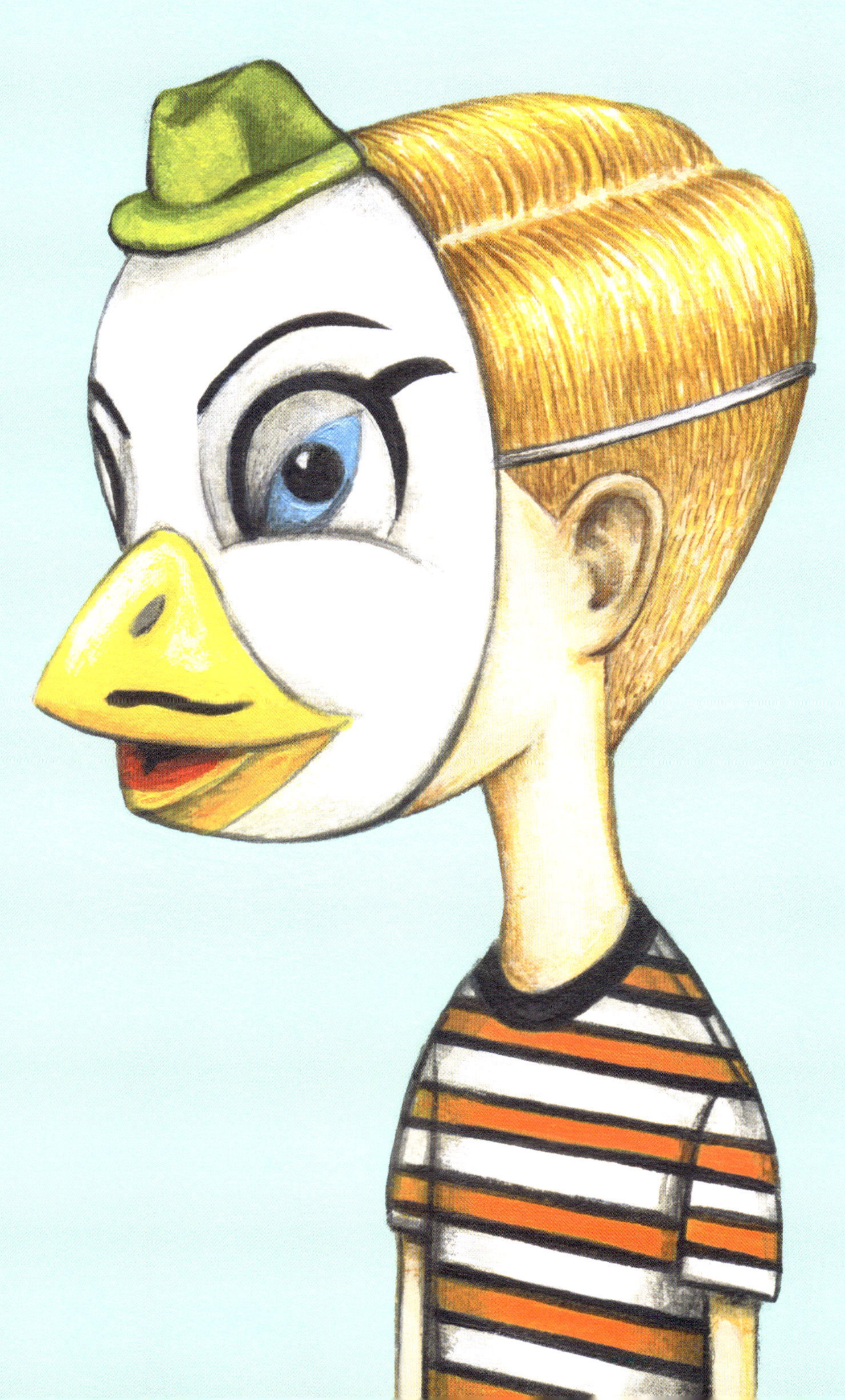

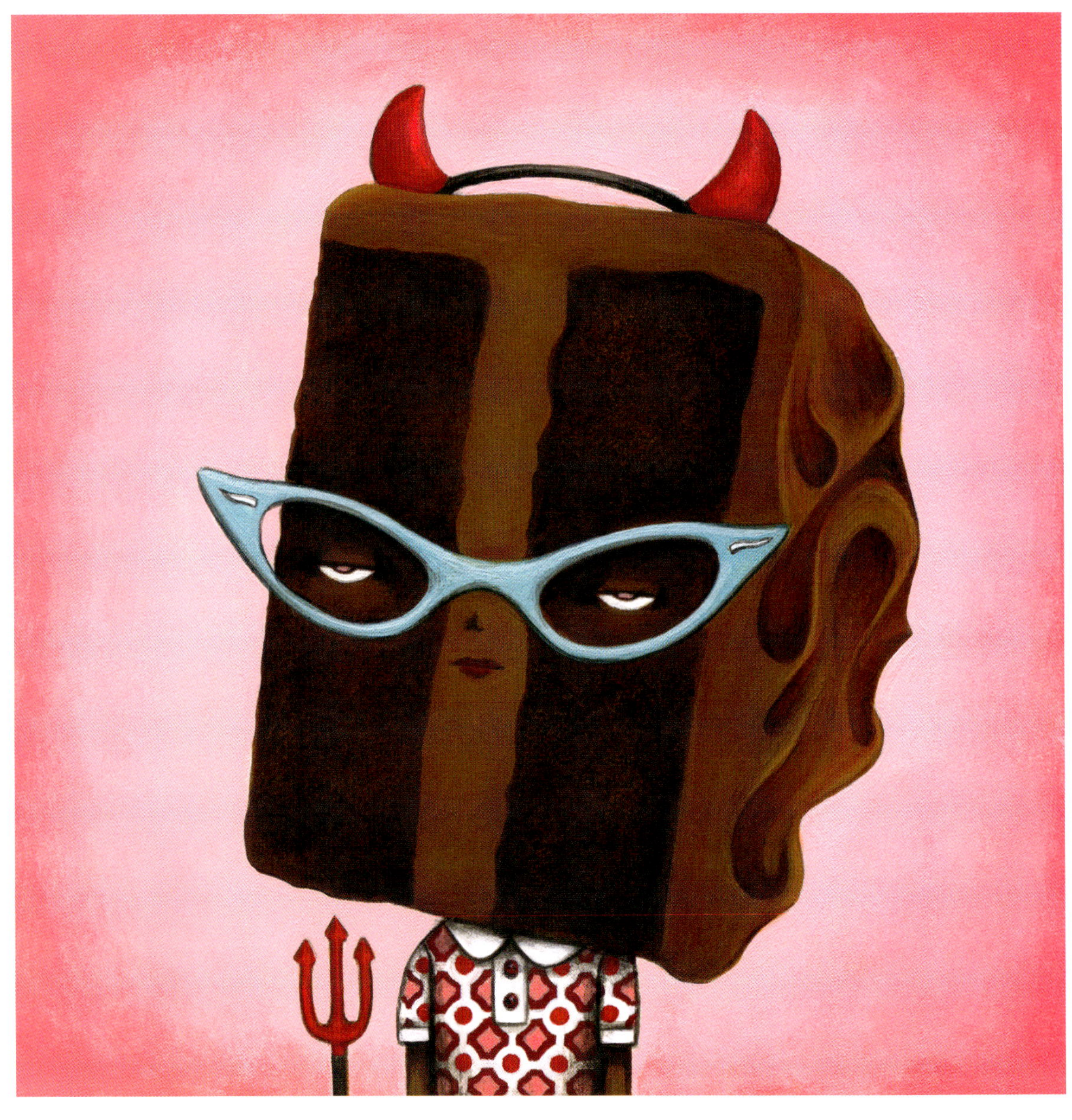

left: Devils Food Cake
right, top: Glazed and Confused With Sprinkles, Strawberry Shortcake, *bottom:* Twist Cone, Glazed and Confused Twist

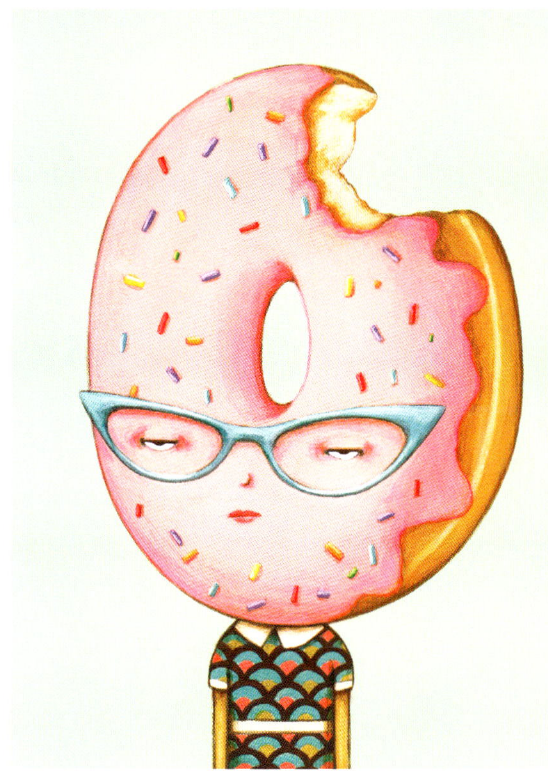

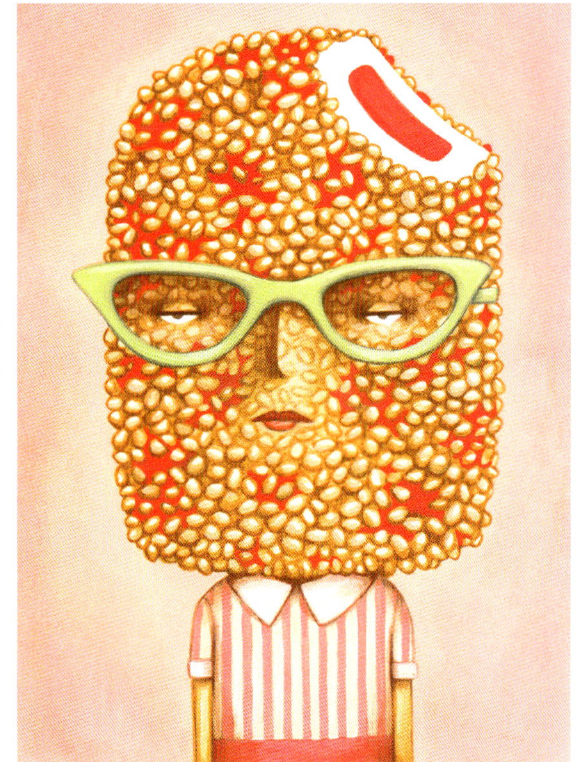

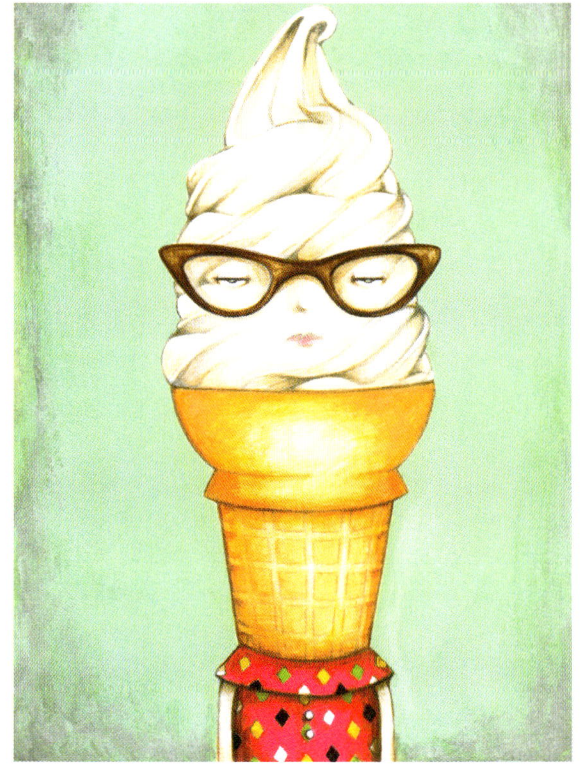

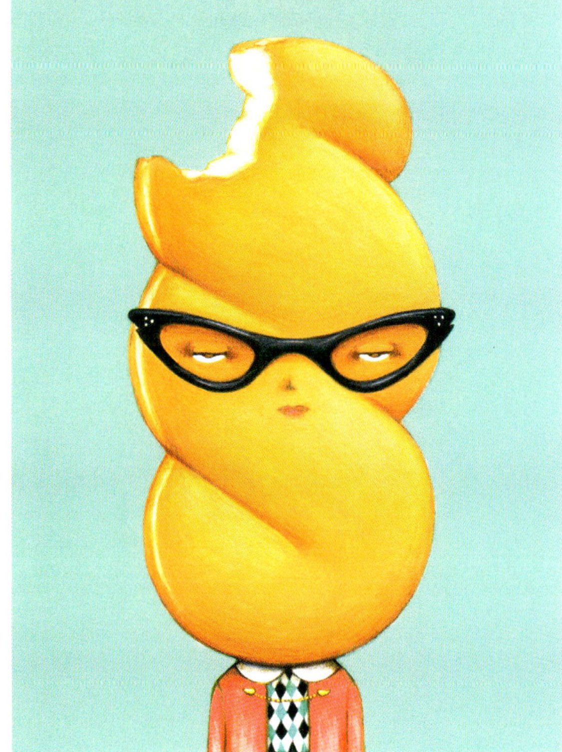

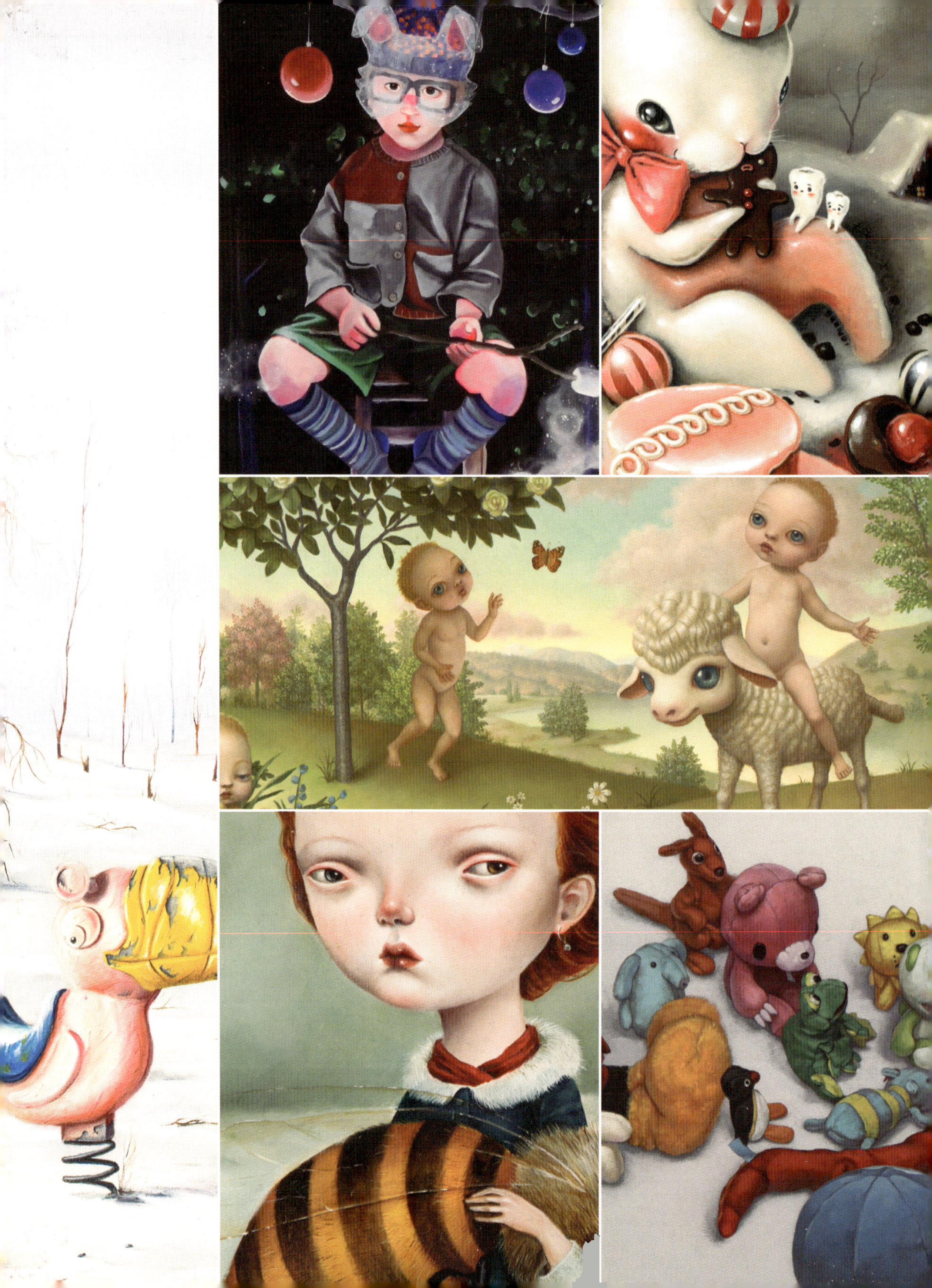